Knowing and Learning Mathematics for Teaching

Mathematics Teacher Preparation Content
Workshop Program Steering Committee

Center for Education

Mathematical Sciences Education Board

National Research Council

NATIONAL ACADEMY PRESS
Washington, D.C.

NATIONAL ACADEMY PRESS • 2101 Constitution Avenue, N.W. • Washington, D.C. 20418

NOTICE: The project that is the subject of this report was approved by the Governing Board of the National Research Council, whose members are drawn from the councils of the National Academy of Sciences, the National Academy of Engineering, and the Institute of Medicine. The members of the committee responsible for the report were chosen for their special competences and with regard for appropriate balance.

This study was supported by Grant No. DUE-9706060 between the National Academy of Sciences and the National Science Foundation. Any opinions, findings, conclusions, or recommendations expressed in this publication are those of the author(s) and do not necessarily reflect the views of the organizations or agencies that provided support for the project.

International Standard Book Number 0-309-07252-2
Library of Congress Catalog Card Number 00-110978

Additional copies of this report are available from National Academy Press, 2101 Constitution Avenue, N.W., Lockbox 285, Washington, D.C. 20055; (800) 624-6242 or (202) 334-3313 (in the Washington metropolitan area); Internet, http://www.nap.edu

Printed in the United States of America

THE NATIONAL ACADEMIES

National Academy of Sciences
National Academy of Engineering
Institute of Medicine
National Research Council

The **National Academy of Sciences** is a private, nonprofit, self-perpetuating society of distinguished scholars engaged in scientific and engineering research, dedicated to the furtherance of science and technology and to their use for the general welfare. Upon the authority of the charter granted to it by the Congress in 1863, the Academy has a mandate that requires it to advise the federal government on scientific and technical matters. Dr. Bruce M. Alberts is president of the National Academy of Sciences.

The **National Academy of Engineering** was established in 1964, under the charter of the National Academy of Sciences, as a parallel organization of outstanding engineers. It is autonomous in its administration and in the selection of its members, sharing with the National Academy of Sciences the responsibility for advising the federal government. The National Academy of Engineering also sponsors engineering programs aimed at meeting national needs, encourages education and research, and recognizes the superior achievements of engineers. Dr. William A. Wulf is president of the National Academy of Engineering.

The **Institute of Medicine** was established in 1970 by the National Academy of Sciences to secure the services of eminent members of appropriate professions in the examination of policy matters pertaining to the health of the public. The Institute acts under the responsibility given to the National Academy of Sciences by its congressional charter to be an adviser to the federal government and, upon its own initiative, to identify issues of medical care, research, and education. Dr. Kenneth I. Shine is president of the Institute of Medicine.

The **National Research Council** was organized by the National Academy of Sciences in 1916 to associate the broad community of science and technology with the Academy's purposes of furthering knowledge and advising the federal government. Functioning in accordance with general policies determined by the Academy, the Council has become the principal operating agency of both the National Academy of Sciences and the National Academy of Engineering in providing services to the government, the public, and the scientific and engineering communities. The Council is administered jointly by both Academies and the Institute of Medicine. Dr. Bruce M. Alberts and Dr. William A. Wulf are chairman and vice chairman, respectively, of the National Research Council.

MATHEMATICS TEACHER PREPARATION CONTENT WORKSHOP PROGRAM STEERING COMMITTEE

Deborah Loewenberg Ball, *Chair*, University of Michigan
Richard Askey,* University of Wisconsin-Madison
Hyman Bass,* Columbia University
Genevieve Knight, Coppin State College
Mark Saul, Bronxville High School
Deborah Schifter, Education Development Center, Inc.
Olga Garcia Torres, Tucson Unified School District

Staff

Rodger Bybee, Executive Director, Center for Science, Mathematics, and Engineering Education (CSMEE)
Joan Ferrini-Mundy, Associate Executive Director, CSMEE
Gail Burrill, Project Director
Bradford Findell, Program Officer
Kirsten Sampson Snyder, Reports Officer
Doug Sprunger, Senior Project Assistant
Danna Brennan, Project Assistant

---

*Member of the National Academy of Sciences

Dedication

James R. C. Leitzel was a member of the Mathematical Sciences Education Board (MSEB) from 1994 to 1997. Jim's contributions to mathematics education are vast and diverse, but one of his principal commitments was to the improvement of teacher preparation and professional development. He was an articulate advocate for the Board's initiatives in this area. Jim served on the Professional Development of Teachers of Mathematics Working Group that contributed to the National Council of Teachers of Mathematics' *Professional Standards for Teaching Mathematics* and was the editor of the Mathematical Association of America's *Call for Change: Recommendations for the Mathematical Preparation of Teachers of Mathematics*. Jim's dedication to teachers and their growth as mathematics teachers also extended to those in his classes at The Ohio State University, the University of Nebraska-Lincoln, and the University of New Hampshire and to the many mathematics educators for whom he became a mentor. Jim passed away in 1998 but left a legacy of concern, care, and nurturing for teachers and teaching. In recognition of his contributions both to the MSEB and to the mathematics education community, we dedicate this book to him.

Acknowledgments

We would like to acknowledge the staff at the National Research Council's (NRC) Center for Science, Mathematics, and Engineering Education (CSMEE) for their efforts in putting the Workshop together. In particular, Doug Sprunger was instrumental in overseeing arrangements for the meeting and in arranging these proceedings for review and publication. Onsite support was also provided by Kirsten Sampson Snyder and Tina Winters.

We are grateful to the members of the Program Steering Committee for their oversight in planning the program for the Workshop. We also wish to acknowledge the speakers and in particular the discussion group leaders for their contributions and leadership that gave substance to the discussion.

This report has been reviewed in draft form by individuals chosen for their diverse perspectives and technical expertise, in accordance with procedures approved by the National Research Council's Report Review Committee. The purpose of this independent review is to provide candid and critical comments that will assist the institution in making the published report as sound as possible and to ensure that the report meets institutional standards for objectivity, evidence, and responsiveness to the study charge. The review comments and draft manuscript remain confidential to protect the integrity of the deliberative process. We wish to thank the following individuals for their participation in the review of this report:

Shelly Ferguson, National Council of Teachers of Mathematics
Kay McClain, Vanderbilt University
Albert Otto, Illinois State University
Tad Watanabe, Towson State University
Laura van Zoost, University of Western Michigan

While the individuals listed above have provided many constructive comments and suggestions, responsibility for the final content of this report rests solely with the steering committee and the National Research Council.

Gail Burrill
Project Director
Mathematical Sciences Education Board

Contents

Knowing and Learning Mathematics for Teaching

Introduction

Content preparation of teachers is a current topic of interest to mathematics educators across the nation. Many experts now agree that reforming teacher preparation in postsecondary institutions is central to sustaining and deepening efforts to provide quality mathematics education for all students (National Science Foundation, 1996; National Research Council, 1996). Traditionally, recommendations about the mathematical content preparation of teachers have taken the form of a list of courses or a list of topics. Yet, research has shown that the number of mathematics courses taken by teachers does not correlate significantly with their effectiveness as measured by student learning (Begle, 1979; Monk, 1994). In other words, what the teachers take from their mathematics courses does not necessarily serve them well in their classroom practice. Recent recommendations about the mathematical preparation of teachers, such as the Conference Board of the Mathematical Sciences' document *Mathematical Education of Teachers* (in preparation), have attempted to move beyond lists of content, stressing the need for knowledge about mathematical connections, communication, modeling, or use of technology, for example. In prac-

tice, however, these recommendations are often realized as courses or sequences of courses organized by mathematical content and taught via a narrow repertoire of approaches, which alone will not be effective for prospective teachers nor for the students they will be teaching.

Despite the plethora of recommendations over the past forty years, questions about what mathematics content teachers need to know, how and where they should come to know the material, what they need to know about the nature and practice of mathematics, and how their knowledge of mathematics relates to teaching practice, though fundamental, are largely unresolved in current research. There is a tremendous need to address these questions systematically, to develop new ways of thinking about the role of content knowledge in teacher preparation, and to identify focused questions for future research involving members of the mathematics education community—mathematicians, scientists, mathematics educators, teacher educators, K-12 teachers, and administrators.

Questions about teachers' knowledge of content are of interest across a range of communities that are concerned with teacher preparation. Some feel strongly that prospective teachers need deep and substantial knowledge of mathematics content; however, there is varying opinion about the level, breadth, and formality of this content. Others are concerned that prospective teachers have content knowledge that will be useful to them in classroom settings with diverse student populations. To some, there is the perception that these two perspectives are mutually exclusive, while others look for a balance. Recently developed standards-based K-5 curriculum materials impose substantial new mathematical demands on K-5 teachers, and developers worry that teacher preparation courses will not adequately prepare teachers to employ these mathematically challenging materials in the classroom or to manage the mathematical discussions that emerge in classrooms when they are used. Thus, one of the two major questions addressed at the workshop was: What is the mathematical knowledge teachers need to know to teach well?

At the same time, professional developers in mathematics education (Ball & Cohen, 1999; Schifter, Bastable, & Russell, 1999; Shulman, 1992; Stein, Smith, Henningson, & Silver, 2000), particularly at the inservice level, are building experience and expertise with professional development materials and tools, including the use of videos, case studies, teacher reflections on practice, mathematicians' commentaries, analyses of student work, and the use of curriculum materials by teachers. While many of these efforts have shown promise with inservice teachers, there is very little experience in the mathematics education or mathe-

matics communities with incorporating such practice-based approaches to teacher development into preservice content courses. Thus, a second question of the workshop was: How can teachers develop the mathematical knowledge they need to teach well?

REFERENCES

Ball, D. L., & Cohen, D. K. (1999). Developing practice, developing practitioners: Toward a practice-based theory of professional education. In G. Sykes & L. Darling-Hammond (Eds.), *Teaching as the learning profession: Handbook of policy and practice* (pp. 3-32). San Francisco: Jossey Bass.

Begle, E. G. (1979). *Critical variables in mathematics education: Findings from a survey of the empirical literature.* Washington, DC: Mathematical Association of America.

Conference Board of the Mathematical Sciences. (in preparation). *Mathematical education of teachers.* Draft report available on-line: http://www.maa.org/cbms.

Monk, D. H. (1994). Subject area preparation of secondary mathematics and science teachers and student achievement. *Economics of Education Review, 13*(2), 125-145.

National Research Council. (1996). *From analysis to action: Report of a convocation.* Washington, DC: National Academy Press.

National Science Foundation. (1996). *Shaping the future.* Washington, DC: Author.

Schifter, D., Bastable, V., & Russell, S. J. (with Yaffee, L., Lester, J. B., & Cohen, S.) (1999). *Developing mathematical ideas, number and operations part 2: Making meaning for operations casebook.* Parsippany, NJ: Dale Seymour.

Shulman, J. (1992). *Case methods in teacher education.* New York: Teachers College Press.

Stein, M. K., Smith, M. S., Henningson, M. A., & Silver, E. A. (1999). *Implementing standards-based mathematics instruction: A casebook for professional development.* New York: Teachers College Press.

Workshop Overview:
Knowing and Learning Mathematics for Teaching

The Mathematics Teacher Preparation Content Workshop, held on March 19-21, 1999, at the National Academy of Sciences, was designed around two central questions:

- What is the mathematical knowledge teachers need to know to teach well?
- How can teachers develop the mathematical knowledge they need to teach well?

Mathematics teacher educators, mathematics education researchers, mathematicians, K-12 school supervisors, and classroom teachers explored these two questions by considering actual tasks of teaching practice, such as remodeling problems, analyzing student work, or managing discussions. For the broader mathematics education community, the papers and reports collected in this proceedings are intended to inform and provoke discussion of these questions and the issues surrounding them.

The Workshop consisted of plenary sessions designed to set a framework for thinking about the questions, concurrent sessions based on specific tasks of teaching that illustrated how the questions might be enacted in the classroom, and panel sessions in which the panelists

reflected on their experiences at the Workshop in the context of their own background. In addition, each participant was assigned to one of ten small discussion groups, with the membership of each group representative of the range of interests and professional responsibilities of the participants. Each group was assigned to respond to one of five over-arching questions. The participants met with a designated leader in these small groups periodically throughout the Workshop to continue their thinking about their response to the assigned question in light of the plenary and concurrent sessions in which they had taken part.

Prior to the Workshop participants were given two tasks to do to lay the groundwork and provide a common platform from which to begin to address issues related to the content knowledge of teachers. They also read Chapters 1 and 4 from Liping Ma's (1999) *Knowing and Teaching Elementary Mathematics: Teachers' Understanding of Fundamental Mathematics in China and the United States* and considered explicit questions about each chapter.

The Workshop began on Friday evening with a reception and a general welcome from Rodger Bybee, Executive

Director of the Center for Science, Mathematics, and Engineering Education. Steering Committee chair Deborah Ball gave a welcome and a brief overview of the Workshop. Following the welcome, participants met in their small groups to discuss the preworkshop reading and to consider, for the first time, the overarching question assigned to their group. The opening session concluded with a panel consisting of Liping Ma, Mark Saul, and Genevieve Knight. Ma described what she meant by profound understanding of fundamental mathematics (PUFM). Fundamental mathematics is a foundation for later learning that is primary because it contains advanced mathematics topics in elementary form and is elementary because it is at the beginning of students' learning. Profound understanding indicates a deep, vast, and thorough knowledge of the subject. According to Ma, teachers with PUFM are able to reveal and represent mathematical ideas in ways that are connected, that display multiple perspectives and awareness of basic ideas of mathematics, and that have longitudinal coherence.

Mark Saul addressed the question, "What is it that is essential to an elementary teacher's understanding of mathematics?" He offered a list not meant to be exhaustive but to stimulate thinking. Saul suggested there are a variety of ways to come by this knowledge, and it is our responsibility as a community to begin implementing some of these. He raised an important question of balance. People who work with teachers must themselves have a profound understanding of the mathematics they are teaching, but too much mathematics presented too quickly can result in disaster. Genevieve Knight described a 1959 text, the *Fundamentals of Freshman Mathematics* by Allendoerfer and Oakley, designed to give a modern

treatment of topics needed to prepare students for calculus and emphasizing the authors' interpretation of essential ideas of fundamental mathematics. Knight questioned which teachers are those who must possess this fundamental knowledge and what is fundamental mathematics. Is it a list of topics, courses, experiences? She charged the group to think about how to create an explicit set of defining properties of what fundamental mathematics means and a well-designed system to determine when a teacher or a student understands.

The first full day of the Workshop began with a presentation by Hyman Bass and Deborah Ball, focused on the task of establishing a classroom culture in which mathematics reasoning is both possible and called for. They posed the question: What lenses do elementary teachers need to see that they as teachers are involved in the development of children's capacity to construct proofs, to understand and follow mathematical proofs, to understand the need for justification, and to be able to distinguish valid justifications from invalid justifications? A videotape of Ball's third-grade classroom gave a concrete example of young children talking with each other about a mathematical idea and reasoning about its interpretation. Bass noted that his ongoing work analyzing the videotapes of Ball's classroom is essentially the same as the focus of the workshop: to look for the mathematics entailed in the core tasks of teaching. Because such tasks involve mathematical decisions, the focus is on discerning what that mathematics is and how to place it into a larger mathematical context. The two examples in the video were used to consider some core elements of teaching: What common knowledge do students have and how can a teacher use this common knowledge to help students understand how to justify a mathematical claim in a meaningful way?

Reacting to the video and the comments by Ball and Bass, Jim Lewis noted that establishing a classroom culture in which mathematical reasoning is called for, such as in the video, places a greater demand on the teacher than would a more traditional approach of demonstrating the process for solving a problem and having children practice. His concern with proper notation and language reinforces the challenges that the teacher faces on a daily basis, deciding when to introduce new mathematical notation and when to couch the discussion in the language of the children. Lewis suggests the mathematical knowledge required to teach in this manner is far superior to the mathematical knowledge that most students have when they are certified as ready to teach mathematics at the elementary school level.

The plenary session was followed by concurrent sessions on what mathematics teachers need to know to teach well. The participants were assigned to two of four concurrent sessions, each focused on the mathematics involved in a particular task of teaching. The session led by Erick Smith looked in depth at one classroom example and the mathematics the teacher needed to know to manage a classroom discussion around the student presentations. The participants in the session addressed the question: How do teachers make mathematical meaning as they develop an understanding of their students' mathematical thoughts; that is, what mathematical knowledge do teachers need to understand the mathematical work of their students?

Virginia Bastable led a session focused on investigating students' mathematical thinking. The session was divided into two components: reviewing a written case study to share observations about the mathematical thinking of the students and reflecting on the experience to make more general statements about the mathematical knowledge needed by teachers to understand this mathematical thinking. Olga Torres engaged participants in remodeling a mathematical task, either to make it simpler or more difficult. In the process, the participants considered issues related to teachers' understanding of mathematical language, the underlying mathematical ideas, and ways of reasoning, and the prior knowledge of both teacher and student. The session led by Michaele Chappell centered on the teachers' mathematical knowledge, skills, and dispositions that matter in examining and analyzing student work. The basis for the discussion was student work on a seventh-grade problem dealing with proportionality.

The day ended with a panel session on the kinds of mathematical knowledge that matter in teaching. Alan Tucker observed that the typical three or six credits in a teacher preparation program seem insufficient for a preservice teacher to pick up all of the knowledge needed to do the tasks featured in the workshop. He suggested that learning to teach must be a process that is continually evolving through the life of the teacher. To make this experience successful, teachers need a foundation for their learning: critical thinking skills that enable them to reason from basic mathematics principles. Tucker concluded by observing that the level of common mathematical knowledge among the public seems to be actually much higher today than in the past and pointed out that the exciting part of being a teacher is to take advantage of and build on what people already know.

Based on the experiences of the day, Deborah Schifter added to Mark Saul's list of what is essential to an elementary teacher's understanding of mathematics.

She suggested that teachers need to be connected with the notion that mathematics makes sense, must be able to work with uncomfortable feelings to come to the place where mathematics does make sense, and must be curious about how mathematics works. She observed that teachers must learn to see the mathematics in the situations they encounter. Gladys Whitehead pointed out that as faculty in community colleges work with elementary majors, they struggle with two concerns: providing teachers with an adequate content base and adequate teaching strategies. Her question was: How do we capture our own experience and pass it on to new teachers? She closed by noting that postsecondary teachers need inservice development and that working with school systems and their teachers can help those in post-secondary revamp their programs for teachers.

The second full day of the Workshop was framed around the two questions: How might prospective elementary teachers be helped to develop the kind of mathematical knowledge they need to teach well? What are alternative and promising approaches to the mathematics education of beginning teachers? Participants were again assigned to two of four concurrent sessions. Using student curriculum materials to help teachers learn mathematics was the focus of the session offered by Shin-Ying Lee and Marco Ramirez. Lee focused on Japanese teachers' manuals as a significant source of information that contributes to teachers' knowledge of mathematics. The manuals provide different aspects of mathematical knowledge and tie the content knowledge to an understanding of how students learn and the common difficulties students have. Ramirez took teachers through a lesson from *Investigations in Number,*

Data, and Space, a relatively new U.S. elementary curriculum created by TERC. The materials focus primarily on the role of the teacher and include only a small set of student activities for each concept. The teachers' manuals suggest questions to ask and point out problems students may encounter and various strategies students may use for a given task.

Carne Barnett discussed how studying case materials enables teachers to learn mathematics. A major goal of the session was to illustrate how a deliberately facilitated case discussion can help teachers acquire an advanced and flexible knowledge of the mathematics content they teach. A second goal was to demonstrate how an analysis of the mathematics in a classroom situation prepares teachers to make informed and strategic teaching decisions. Jill Lester, Virginia Bastable, and Deborah Schifter illustrated the development of mathematical content knowledge through a discussion of programs and practices from Developing Mathematical Ideas, a mathematics inservice program for teachers. Participants worked through a case on number and discussed how this provided the opportunity for preservice and inservice teachers to learn mathematics. Bradford Findell and Deborah Ball offered an analysis of video and its role as a delivery mechanism for helping teachers learn mathematics. The goal of the session was to consider how video can be used to provide opportunities for teachers to engage in mathematics content. The session was organized around two video clips: a 5-minute teacher-directed class discussion taken from VideoCases for Mathematics Professional Development project and the beginning of a 30-minute lecture prepared as part of a 51-video course, Gateways to Arithmetic by Herb Gross, for prospective elementary teachers.

Participants discussed the advantages and disadvantages of each case as an opportunity to learn mathematics.

The closing panel discussed how teachers come to learn the mathematics they need to know to teach well. Richard Askey used an analysis of problems presented in textbooks to illustrate his view of important mathematics teachers should know and be able to do. He discussed the mathematics in different texts and how the need for deep knowledge of mathematics is reflected in teachers' manuals. Carol Midgett described the learning of mathematics from her own experience as a teacher, attributing much of her growth in understanding mathematics to professional activities outside of the classroom. She indicated that the Workshop was important because it provided the opportunity for people from all levels of educational practice to work together in their common struggle to deal with the complexity of teaching and what mathematical knowledge it takes to teach well. Alice Gill reemphasized that teachers need to know mathematics and to know it well. She urged the Workshop participants to keep in mind not only the mathematics but also where the teachers are and what additional supports they may need. James Lightbourne closed the panel with reflections on the importance of helping teachers come to learn mathematics in the ways described during the Workshop. He mentioned several National Science Foundation programs as other possibilities for promising ways to develop this teacher knowledge. Joan Ferrini-Mundy, the panel moderator, suggested potential sites of practice other than those featured at the Workshop that could be vehicles for learning mathematics and offered an initial set of reasons why sites of practice are useful as ways to develop teacher knowledge.

Deborah Ball closed the Workshop by observing that it was not designed to provide answers to the many questions about teacher content knowledge but to serve as an intellectual resource for the participants to use in framing their own work. She encouraged the participants to try some activities based on the thinking of the Workshop, centered on core tasks of teaching, document the results, and share them with their colleagues. In this way, she suggested, the field can begin to move forward in a real analysis of what mathematics teachers need to teach well and how they come to learn that mathematics.

Pre-Workshop Tasks

Before coming to the Workshop, participants were asked to do two tasks and to bring their thinking to the workshop. The tasks below were developed as part of research conducted at Michigan State University (Ball, 1988; Kennedy, Ball, & McDiarmid, 1993). Participants were asked to consider how they would

Figure 1. Homework Tasks

Task 1
Let's spend some time thinking about one particular topic that you may work with when you teach, subtraction with regrouping. Look at these questions ($52 - 25$, $91 - 79$, etc.). How would you approach these problems if you were teaching second grade? What would you say pupils need to understand or be able to do before they could start learning subtraction with regrouping?

Task 2
Imagine that one of your students comes to class very excited. She tells you that she has figured out a theory that you never told the class. She explains that she has discovered that as the perimeter of a closed figure increases, the area also increases. She shows you this picture to prove what she is doing.

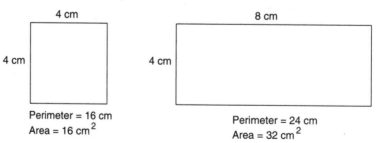

4 cm

Perimeter = 16 cm
Area = 16 cm^2

8 cm

Perimeter = 24 cm
Area = 32 cm^2

How would you respond to this student?

approach the tasks and how they would want elementary teachers to approach them. They were also asked to reflect on the mathematical knowledge, skill, and even sensibilities that their approach would require of a teacher.

Participants were also asked to read material from Chapters 1 and 4 of Liping Ma's book *Knowing and Teaching Elementary Mathematics*. Ma used the two tasks above to interview Chinese elementary teachers and then compared the Chinese teachers' responses to those obtained by the Michigan State researchers who had interviewed U.S. teachers. Participants were given the following questions concerning the Ma excerpts.

CHAPTER 1

1. Ma raises the issue of vocabulary and appropriate word choice in teachers' mathematical talk with students. How does this play out in both the teachers' grasp of mathematics and how the students came to understand the mathematical concept?
2. Ma quotes Jerome Bruner (1977) on the notion that the more fundamental the concept, the greater the applications. How is this idea reflected in the different approaches used by the teachers? What does this indicate about the mathematics teachers must know in order to be effective teachers?
3. Ma describes two ways of thinking about knowing a mathematical concept: as a sequence of steps leading to the concept or as a package of knowledge whose elements contribute in different ways and at different

points to the knowing. With which of these ways are you most comfortable? Select another topic and try to analyze it from both perspectives.

CHAPTER 4

1. Is there any indication of how attitude towards mathematics affected the teachers' approaches both to the problem and to how they responded to the question?
2. Read the responses of the teachers carefully. Can you categorize the responses according to the level of the teachers' mathematical understanding?
3. Ma writes that only teachers with mathematical inquiry themselves can foster this in their students. Do you agree? How do the teachers interviewed display mathematical inquiry?

REFERENCES

Ball, D. L. (1988). *Knowledge and reasoning in mathematical pedagogy: Examining what prospective teachers bring to teacher education.* Unpublished doctoral dissertation, Michigan State University, East Lansing.

Bruner, J. (1977). *The process of education.* Cambridge, MA: Harvard University Press.

Kennedy, M. M., Ball, D. L., & McDiarmid, G. W. (1993). *A study package for examining and tracking changes in teachers' knowledge* (NCRTL Technical Series 93-1). East Lansing, MI: The National Center for Research on Teacher Education.

Ma, L. (1999). *Knowing and teaching elementary mathematics: Teachers' understanding of fundamental mathematics in China and the United States.* Mahwah, NJ: Lawrence Erlbaum.

Teachers' Understanding of Fundamental Mathematics

Following the small-group discussions on the preworkshop assignment from Liping Ma's book *Knowing and Teaching Elementary Mathematics* (1999), a panel set the stage for thinking about the two overarching questions that were the focus of the workshop:

- What is the mathematical knowledge teachers need to know to teach well?
- How can teachers develop the mathematical knowledge they need to teach well?

PANELISTS

Knowledge of Fundamental Mathematics for Teaching
  Liping Ma, Stanford University

Elementary Teachers and Essential Mathematical Knowledge
  Mark Saul, Bronxville High School

What Is Fundamental Mathematics?
  Genevieve Knight, Coppin State College

Knowledge of Fundamental Mathematics for Teaching[1]

Liping Ma, Cathy Kessel

What mathematical knowledge do elementary teachers use in teaching? About 10 years ago, Deborah Ball and her colleagues at Michigan State University carried out a research project to address this question (Ball, 1988; Kennedy, Ball, & McDiarmid, 1993). Teachers were asked how they would respond to classroom scenarios in which mathematical ideas played crucial roles. As a graduate student, the first author of this paper worked on this project and was struck by the teachers' responses. Her memories of elementary teaching in China suggested that Chinese teachers would react quite differently.

She investigated this suspicion in her dissertation research, asking Chinese elementary teachers the same questions that had been asked of U.S. teachers. To analyze the responses of both groups of teachers, she developed the notion of profound understanding of fundamental mathematics (PUFM). Fundamental mathematics is a foundation for later learning. It is primary because it contains advanced mathematical topics in rudimen-

tary form, and it is elementary because it is at the beginning of students' learning. Profound has three related meanings— deep, vast, and thorough—and profound understanding reflects all three. A deep understanding of fundamental mathematics is defined to be one that connects topics with ideas of greater conceptual power. A broad understanding connects topics of similar conceptual power. And thoroughness is the capacity to weave all parts of the subject into a coherent whole. Profound understanding of fundamental mathematics is an understanding of fundamental mathematics that is deep, broad, and thorough.

Teachers with PUFM are able to reveal and represent ideas and connections in terms of mathematics teaching and learning. Such teaching and learning tends to be connected, display multiple perspectives, demonstrate awareness of basic ideas of mathematics, and have longitudinal coherence. Like a taxi driver who knows a road system well, teachers with PUFM know many connections among past, present, and future under-

---

[1]The essence of this paper was contained in the remarks of Liping Ma at the opening panel session of the Workshop.

standing of mathematics. They know how to guide students from their current understandings to further learning and to prepare them for future travel. Such teaching and learning is possible because the road system of fundamental mathematics has depth, breadth, and thoroughness, allowing teachers to connect student understandings with topics to be learned.

This is not the case in the United States, where knowing elementary mathematics is sometimes, perhaps often, construed as knowing how to add, subtract, multiply, and divide whole numbers and fractions.[2] In terms of content, this characterization is insufficient—at the very least, elementary mathematics concerns geometry as well. But for Chinese teachers with PUFM, it is insufficient in another way. Those in Ma's study would say, "It is not enough to know how, one must also know why." The attitude expressed by this saying may affect a teacher's own knowledge—if knowing how is insufficient, one must find a rationale for mathematical procedures. Moreover, it may affect a teacher's goals for students—if knowing how is insufficient, students must come to understand why. In contrast, a teacher without this attitude may still know how and why, but not think it important that students know both. Or a teacher without this attitude may know how, but not why—and may not be able to answer students' questions, nor see the importance of student questions. Thus a teacher's attitude may affect not only the mathematics the teacher knows but also the mathematics the teacher teaches.

Other mathematical attitudes displayed by Chinese teachers include the following: claims must be justified with mathematical arguments, it is desirable to approach the same topic in multiple ways, and it is desirable to preserve the consistency of an idea in different contexts. Such attitudes may affect a teacher's knowledge by contributing to its coherence and connectedness—and also affect a teacher's teaching.

These fall in the category of what Jerome Bruner (1977) calls basic attitudes and considers as one aspect of the structure of a discipline. Another aspect of disciplinary knowledge identified by Bruner is basic principles. In the case of elementary mathematics (and perhaps all disciplines), basic attitudes have a symbiotic relationship with basic principles. For example, justifications in elementary mathematics often draw on the distributive law. Solving a fraction problem in multiple ways might draw on relationships between a fraction and a division, division as the inverse of multiplication, or relationships between fractions and decimals. In the base-10 system, noting the consistency of the relationship between 10 and 1, 100 and 10, and so on leads to the idea of the rate of 10: Each unit of higher value is composed of 10 or powers of 10 lower value units. This leads to the more general principle of the rate of composing a higher valued unit—the rate is 10 in the base-10 system, but there are other possibilities. For instance, the binary system has a rate of 2.

Like basic attitudes, basic principles may play a role in teaching, as well as knowing, mathematics. They may appear as parts of what Chinese teachers call a "knowledge package" for a given topic—a network of conceptual and procedural topics that support and are supported by

---

[2]This perception of what it means to know elementary mathematics has been challenged by many in the U.S., in particular by the writers of the various National Council of Teachers of Mathematics *Standards*.

its learning. An experienced Chinese teacher said

> You should see a knowledge "package" when you are teaching a piece of knowledge. And you should know the role of the present knowledge in that package. You have to know that the knowledge you are teaching is supported by which ideas or procedures, so your teaching is going to rely on, reinforce, and elaborate the learning of these ideas. (Ma, 1999, p. 18)

To see a topic to be taught as part of a package of knowledge, rather than in isolation, requires a way of thinking that may not be common in the United States. When U.S. elementary teachers were asked how they would respond to a student's mistake in calculating 123×645, they focused on the given problem. When Chinese teachers were asked the same question, about 20% made comments such as

> This mistake should have happened when students learn multiplication by two-digit numbers. The mathematical concept and the computational skill of multidigit multiplication are both introduced in the learning of the operation with two-digit numbers. So the problem may happen and should be solved at that stage. (Ma, 1999, pp. 45-46)

This reflects a general principle in the organization of knowledge packages: Not all topics receive equal emphasis. Some are considered key pieces, and teachers take particular care that students understand them. Two-digit multiplication is a key piece for the three-digit multiplication package because the simplest form of the "moving over" idea involved in multidigit multiplication occurs in the two-digit case. Such attention to an idea in its first and simplest form allows teachers to pay less attention to later and more complicated forms. One Chinese teacher in the study put it this way, "To tell you the truth, I don't teach my students multiplication by three-digit numbers. Rather, I let them learn it [on] their own."

Figure 1 shows a model of the knowledge package for subtraction with regrouping derived from interviews with Chinese teachers. [Here "regrouping" includes more than "borrowing." Instead, the intended meaning is that some digit in the base-10 representation needs to be decomposed to make the computation. For example, in computing $15 - 7$, one can't simply work with the digits 1, 5, and 7. Instead, one needs to decompose the 1 as 10 ones and group some or all of the 10 ones with the 5 (e.g., 2 ones might be grouped with the 5).]

The topic under discussion appears in a rectangle surrounded by other topics that occur in the curriculum (in ovals), and basic principles (in rectangles with rounded edges). Key pieces of the package have thick borders.

The central sequence in the subtraction package goes from the topic of addition and subtraction within 10, to addition and subtraction within 20, to subtraction with regrouping of numbers between 20 and 100, then to subtraction of large numbers with regrouping. "Addition and subtraction within 10" is addition with sums of 10 or less and subtraction with minuends of 10 or less, which don't require carrying or regrouping. For example, $10 - 4 = ?$ has a minuend of 10, and requires no regrouping. A related addition problem $4 + 6 = ?$ has the sum of 10, and requires no carrying. "Addition and subtraction within 20" is addition with sums between 10 and 20 and subtraction with minuends between 10 and 20.

Three levels of subtraction with regrouping problems are related to this central sequence:

Figure 1. The Knowledge Package for Subtraction

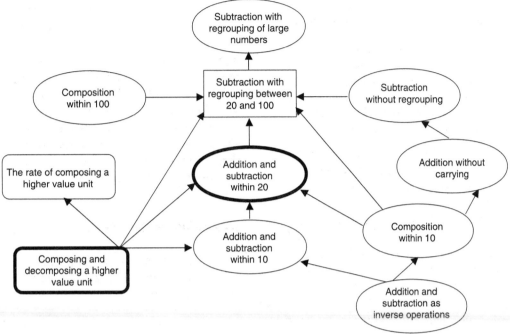

From Ma (1999). Used by permission of Lawrence Erlbaum Associates.

- minuends between 10 and 20, e.g., 15 – 7;
- minuends between 19 and 100, e.g., 53 – 25;
- minuends with three or more digits, e.g., 203 – 15.

Each of these levels concerns a new idea and a new skill:

- decomposing a ten;
- splitting a ten from several other tens, then decomposing it;
- successive decomposition, e.g., decomposing 1 hundred as 10 tens, then 1 ten as 10 ones.

The different levels of regrouping problems correspond to pieces of the knowledge package shown in Figure 1.

However, other necessary pieces of knowledge do not occur as separate topics in the curriculum. Instead, students' learning of curriculum topics supports and is supported by knowledge of basic principles: composing and decomposing a higher value unit, the rate for composing a higher value unit, and addition and subtraction as inverse operations.

How do teachers help students focus on these basic principles? Teacher Mao (a pseudonym), speaking from thirty years of experience, described how questions can play a role in student learning:

> What is the rate for composing a higher value unit? The answer is simple: 10. Ask students how many ones there are in a 10, or ask them what the rate for composing a higher value unit is, their answers will be

the same: 10. However, the effect of the two questions on their learning is not the same. ... When you require them to think about the rate for composing a higher value unit, you lead them to a theory that explains the fact as well as the procedure. Such an understanding is more powerful than a specific fact. ... Once [students] realize that the rate of composing a higher value unit, 10, is the reason why we decompose a ten into 10 ones, they will apply it to other situations. (Ma, 1999, pp. 10-11)

Teacher Mao's description illustrates how attitude toward mathematics may affect a teacher's choice of questions. Both questions, "What is the rate for composing a higher value unit?" and "How many ones are there in a 10?" have the same answer. But a teacher with the attitude that one must know why as well as how chooses the question that leads toward an understanding of the basic principle. This choice reflects the kind of knowledge that the teacher wants students to learn. But, as Teacher Mao says, this knowledge can be applied in other situations, so this choice also affects students' future learning.

Teacher Mao's description suggests that answering the question "What mathematical knowledge do elementary teachers use in teaching?" has two aspects: what to teach and how to teach it. The two aspects are often considered as separate—content and pedagogy—and taught to prospective teachers as separate subjects—mathematics and methods. But, just as a mathematical attitude toward elementary mathematics makes it more than a collection of disconnected procedures, the "knowledge package" way of thinking about teaching elementary mathematics makes knowledge for teaching more than content plus pedagogy. Instead, Teacher Mao and other Chinese teachers show us that content and pedagogy may be two sides of the same coin. Whether this coin will ever become common currency in the United States will depend not just on the individual efforts of teachers, but also on the way those teachers are prepared and supported—by their colleges and universities, their working conditions, and the depth, breadth, and thoroughness of the mathematics they teach.

ACKNOWLEDGMENTS

We thank Rudy Apffel, Gail Burrill, Sue Helme, and Cherisa Yarkin for their comments on this paper.

REFERENCES

Ball, D. L. (1988). *Knowledge and reasoning in mathematical pedagogy: Examining what prospective teachers bring to teacher education.* Unpublished doctoral dissertation, Michigan State University, East Lansing.

Bruner, J. (1977). *The process of education.* Cambridge, MA: Harvard University Press.

Kennedy, M. M., Ball, D. L., & McDiarmid, G. W. (1993). *A study package for examining and tracking changes in teachers' knowledge* (NCRTL Technical Series 93-1). East Lansing, MI: The National Center for Research on Teacher Education.

Ma, L. (1999). *Knowing and teaching elementary mathematics: Teachers' understanding of fundamental mathematics in China and the United States.* Mahwah, NJ: Lawrence Erlbaum.

National Council of Teachers of Mathematics. (1989). *Curriculum and evaluation standards for school mathematics.* Reston, VA: Author.

Elementary Teachers and Essential Mathematical Knowledge

Mark Saul

One learns to dread certain moments in the classroom, moments which are as awkward as they are inevitable. Among those I dread the most is a question which eventually occurs to someone in the class: "What's the last math we have to learn?" I don't have a good answer for this one. I've tried to tell students of the joy of mathematics, that I look forward to learning more math the same way I look forward to a good meal, and that there's always more math. But these last four words somehow never go over well. Instead, the news is perceived as a bombshell: your travails are never really finished. There's always more math.

It's these same four words that define the problem in talking about the mathematical background of elementary school teachers. Where does one stop? How much mathematics must an elementary school teacher know? The facile answer is: as much as possible, and the more, the better. Liping Ma's book gives a more sober view of the situation. She tells us, among other things, that even in elementary arithmetic, there is a depth to the knowledge necessary to teach, and that one could spend years simply acquiring this depth. So we are led to ask a more careful question: what is essential to an elementary teacher's understanding of mathematics? Here is a quick and tentative list. It is not meant to be exhaustive but rather to stimulate inquiry. Which items are most central to the elementary teacher's life? Which are less important? Which are described too generally, or too specifically? What's left out?

A deep knowledge of arithmetic, of at least the rational numbers, is certainly essential to an elementary teacher's background. How this deep knowledge is acquired and exactly what it consists of are not simple questions and certainly do not belong in a list such as this one. However, it is not hard to see that a knowledge of arithmetic algorithms is close to the center of arithmetic. Whether these algorithms are carried out mentally, with paper and pencil, with manipulatives, or with a calculator, and in what proportion these and other methods should be combined, are again issues worthy of much more discussion.

The study of algorithms leads to the issue of algebra. How much algebra must elementary teachers know? We can make a distinction here. One view of algebra is as "generalized arithmetic" (the phrase is Newton's), and it seems to me important that elementary school teachers (indeed, elementary school students) know about the use of variables to stand for numbers, and of algebraic expressions as a record of the results of binary operations on numbers.

There is a higher conception of algebra, which is still on an elementary level and which may or may not be appropriate to the education of elementary teachers. This is the conception of algebra as the study of the field of rational expressions (not just rational numbers), an insight which is the contribution of I. M. Gelfand (Gelfand & Shen, 1993). The notion that variables can stand for algebraic expressions, and not just rational numbers, is the beginning of another level of the learning of algebra, which may or may not be central to the work of the elementary school teacher.

It seems to me that elementary teachers must also know something about geometry. I am not referring to the usual taxonomies of geometric figures that one finds in elementary texts, nor to the various algebraic formulas that describe geometric figures. Rather, I am thinking of how figures are imbedded in (Euclidean) space, how they relate to each other, and how they move (that is, the study of geometric transformations). Again, I think of the words of I. M. Gelfand, who once commented to me that Descartes and Hilbert shaped the study of geometry in the schools: Descartes by introducing coordinates and algebraic methods, and Hilbert by modernizing and perfecting the axiomatic method of Euclid. Geometry can also be considered as a set of models of space, how objects are located in space, and how they move in space.

Another part of mathematics which I would offer as fundamental to the education of elementary school teachers is the language in which mathematics is expressed. This is largely the language of set theory: union, intersection, the null set, quantifiers, negation, but also functional notation and the idea of an isomorphism as a structure-preserving function.

Related to the language of mathematics is a set of concepts I call the nature of mathematics, that is, the notion that mathematics is logic-driven. Teachers (and indeed any educated person) ought to know what an axiomatic system is, what existence and uniqueness of an object mean, what it means to assert that something is possible or impossible (and not just very difficult), and what it means in mathematics to construct an object. Perhaps more important, teachers should understand the nature of mathematical truth. It is not dogmatic, as is theological truth. It is not conventional, as is political or moral truth. I am in danger of embracing here one particular philosophy of mathematics, or rather of rejecting certain others. This is not my point. What I mean to say is that the nature of mathematical truth, however conceived, ought to be discussed at some point in the training of elementary school teachers.

Any list such as the one I've just given raises more questions than it answers. One of the most important is: how does such a list for elementary school teachers differ from a similar list for the general public? Or does it? How should the body of knowledge outlined above be shaped to fit the needs of the elementary teacher? Liping Ma (1999) notes that much of the "deep knowledge" of the Chinese teachers she interviewed was acquired during their own elementary and middle school education. Our problem is that we need to start this cycle in motion.

A related question is: how should the elementary schoolteacher come to know about these ideas? Hyman Bass has commented in his conversation, for example, that a close study of arithmetic would eventually lead to a consideration of the other essential topics of mathematics. It seems to me that it would take great art to make this happen. Nonetheless, it may be a fruitful approach.

There are certainly other fruitful approaches. The important thing to note is that this process of bringing mathematical knowledge to teachers must be thought about carefully. We must not stray, either to the left or to the right. There are two important and common errors. Vladimir Retakh, a colleague who teaches at the university level, once commented to me: "Some people think that if you have passed Calculus II then you are ready to teach Calculus I." This is certainly erroneous. The message here is that people working with teachers must themselves know considerably more mathematics than they are teaching.

But can one have too much mathematics? Another common error in working with teachers is to provide too much mathematical information, too quickly, and in the wrong way. The situation is something like the bursting of a dam: a powerful and useful force is dissipated and rendered destructive. To continue the metaphor, we must have a sluice or spigot to regulate the amount and direction of mathematics begin dispensed. This regulator, of course, is knowledge of pedagogy, the pedagogy of teacher education.

It's a difficult process and requires a synergism that, I think, is evident in this group of people. And still it is difficult. Working with teachers involves a synthesis of mathematical and pedagogical knowledge that we are just beginning to achieve. We have a long road ahead, but also an exploration that can only get more exciting as it unfolds.

REFERENCES

Gelfand, I. M., & Shen, A. (1993). *Algebra*. Boston, MA: Birkhäuser.

Ma, L. (1999). *Knowing and teaching elementary mathematics: Teachers' understanding of fundamental mathematics in China and the United States*. Mahwah, NJ: Lawrence Erlbaum.

What Is Fundamental Mathematics?

Genevieve Knight

Forty years ago, Allendoerfer & Oakley (1959) published a textbook titled *Fundamentals of Freshman Mathematics*. The purpose was to give a modern treatment of those topics in mathematics that were needed to fill the gap between intermediate algebra, analytic geometry, and calculus. The book was influenced by the recommendations of many who were working even then to implement a reform of the mathematics curriculum. In the "To the Student" messages, students were challenged to master the language and essential ideas of elementary mathematics. When the students finished the book, they should have been prepared to study more advanced ideas of calculus, differential equations, and modern algebra that are the keystones of modern scientific and engineering developments. Notice the use of the words "elementary mathematics" and "fundamentals of freshman mathematics."

The panelists were asked to address teachers' understanding of fundamental mathematics. But first, we need to consider some questions. What teacher groups are the focus? Are the teachers elementary generalists? Mathematics teacher education majors? K-4 teachers with an area of concentration in mathematics? Non-teacher focused majors? What is fundamental mathematics? Is it a collection of topics? Courses? Experiences? Has the mathematics community agreed what constitutes fundamental mathematics?

According to Ma (1999), fundamental mathematics is elementary, foundational, and primary. It is elementary because it is at the beginning of mathematics learning. It is primary because it contains the rudiments of more advanced mathematical concepts. It is foundational because it provides a foundation for students' further learning in mathematics.

In Liping Ma's work, she refers to the mathematics for elementary teachers that is really conceptual understanding, fundamental to shaping the foundation for young learners to mentally assemble discrete units of knowledge to form units of units that eventually generate complex structures in abstract mathematics. Teachers recall their own early experiences that gave meaning to mathematics for them. Hence, they engage their students in activities that generate conceptual understanding. Teachers take part in discourse with students to verify that valid conclusions are supported by correct understandings of the mathematics. Ma's summaries also indicate that teachers who conceptually understand this fundamental mathematics produce students who themselves exhibit conceptual understanding, have the ability to learn and to reason, and are able to achieve.

It is crucial that we begin to give some reflective thought to what is meant by fundamental mathematics. If we are to promote teacher understanding of fundamental mathematics, we must have (a) an explicit set of defining properties of what is meant by fundamental mathematics and (b) a well-designed system that allows us to determine when a teacher or student "understands."

As a community, we need to examine what is fundamental mathematics and collectively promote research that will enable us to prepare elementary teachers to teach for student understanding. As we engage in conversations over the next few days, let us attempt to share best thoughts and practices. All of the voices actually engaged in the educative process *must* be heard. The list of participants represents a wide range of people who value education and have many experiences to share. Our focus is what mathematics should teachers know and be able to do so that students can learn, understand, and achieve. Tonight, think about the words Liping Ma used to describe her research. Organize your operational definitions, come ready to communicate, and bring closure to the conversation on Sunday.

REFERENCES

Allendoerfer, C. B., & Oakley, C. O. (1959). *Fundamentals of freshman mathematics.* New York: McGraw-Hill.

Ma, L. (1999). *Knowing and teaching elementary mathematics: Teachers' understanding of fundamental mathematics in China and the United States.* Mahwah, NJ: Lawrence Erlbaum.

RECONSIDERING THE MATHEMATICS THAT TEACHERS NEED TO KNOW

The first full day was devoted to consideration of teacher knowledge of mathematics. What mathematical knowledge does it take to teach well? What mathematics is crucial to the work of elementary school teaching? What can we learn from a closer look at the mathematics teachers have to teach and analyses of the core tasks and mathematical problems that they have to solve in the course of their work?

Such tasks include examining, interpreting, and evaluating student work; analyzing and modifying mathematics problems; designing follow-up problems (for example, homework); producing an explanation of a mathematical idea; and managing a class discussion around a mathematical idea. These were studied at the Workshop through videotapes of classroom lessons, copies of student work, and studying student thinking about mathematics.

Investigating Teaching Practice: Setting the Stage

The first session used videotapes of excerpts from an elementary classroom to establish a framework for thinking about creating a classroom climate where mathematical reasoning is the norm and how this is reflected in the mathematical content teachers need to know.

PRESENTERS

What Mathematical Knowledge Is Entailed in Teaching Children to Reason Mathematically?
Deborah Loewenberg Ball, University of Michigan
Hyman Bass, Columbia University

Reaction to the Presentation by Deborah Ball and Hyman Bass
James Lewis, University of Nebraska

What Mathematical Knowledge Is Entailed in Teaching Children to Reason Mathematically?

Deborah Loewenberg Ball, Hyman Bass

INTRODUCTORY COMMENTS BY BALL

Consider the task of establishing a classroom culture in which mathematical reasoning is both possible and called for. The wording of this task is part of the popular rhetoric these days, but our goal is to think about the task from a mathematical perspective. The idea of classroom culture is ubiquitous in elementary school teachers' talk. Everybody talks about creating classroom climates or cultures in which students feel comfortable and safe and talk to each other. What does it mean to think about the mathematical resources involved in creating a mathematical classroom culture, not just the generic idea of classroom culture? Mathematical reasoning is also something that everybody talks about. It is in the NCTM *Standards* (National Council of Teachers of Mathematics [NCTM], 1989). It is in every text you look at, but people mean different things by these words. Here, too, we want to probe what it means to look at children's mathematical reasoning, thinking about it mathematically.

There are many other perspectives that bear on mathematical reasoning: cognitive perspective, socio-cultural perspectives, perspectives that look from the bottom up at how children reason. Those are all valuable, but we want to focus on what it means to look at children's mathematical reasoning as emergent mathematical justification. What lenses do elementary teachers need to understand that what they as teachers are involved with is the development of children's capacity to construct proofs, to understand and follow mathematical proofs, to understand the need for justification, and to be able to distinguish valid justifications from invalid justifications? This is not discordant with discussions about classroom culture or mathematical reasoning but means reflecting about these phrases in combination with each other and specifically thinking about them from a mathematical perspective.

We're going to show you two different pieces of videotape—one very basic and one more complicated. Both are from my third-grade classroom.

The purpose of looking at this tape is to give a concrete example of young children talking with each other in a group about a mathematical idea and analyzing how these ideas are crucial to the resources required to teach. What do the videos cause you to see about the classroom and what do they make you think about the mathematics that teachers might need to know to establish and maintain a classroom culture in which mathematical reasoning is central?

We invite you to think about the tape, to make comments, and to talk to each other.

INTRODUCTORY COMMENTS BY BASS

I came into the work as a mathematician, and my role is essentially the same as the assignment for the workshop, to look for the mathematics entailed in the core tasks of teaching, the kinds of problems a teacher has to solve, design of lessons, interpretations of student thinking and work, and how to assess whether to pursue an idea or return to the lesson plan. Many of these decisions entail mathematical knowledge and considerations, and the idea is to try to discern what that mathematics was, to place it in a larger mathematical context. The problem is how to look at these core tasks of teaching.

The idea of doing this is compatible with the work of a university mathematician. The courses that we teach—for example, our calculus courses—are, in fact, designed to serve professional communities, like engineers, or economists or biologists. We do, in fact, look at how, in practice, they use mathematics, and we design curricula to meet those needs. Somehow, however, in teaching teachers about mathematics, we don't seem to have looked carefully at how the mathematics is actually used in practice. We treat it as a disembodied subject matter to be imported by the teacher, and the very complicated and difficult process of importation, which entails considerable knowledge in its own right, is not part of

the picture. So, the method used here was to start with a site of practice, analyze mathematics in use, and pull out curricular and epistemological ideas from that use.

As a mathematician, this was new for me, because I'm accustomed to analytical reasoning where the truth of things ultimately derives from the meanings of the words. Here I had to pay attention to data and try to justify claims not by deduction but by evidence from those data. I took that quite seriously; and, at the outset, I fully expected to come up with a list of mathematical topics which I would embed in somewhat larger recognizable domains of mathematics as interesting packets of knowledge that would be helpful for teachers. What I want to emphasize is that we're paying attention to something that is not a mathematical topic in the typical sense. It was not drawn from rhetoric of the standards or from my own inclination to pay close attention to the importance of proofs. Rather, it was something that was driven by observation of the data, by looking at what was actually happening in this particular class and giving more specification to what these words mean.

We have two objectives. One is to explain what it means to create a community of reasoning among a class of third-graders and, secondly, to find out what mathematical resources a teacher might bring into play to create such a community. Now, that may be a characteristic of this particular class, but the presumption, I think, in any research of this kind is that close observation of a complex enactment of teaching suggests principles that are applicable much more broadly. In a way, one of the surprising and, to me, very satisfying outcomes was that the description of mathematical reasoning we found appropriate to third-graders—and I emphasize that this was based on observation—was completely consonant with the way you would describe mathematical reasoning among professional mathematicians.

Let me now turn to some of the ideas we found. This is a conceptual framing, and again I want to emphasize that it was drawn from the data. What is reasoning? It's one of the principal instruments for developing mathematical understanding and for the creation of new mathematical knowledge. We're thinking here of the reasoning of justification, warrants for claims, as opposed, for example, to the reasoning of the inquiry in discovery. Such reasoning, in our view, requires two foundations. One is a body of prior knowledge, either inherited or assumed, on which to stand as a point of departure. You can't get something for nothing. You have to buy it with some sort of currency. And this foundation furnishes the elementary bonds in chains of reasoning. The other is the linguistic medium and the elementary and often unarticulated rules of logic with which to formulate claims and the networks of relationships that are offered to justify them. A classroom dedicated to creating a culture of shared mathematical reasoning has both of these foundations: the basic common knowledge and the linguistic structure and conventions for mathematical communication. Both of these must be made part of the community consciousness of students, as well as the teachers.

First, let's talk about the basic common knowledge. This is defined relative to the community of reasoners. If these were professional mathematicians, this base might consist of an axiom system for some mathematical structure like Euclidean geometry or group theory, simply admitted as given, plus a body of previously developed and publicly accepted mathematical knowledge derived from these axioms. In

another setting, a university instructor who lists prerequisites for a course is defining part of the presumed common knowledge in the environment of that course.

In a third-grade classroom of children with diverse backgrounds, this base of common knowledge is at first not wholly known or formed. It is determined and shaped through ongoing empirical inquiry, observation, and orchestration by the teacher. The children's knowledge comes from a mix of prior experience and mathematical learning, and it grows through the learning in the classroom. The crucial issue is the following: How can one justify a mathematical claim? One way is to simply assert it dogmatically with whatever force of authority its advocates can evoke; and, in fact, this is a course open to and often taken by teachers of young children. But that route is the antithesis of what we mean by mathematical reasoning. On the other hand, the process of reasoning itself typically consists of a sequence of steps, each of which has the form of justifying one claim by invocation of another, to which the first claim is logically reduced. This process, which merely transforms one claim into another is not a vicious circle because the reduced claim is typically of a more accessible and elementary nature, and in a finite number of steps, one arrives at a claim which requires no further warrant. Why? It's universally persuasive in the reasoning community because it's part of the base of common knowledge. Thus, the base of common knowledge defines the primordial steps requiring no further warrant, which form the kind of stepping stones of an argument. As we like to say, it defines the granularity of acceptable mathematical reasoning in that particular environment. The base of common knowledge consists of knowledge of certain facts and concepts, of the meanings of mathematical terms and expressions, of procedures and resources for calculations and problem solving. It is always present in either latent or active forms, and it may be passive and only implicit in either the students' or the teachers' talk. It plays a role for both teachers and students in a classroom where mathematical reasoning is expected.

First, consider the teacher. The teacher must both uncover and build students' common mathematical knowledge. Being attuned to the class's base of common knowledge, it is crucial to understand where the students are and where they're prepared to head. The teacher's explanations, for example, depend on a close coordination with students' current base of accepted knowledge. At the same time that such coordination is important, teachers also must work to establish and extend this base of common knowledge. Decisions about when to introduce a term or an idea, when to make a distinction, and when to raise a challenge—all of these are fundamental in helping students to build and extend what they know. Working to extend not only individual students' knowledge but also what is commonly accepted among them is central to the teacher's work.

Next, what about the students? What importance does it have for students? We see two dimensions in this. First, when a child or the teacher reasons before the class, the elements on which the argument is built are presumed to be part of the base of common knowledge. Whether this knowledge is, in fact, common is an empirical question and one of active concern to an investigation by the teacher. The plausible presumption of its commonality is a working premise of the reasoning, and this very process of reasoning, with suitable interventions by the teacher,

can, in fact, help plant such presumed common knowledge into the common base when it's not already solidly there. Independently of this empirical question, an important objective of the teacher is to encourage children to build mathematical arguments on the basis of presumed common knowledge, for this is an important part of teaching them what it means to reason mathematically. In the course of this, the teacher also wants to make the evolving base of common knowledge a part of the class' consciousness—that is to say, to make it common.

So, now let me turn to the other component of this construct, mathematical language. We understand language in a very broad and inclusive sense, comprising all of the linguistic infrastructure that supports mathematical communication, with its requirements for precision, clarity, and the economy of expression. It includes the nature and role of definitions in mathematics, the nature and rules for manipulation of symbolic notation, and the compression of concepts afforded by their uses. It is important to recognize disagreement that stems from divergent or unreconciled uses of terminology from disagreement that is rooted in substantive and conflicting mathematical claims. The ability to do this requires a sensitivity to the nature and role of language in mathematics. We're concerned, as well, with the transformation of mathematics embedded in experiential settings, described informally with common language, into more formal mathematical expression susceptible to efficient mathematical manipulation. We emphasize that mathematical language is not simply an inert canon inherited and learned from a distant past. It is, as well, a medium in which learners, as mathematicians, act and create. Notations are introduced to reduce computation and manipulation to manageable proportions. How and when to do this is an important skill and one needing and deserving to be taught. Definitions are not simply delivered names to be memorized. They are seeded or conceived in concepts; they gestate through active investigation and reflection, and when they come to term, they are born out of a need to describe a rich or important idea in need of easy reference to facilitate its entry into common discourse. These are what we call emergent definitions. The decision about what to name and when and how to name it calls for a developed mathematical sensibility and discrimination, one that teachers of mathematics at entry level would be well served to acquire. Another persuasive role of definitions, not always recognized as such, arises when a notion given meaning in one context is then given expanded meaning in an enlarged context, a process that we refer to as expanding definitions. This raises important questions about the criteria, usually left only implicit, by which such extensions are made.

Now, all of this may seem fairly esoteric and a bit simplistic to mathematicians, but let me illustrate how these notions can play out in the early grades. Take, for example, the study of number—basic number systems. The children typically first encounter whole numbers, and they may have some informally developed sense, say, of even and odd, and they probably could quickly decide correctly whether a given small whole number is even or odd. At first, they usually have no formalized definition of these notions and typically lack, for example, the unit-digit criteria for recognizing evenness or oddness. Eventually, they may be led to some working definition, say, of even numbers as those that can be evenly divided into two groups with none left over or, for example, that the numbers

alternate: even, odd, even, odd, etc. Perhaps they can be made to see that the unit digit controls this property. Later, when first introduced to positive and negative integers, they may be asked the question of whether zero or negative 3 is even or odd. Now, is this a question of finding mathematical truth? Mathematically, the answer is no, because at the moment, these notions don't have meaning in that environment. For them, at this moment, evenness or oddness of these numbers has yet to be defined. The issue is, rather, how should these notions be defined for such numbers and by what criteria.

One can try to apply a working definition of even in this larger number domain, but then various questions arise. Does the working definition of even make sense? What does it mean to divide negative 6 into two equal parts? Or there may be several equivalent definitions of even for whole numbers. In fact, there are. You can divide numbers into two equal parts, or you can separate them into pairs, with none left over, or you can apply the alternating definition. These are all quite distinct but in significant ways mathematically equivalent. So, if there are several definitions for even numbers, do these generalize to give a common notion for integers, and if so, should one prove this, and if not, how should one prioritize them?

Do evenness and oddness have reasonable meaning for fractions? Is one-and-three-quarters even or odd? The same questions are posed. We don't assign a meaning there and for exactly these kinds of reasons. What would the alternating definition mean for fractions? What would dividing into two equal parts mean in that setting? We don't encounter that. The decisions have already been made for us. We don't enter that domain, but if we did, we would see that these issues of expanding definitions do present themselves.

So, these notions have, at the moment, not yet been defined, and how should they be defined? To derive definitions, one course is to derive them from some model used to represent integers—for example, money and debt or an elevator building with many basements or a frog leaping back and forth on the number line. Alternatively, one might try to extend the operation to consider another mathematical notion, not only evenness or oddness but the very operations of arithmetic. Once you've defined what negative numbers are, what should addition and multiplication mean for them? At the moment, the issue is not what they are and how to discover what they are but, rather, how should one define them, and the criteria by which that's done involves significant mathematical considerations. It's not simply a matter of arbitrary convention.

Implicitly, the sort of criteria we use are those of preserving certain patterns of regularity. For example, the alternating definition extends in a very natural way to the negative numbers, but the notion of dividing something into equal parts or an equal number of pairs, or a whole into number of pairs with nothing left over, presents a different way of prolongation to the other domain. For example, when extending the notion of addition to negative numbers, you might want to preserve certain mathematical properties like the distributive law with respect to multiplication and addition, but arguments made about arithmetic with negative numbers, which invoke those properties, have tacitly made the presumption that the definition must be made in such a way as to preserve those properties, just as using exponential notation when the exponent is no longer an integer or a rational number

raises the question of what meaning should be assigned to it. You want to do this in such a way that you preserve the usual laws of exponentiation.

So, these are simply some illustrations of why questions of mathematical language, which at first may seem fairly sterile of content and seem to be merely a matter of convention, in fact involve, in the way one evolves and constructs such language, substantial mathematical issues. We're not trying to suggest in any sense that we think of this as something that happens without consideration for the mathematics and the tasks in which children are apt to engage.

I wanted to set the context about the sort of work students have been doing before we watch the tape, because you'll see their work on one of these problems. There are two clips from the same lesson, both taught early in the school year. So, you can see the beginning of efforts for the students to make mathematical justifications to one another. This is not a case of looking at a classroom that has a well-established culture yet, but you can see it beginning to emerge.

One of the problems the students worked on the first or second day of class was the coin problem, which is taken from the *Curriculum and Evaluation Standards* (NCTM, 1989, p. 24): "I have some pennies, nickels, and dimes in my pocket. I put three of the coins in my hand. How much money could I have?"

Another problem students did subsequent to that was a permutations problem involving taking the digits of the date, September 12 and the questions, how many 3-digit numbers can you make with the digits 9, 1, 2. They also worked with 2-digit and 4-digit numbers, and there, too, they were beginning in both of these problems to consider the question not just of answers but of how many solutions there were. How could you establish that you had all of the solutions? You can see some of the potential in these problems for creating the need for mathematical justification.

We're going to watch the problem, "Write number sentences for 10."

One issue is how problems get framed: What language is used; why number sentences; what does this actually mean. When I show this problem to people who aren't familiar with elementary classrooms, they actually don't know what the problem means and they don't like the wording of it very much at all. They would prefer the problem to say something like, "write arithmetic expressions that equal 10." The whole question about how you word things for students and when and how you make decisions to use different forms of mathematical language, less formal, more children-like is important. On the videotapes, you'll see cases both of following children's mathematical language and introducing more formal language.

So, this issue about language has to do with all the judgments that go into deciding when to use what kind of language. We're not advocating a particular point of view about that. We're simply saying that's an example of a site in which teachers reason and make decisions about the precision of mathematical language.

At first, students simply wrote two elementary problems, such as six plus four equals 10 or five plus five equals 10. They were only doing addition and only using two elements. After they've produced a few of these working by themselves, we collect some solutions, and the class is asked to think of some solutions to the problem that involve more than two numbers. As you view the video, consider the way in which the base of common knowledge and mathematical language

are brought to bear. It may allow you to see something about a class discussion that you might not otherwise see.

This classroom is in a school close to Michigan State University in which the children come from many different countries and speak many different languages. The question of language is interesting simply because it's also a very multicultural classroom. There are children who are second-language speakers, some of them quite limited English speakers. The class is the only third grade in the school. There are 19 students at this point in the year, which is just a function of how many third-graders there are in the school. Sometimes the classes were as large as 30 or 32. Sometimes they were as small as 17 or 19. The school was a very mobile environment. Children were coming in and out of the class, leaving the class, entering the class all throughout the year. It was not a stable kind of teaching environment.

At this point in the session, participants watched the videos. See Appendix E for transcripts.

I just want to make a couple of comments about this episode. It illustrates perfectly the early use of what we're calling the base of common knowledge of the children at that grade level to define, in this instance, the accepted granularity of reasoning and to have a child model, with the teacher's guidance, what it means to prove and communicate the proof of a mathematical claim. Kip, seizing the teacher's challenge to make sums with more than two terms, goes almost to the limit with his expression, one plus one plus one plus one plus one plus one plus one plus three equals 10. He probably got tired of repeating ones at the end and so finished off quickly with the three. Now, one objective of this task was to open up the children's knowledge of, and skills with, basic arithmetic. The immediate verification of Kip's formula was not something to be presumed within easy reach of the children—that is to say, not part of their basic common knowledge. Perhaps for a fifth-grade class, this judgment would have been different. A young child's initial sense of addition comes from counting, which is adding one term at a time. Adding many terms at once or adding two terms both larger than one is a more complex operation, not only for children but also mathematically. Thus, once Kip's dramatic formula was presented to the class, the culture of reasoning demanded that it be justified or proved in a manner appropriate to children at this level, and as a move toward creating the culture of reasoning, the teacher had the children publicly honor this mandate.

When Ranya is called upon to explain why Kip's formula equals 10, she first just recites the equation. The teacher presses on with, "But how could you prove that to someone who wasn't sure," introducing in the process the mathematical term "prove," which is a significant mathematical term that is later adopted as part of the children's vocabulary. Ranya replied that she counted, and she was then pushed further to make this counting public. "There's one, and the next one is two, and the next one is three," et cetera. In fact, it was presumably by this counting that Ranya had proved to herself that the formula was valid, and the teacher now required that this reasoning be made public to persuade the class, as well. The teacher then publicly validates Ranya's performance, and she later appeals to it as one of the early benchmarks for what it means to explain something in mathematics and not just to assert it.

Do students have the common knowledge that one plus one plus one . . . plus three is 10? At the beginning of the school year, what the children know and don't know about basic arithmetic is not really known to the teacher. The question is what is a safe level of assumption about their knowledge, and certainly, everyone, I think, would agree that counting by one is something that could be presumed of everyone.

In the second example, which is more complicated, the basis of the student argument is that you can add any number to the sum and subtract that same number from the sum and you get the same result. For example, any number plus a lot of zeros minus that same number plus 10 equals 10. There's a predictable result.

To contextualize this segment a bit, this is in September, at the beginning of the school year, and this is the third of several tasks that had been presented to the class. The first one was the coin problem; the second one was the permutation problem.

One thing to keep in mind is what was the purpose of these early tasks? One, since there was not a clear knowledge by the teacher about what the students knew and what their level of facility with the curriculum of the course was, the task had to be accessible to children with a variety of levels of knowledge and skill and, at the same time, challenging. There should be entry points with different levels of mathematical sophistication and challenge. Second, the tasks should involve some serious mathematics and engage the children in some of the material that would be part of the course. Third, the tasks should provide context in which to develop this culture of mathematical reasoning. Overall, the tasks were designed to expose some of the basic common knowledge which the teacher was in the process of trying to discover.

Thus, the tasks provided not only work for the kids but also work for the teacher to discover what they knew. The first two problems, the coin problem and the permutation problem, were problems of a combinatorial character, and one important feature was that they admitted multiple solutions. In both of those problems, the number of solutions was finite, and the students could empirically generate lists of answers, until finally, they exhausted them all. When asked whether they had all the solutions, the students decided empirically that they did. When asked why, they would say, "Well, we keep coming up with the same answers over again," or, "I looked at so-and-so's list and she didn't have anything that I didn't have already." Essentially they were making an empirical argument, a kind of scientific or probabilistic claim, not a mathematical argument. It was the first encounter as a class with the challenge to try to mathematically prove a claim, "do you have a full set of possible solutions to this problem?"

In that sense, the third problem was different in two important respects. First, this was a problem not only with multiple solutions but with infinitely many, and so, it presented an opportunity to see how the students encountered the notion of the infinite and what their disposition would be toward that. Second, unlike the combinatorial problems with coins and with permutations, the terrain of the problem was the central domain of arithmetic, which is what the mathematics curriculum is about at that level. Making up number sentences that equal 10 opens the doorway to essentially all the arithmetic operations and all the things the curriculum wants to do with them. In some sense, the students in this process are not only going to expose what they know and so define this sort of basic common knowledge but begin to show the edges of their common knowledge. They'll make constructions where they falter and, in some sense, identify the point where the teachers wants to then develop the curriculum to expand what this basically is all about.

REFERENCE

National Council of Teachers of Mathematics. (1989). *Curriculum and evaluation standards for school mathematics.* Reston, VA: Author.

Reaction to the Presentation by Deborah Ball and Hyman Bass

James Lewis

We have all been charged with spending the day exploring the question, "What mathematical knowledge does it take to teach well?" The answer to that question depends, in part, on how a teacher approaches teaching. If the task at hand is learning to divide fractions, solving, for example, the problem $1\frac{3}{4}$ divided by $\frac{1}{2}$, it takes far less mathematical knowledge to tell students to "invert and multiply" than it takes to make sure students understand why this procedure leads to a correct answer.

In their presentation, Ball and Bass are interested in a slightly different question, namely "What mathematical knowledge does it take to teach children to reason mathematically?" One obvious answer is that it takes quite a bit more mathematical knowledge, and this is certainly underscored by the videotapes that were shown as part of the presentation.

Watching the tape of Deborah Ball teaching a class of third-grade students, it becomes clear that she is attempting to establish a classroom culture in which mathematical reasoning is called for. In her classroom, she changes the core question from "What is the answer?" to "Why is the answer correct?" There is no

doubt that this places a much greater demand on the teacher than would a more traditional approach of demonstrating a process for solving a problem and then having children practice very similar problems until they have mastered the technique. It seems to me the contrast is a bit like the difference between an outdoorsman walking through a familiar wooded area and a tourist hiking an unfamiliar trail. The tourist, and the elementary teacher with minimal knowledge of mathematics, is quickly lost once "off the trail."

In her presentation, Ball identified three responsibilities that a teacher must accept if the teacher is to help students reason mathematically. The teacher must

- uncover the students' current base of common knowledge;
- establish and extend the students' base of common knowledge; and
- model and guide the construction of acceptable mathematical arguments.

An analysis of the videotape of Ball in her third-grade classroom shows her efforts to be sure that the students have a base of common knowledge and that the students have access to a common language. At the beginning of the videotape, Ball asks her students to "think of a number sentence that uses more than two numbers" and to "make a number sentence that equals 10, but has more than two numbers *adding* to 10" (emphasis mine). I saw that as two separate questions, but Ball's students seemed to have no trouble interpreting the charge to be a search for various expressions that equal 10.

The answer offered by one of the students was to add one to itself a sufficient number of times to get 10. Ball immediately challenges the class to explain why the answer is 10. When one student essentially repeats the assertion that "one plus one plus one . . . equals 10," Ball points out that the student has only read the answer, not given a justification for the answer.

Later, when one student says that "100 divided by 10 equals 10," the class is again challenged to explain the answer. One answer offered is, "Lin said her mom taught her . . . about dividing by." Relying on what mom said is also found to be an insufficient explanation. At this point on the videotape a number of students offer ideas that appear to have some depth of understanding behind them (e.g., since 10 times 5 equals 50 then surely 50 divided by 5 equals 10). At this point, Ball records one of the assertions the students have been discussing (50 divided by 5 equals 10), but she stresses that the idea does not yet belong on the list of facts that everyone understands as part of the class's base of common knowledge.

In a later class, Ball introduces the term "conjecture" and offers the class a definition of the term. She uses one of the student's number sentences as a conjecture and leads the class in a discussion of why the conjecture is correct. The basic idea under consideration by the class is that not only is $(200 - 200) + 10 = 10$ but that one can replace 200 by any other number in this sentence and get another number sentence that equals 10. (Note: I can't resist adding the parenthesis signs but the students seem comfortable with expressions like $200 - 200 + 10$ and everyone seems to know what to do.)

My concern with proper notation reinforces some of the challenges that the teacher faces on a daily basis. The teacher must be able to hear what a student is saying (or might be saying); the teacher must decide what is mathematically significant in the discussion; and the teacher must decide when to introduce new mathematical notation and when to couch the discussion in the language of the children. This particular videotape is rich in concepts such as the term conjecture, the discussion about what does or does not constitute a proof, and the basic language of mathematical reasoning used in the classroom. At the same time, there is a tolerance of imprecise language used by the children that would be unacceptable in my college classroom.

At the end of the videotape showing in this session, Ball is clearly modeling and guiding the "construction of acceptable mathematical arguments" when she introduces the concept of a variable and the sentence $(x - x) + 10 = 10$ as being valid for any value x.

I found the videotape of Deborah Ball teaching third-grade students to be fascinating. She clearly was establishing a classroom culture that called for mathematical reasoning, and her students demonstrated a sophistication regarding the need to prove statements rather than accept them on faith. As a mathematician teaching at the university level, I have very little knowledge of third-grade classrooms, but I suspect that similar classrooms are in short supply. I am also convinced that the mathematical knowledge required to teach in this manner is far superior to the mathematical knowledge that most of our students have when we certify them as ready to teach mathematics at the elementary school level.

Investigating Teaching Practice: What Mathematical Knowledge, Skills, and Sensibilities Does It Take?

These sessions were designed to focus on looking at practice as a way to identify the mathematical knowledge needed by teachers. Participants took part in two of four concurrent sessions. In each session, they engaged in activities to help them see how teacher knowledge of mathematics is related to investigating tasks that teachers do in the practice of teaching. In each session, the objective was to work through the task as a teacher would, then reflect together about the mathematics teachers need to use in the context of doing the tasks.

SESSIONS

Analyzing Student Thinking
  Virginia Bastable, SummerMath for Teachers

Remodeling Mathematical Tasks
  Olga G. Torres, Tucson, Arizona Public Schools

Analyzing Student Work
  Michaele F. Chappell, University of South Florida

Managing Class Discussion
  Erick Smith, University of Illinois-Chicago

Analyzing Student Thinking

Virginia Bastable

SESSION GOALS

This session was designed to allow participants the opportunity to participate in one of the tasks of teaching and to analyze the kind of mathematical understandings, skills, and dispositions this task demands. For this session, the task of teaching being investigated was analyzing students' mathematical thinking.

The overarching questions posed to the participants were as follows:

- *What mathematical knowledge does a teacher need in order to follow, analyze, and evaluate the mathematical thinking of his/her students?*
- *What is the nature of the mathematical thinking that teachers must do as they make hypotheses about their students' mathematical ideas?*

OVERVIEW

The session was divided into two main components. The first part provided an opportunity for participants to follow the mathematical thinking of students as expressed in a teacher-written narrative. Participants read a five-page case titled

"Can you divide 39 into 5? Revisited" and discussed a set of focus questions in both small and large groups. During this part of the discussion, the conversation was designed to allow participants to share and debate their ideas about the mathematical thinking of the students described in the print case.

The second component of the session was an opportunity to reflect on the experience to make more general statements about the kinds of mathematical knowledge required to do this kind of work. After the discussion based on the print case, participants were given five minutes to write about their experience based on this prompt: What kinds of mathematical knowledge, skill, and sensibilities did you call upon as you worked to understand the mathematical thinking of the children in the print case? The session concluded with a discussion of this question.

ACTIVITY
CASE STUDY: 39 ÷ 5 OR 5 ÷ 39

The action of sharing provides a context in which children can learn about the meaning of division. It also allows them to sort out some of the complexities of dividing whole numbers: What happens when the numbers don't divide evenly? Is it even possible to divide a larger number into a smaller? What sense could that possibly have?

In this activity, we visit the same class twice as it explores what $5 \div 39$ might mean. In the spring of fourth grade, the students think about the question only in terms of whole numbers. What contexts are modeled by $5 \div 39$ and what would be the result of dividing 5 by 39? When they return to the question several months later as fifth-graders, they are ready to consider their answer in terms of fractions. But their explorations now raise a new set of fascinating questions. The class struggles with the question as described by the teacher.

Participants read the scenario below, "Can You Divide 39 into 5? Revisited." They were asked to consider these questions:

- As you read about these students' discussions, what are the ideas about division that are highlighted for you?
- What new ideas must be entertained as the children extend their work to the realm of fractions?
- And what ideas are you left to work through for yourself?

Can You Divide 39 Into 5? Revisited

[A Teacher's Reflection on a Lesson (Schifter, Bastable, & Russell, 1999, pp. 77-82)]

This year I am in the fortunate position to have moved up a grade together with my class. The children I had last year in fourth-grade are with me again this year as fifth-graders. I am very pleased. They are delightful children, a pleasure to be with two years in a row. At the beginning of the year, we had much less work to do to establish norms of being in class together; there was already a sense of community among us. The several children who were new needed a couple of weeks to catch on, but they had good models in their classmates. This is especially helpful since we have some difficult circumstances in which to work. For example, I have a class of 28 children that is very unbalanced genderwise: 21 boys and 7 girls! If I had been meeting this group for the first time, we would have had to do a lot of work to make sure that the girls had a voice in the class. I still have to be careful, but in general the girls feel at ease, even if they are in the minority.

As far as math class is concerned, most of us already knew what it means to have a mathematical discussion. And it's fascinating to me to have the opportunity to see how ideas develop from one year to the next.

In November we were working on division. We had just finished a few sessions in which we looked at remainders in different contexts and saw them expressed as decimals or fractions. We also considered contexts in which it made sense to round up or down to the next whole number. Now I wanted to explore an extension-situation in which there are more sharers than the number of items to be shared.

I asked the class to think about 3 kids sharing 2 candy bars. Just as the discussion began, Joe looked puzzled and recalled a conversation that we had last year. He claimed that the class reached the conclusion that we couldn't divide a larger number into a smaller number. As he presented the facts of last year's discussion, others began to nod. They were recalling the conversation and the contexts we used in our $5 \div 39$ controversy. Now they were looking at me accusingly. How could I be asking them to divide 2 candy bars among 3 kids if we already "knew" that we couldn't do it.

From *Developing Mathematical Ideas, Number and Operations, part 2: Making Meaning for Operations Casebook*, by Schifter, Bastable, & Russell. © 1999 by Dale Seymour Publications. Used by permission.

This situation again raised the issue for me of leaving students in the middle of a misunderstanding. Would they have understood any more if last year I had told them that you can divide 39 into 5? Would they have been as invested in today's discussion? Were they now having an intuitive sense that we could do it?

Although it was not my planned entry point into this new division piece—I had intended to work with easier numbers—we stuck with 5 ÷ 39 because the class had an investment in it. I began by writing on the board "5 ÷ 39" and "39 ÷ 5."

> ANTHONY: I think that 39 ÷ 5 will be 7 remainder 4, but I think that 5 ÷ 39 will make a decimal number.

I wonder if he is thinking of a number less than one and I wonder why he went to a decimal rather than a fraction. I was surprised because fractions "look" more like "less than one" than decimals do—at least they do to me.

> JACK: I think that you will end up with a fraction of a number because, well, because, 5 and 39—you can't divide 5 by 39 equally. I think it's going to be a number below 0.

I think that Jack is headed in the right direction, especially when he says "a fraction of a number." I wonder aloud about the answer being a fraction number and then about the idea that it would be below 0. I believe that if I had stuck with my original 2 ÷ 3 problem in the candy-bar context, this might have been easier to visualize. But I don't know if the students would have been so invested; they have a sense of ownership over the 5 and 39 problem.

> AL: I agree with Anthony but not with Jack. We had some story problems where the answers were decimals, but they were not below 0. I think we could say that 39 ÷ 5 could be a decimal number. [Al goes to the board and shows how he solved for a quotient of 7.8. I think that this is what Anthony means.]

Anthony says that this is not what he means, but indicates that he doesn't feel ready yet to explain. Al used decimals to solve 39 ÷ 5, but did not try 5 ÷ 39 and did not address the crucial point of using a decimal to name a number smaller than 1. I'm pretty sure that this is where Anthony's going, but I respect his decision to remain quiet for now.

> DARREL: I think 39 can't go into 5. I mean it can go into it, but it's going to be a fraction; it's got to be a fraction. A larger number into a smaller number—5 can go into 39, but there's a remainder. No, it's not a remainder; it's not a number.

I really don't get what Darrel is saying. Does he think that fractions or decimals are only remainders? Why does he think that it's not a number?

> GONSON: I agree with Anthony and with Jack because 39 divided by 5—5 divided by 39. . . .

Gonson repeats the two problems four or five times. There's something that he's trying to sort out. However, the numbers removed from context clearly have little meaning for him.

> JOE: 5 divided by 39 is going to be a smaller number. You got 39 people and 5 candies.

I stop to ask the class which one of the notations—"39 ÷ 5" or "5 ÷ 39"—expresses Joe's story. I want to see if we are at least making a connection between the context and the correct notation. Most of the students didn't get that last year.

Raymond chooses the correct notation and explains that the answer would be pieces of candy bars. (YES!)

> RAYMOND: So, if each kid was going to get equal shares, they would have to cut the 5 candy bars into little equal pieces.

> TEACHER: Can you name those equal pieces?

> RAYMOND: They might be candy bars.

TEACHER: Can you name the fraction that they might be?

RAYMOND: [After a long pause] They wouldn't be able to do it.

(DARN!)

We stop now to take a class poll. How many people think that you can do the problem 5 ÷ 39 and how many think no, you can't. The results: Yes, 13; No, 15.

After a pause, Joe says that he wants to change his "no" to a "yes." He starts to explain that you cut each bar into 7 equal pieces and then asks if he can go to the board. He draws circles to show the 39 people and then draws 5 rectangles for the 5 candy bars. He shows that partitioning 2 candy bars into sevenths will yield 14 pieces and then, without making the lines, indicates that partitioning 4 candy bars will produce 28 pieces. He pauses and sees then that the fifth candy bar will give him a total of 35 pieces. He then draws in lines to show that he has cut it into 11 pieces. Now he's satisfied because he has a total of 39 pieces.

Cynthia quickly responds that this representation couldn't be correct because it isn't equal shares. She seems sure of it. There are 4 rectangles with sevenths and only one with elevenths. "That's a problem," she says.

As Cynthia talks, Valerie goes to the board and points to the elevenths.

VALERIE: Nobody would want one of these small pieces. I think there's something about Joe's solution that feels right, but something also seems wrong.

MARIBEL: I think that Joe is on the right track because each person would only get a really small piece, not anywhere like a whole candy bar. But Valerie is right, too, because the shares that he drew aren't the same for each person.

LINDA: If I cut each of the 5 candy bars into 39 pieces and then give each kid one piece from each candy bar, you could have each kid have $\frac{5}{39}$ of a candy bar.

Linda wants to go to the board and draw hers. She draws 5 rectangles divided up into 39 equal boxes. She is displaying some confidence and some clear mathematical thinking that I have not seen before.

ANTHONY: I think the same thing, that each person will get one piece from the first candy bar and one piece from the second and then from each one after that and will end up with 5 little pieces, so 5/39.

AL: I was thinking that if you wanted you could take 5 from each candy bar over and over again until you were done, but I think that I know that because of the drawing that Linda did.

Al has learned something from the discussion; Linda's work made an impact on him. I'm glad to hear him acknowledge her.

We ended the discussion right there on that day but continued a few days later. Since I happened to have three visitors on that day (three colleagues from the professional development project I'm in), I divided the class into four groups. Each group worked with an adult to come up with a way to show 5 ÷ 39. Time passed very quickly, and we had little time for groups to report back to the whole class.

Joe and Cynthia said that they didn't really have a name for their solution, but they were ready to defend their thinking. Cynthia went to the board and drew the following diagram:

1	2	3	4
5	6	7	8

9	10	11	12
13	14	15	16

17	18	19	20
21	22	23	24

25	26	27	28
29	30	31	32

33	34	35	36
37	38	39	

It was time to end class. Time was short but we were clearly not finished yet. Jack looked at Cynthia's diagram and asked what forty fortieths has to do with 5 ÷ 39. I asked the students to think about that for their homework.

When we returned to the problem the next day, people were feeling refreshed again, ready to take on Cynthia's diagram. While her drawing helped some of the students picture the problem, it raised even more questions:

- What is the last piece called? Is it "$\frac{1}{8}$" or "$\frac{1}{40}$"?
- What's the whole?
- What happens if the last piece is divided into 39 pieces? What if it is divided into 40 pieces?
- Do we know what $\frac{5}{39}$ means?
- Is "slightly more than $\frac{1}{8}$" a better answer than $\frac{5}{39}$ because it's clearer even though it's less exact?
- When we say $\frac{1}{8}$, it's $\frac{1}{8}$ of what? When we say $\frac{1}{40}$, it's $\frac{1}{40}$ of what?
- If we cut the last piece into fortieths, each person gets $\frac{1}{8}$ and $\frac{1}{40}$ of $\frac{1}{8}$. What happens to the extra fortieth? Do we keep on dividing it? (This is where we discussed the "piece," the "sliver," and the "crumb.")

Some of these questions I need to sort out for myself.

FOCUS QUESTIONS

1. Consider the arguments of Anthony, Jack, Al, Darrel, Joe, and Raymond. What might each of them be thinking about division, decimals, about fractions, about what a number is? What is correct about their thinking? What ideas might they be missing?
2. Joe changes his mind from his earlier comments. Explain what it is that Joe now understands? What is he missing?
3. Valerie, Maribel, and Linda offer ideas. Explain the mathematics you see in each case.
4. Joe and Cynthia offer a different kind of representation for the 5 ÷ 39 problem.
5. What is correct about their diagram? What is confusing about it?
6. What is revealed about the students' thinking by the questions that are posed at the end of the text?

DISCUSSION SUMMARY

In the first part of this discussion, participants considered the mathematical thinking of the students represented in the print case. The conversation had several dimensions:

- clarifying exactly what was said in the print case;
- making hypotheses about what aspects of mathematics the students understood;
- making hypotheses concerning the source of the students' confusion;
- locating the mathematical logic in the student's thinking.

The group also spent part of the time discussing the pedagogical aspects of the case.

The issues raised during this part of the discussion were specifically tied to the mathematics of the case and might not at first glance seem to be relevant to the larger question of what kinds of mathematical knowledge and sensibilities are needed for effective mathematics teaching. However, the groups' responses to the more general question were based on the specific issues raised during the case discussion, and, therefore, they are included in this report.

The list provides a description of the mathematical issues considered by the class described in the print case. For a particular mathematical situation, this list illustrates the range of mathematics and knowledge about the nature of mathematics and mathematical reasoning that a teacher must have to negotiate this kind of classroom conversation. I invite the reader to participate in a second level of conversation while reading the list and to ask what it indicates about the nature of mathematical understanding teachers need to have.

- Division can be interpreted as partitioning, as repeated subtraction, or as a missing factor.
- The answer to a division problem can be expressed as a fraction.
- Interpreting remainders in a division situation is dependent on the context.
- Fractions can be interpreted as parts of wholes, as answers to division problems, as units of measure, or as missing factors.
- While $5 \times \frac{1}{39}$ is numerically equivalent to $\frac{5}{39}$, these two expressions can represent different ideas.
- A numerical problem may have multiple representations.
- Representation is both a tool for expressing ideas and a tool that allows ideas to be manipulated.
- The transfer from an abstract problem to a concrete situation that exemplifies the problem can be a support for learning.
- When an abstract problem is related to

a concrete situation, there must be consistency between the real life example and the mathematical model.
- The nature of the inverse relationship between multiplication and division seems more complicated when remainders are expressed as whole numbers.
- Smaller numbers may have made the problem so easy that the mathematical issue (examining what happens when a smaller number is divided by a larger number) would not have been addressed or even encountered.
- Analysis of why a particular approach was incorrect was instrumental in developing a correct approach. The students' mathematical arguments examining what was wrong with the first-offered solution provided the means to refine the solution.

It is important to acknowledge that the discussion of issues was rich, energetic, and quite interesting. In fact, with both groups it was hard to turn our attention away from the specifics of the case to the more general question. To provide material for the second part of the discussion, group members were asked to write for a few minutes reflecting on this question, "What mathematical knowledge, disposition towards mathematics, and mathematical understandings, did you call upon in order to participate in this activity of examining children's mathematical reasoning?" The conversation then continued but, because of the participants' written reflections, with a more general question now on the table: "What kinds of mathematical sensibilities do teachers need to have in order to be able to engage with their students in these ways?"

In some ways, the second-level conversation was still grounded in the content of the particular set of mathematical ideas that had been discussed earlier; but, even so, it is still useful to consider some of these statements as particulars of more general principles. As you read the following list of mathematical sensibilities and knowledge needed by teachers compiled by the groups, I again invite the reader to participate in the task we had before us. Use the list as an opportunity to formulate responses to these questions: " What kind of mathematical knowledge is necessary for teachers to be able to engage with their students' mathematical thinking? What understandings about the nature of mathematics and mathematical reasoning must they have?"

- Have a variety of mental images of $5 \div 39$; specifically, both a measurement and partitive view of division.
- Understand the connections (both what is the same and what is different) between the computation $5 \div 39$ and the number represented by $\frac{5}{39}$.
- Understand the conceptions underlying $\frac{5}{39}$ and 5 times $\frac{1}{39}$ can be very different, even if these two express the same numerical value.
- Understand numbers between 0 and 1.
- Realize that mathematical generalizations are true only for a given domain and that statements that are true for one set of numbers may not be true for another. (For example, "You can't divide a smaller number by a larger number" is in fact true for the domain of whole numbers.)
- Understand that mathematical generalizations must be revisited (and often revised and extended) as the domain under consideration expands.
- Take into account one's own (or the teacher's) beliefs about mathematics.

REFLECTIONS

As I examined these lists and reflected on the discussions, I noted that ideas about the nature of mathematics and mathematical reasoning were prominent. While the lists clearly contained significant mathematical content, that content was described within statements of mathematical relationships and mathematical connections. Beliefs about the nature of mathematics were seen as equally important. Expressed in general terms, our discussions implied that to engage effectively with their students' mathematical thinking, teachers must do the following:

- *View mathematics as the development of ideas that are interconnected.* For example, as we worked to follow the student thinking, we explored the connections between division and fractions, the inverse relationship between multiplication and division, and the similarities and differences between the set of whole numbers and numbers that are between 0 and 1. This leads to the following implications for teacher preparation: Mathematical content should not be separated into individual topics; the ways preservice teachers encounter mathematics as learners is significant; and understanding how an idea develops over time (and across grade levels) is necessary.
- *Recognize that building mathematical knowledge is an iterative process of making, testing, and revising generalizations.* For example, in our discussion we noted that statements, such as "You can't divide a larger number into a smaller number" or "You can't take a larger number from a smaller one" are not absolutely true or false but rather apply over some domains and not

others. This leads to the following implications for teacher preparation: Preservice teachers need experiences to identify the mathematical generalizations they hold and to examine them over a variety of number domains; preservice teachers need the opportunity to experience learning mathematics as a series of ever expanding generalizations, understanding the assumptions in each.

- *Recognize the power of mathematical reasoning; that is, have the expectation that mathematics is a coherent field that makes sense and is derivable by reason.* One caveat: Some mathematical symbols and forms are agreed on by convention and therefore need to be communicated directly. For instance, in our discussion we noted that the meaning of the division sign is something that is a convention. There are mathematical ideas to be worked through regarding the meaning of division, but there is also a convention by which division calculation is indicated as in $39 \div 5$ and $5 \div 39$. For example, in our conversation analyzing the flow of the class discussion in the print case, it was noted the first student solution that was offered was incorrect; however, the mathematical analysis of what was incorrect in the solution moved the class along to a deeper understanding. This leads to the following implications for teacher preparation: preservice teachers need to become aware of and develop their own abilities as mathematical reasoners; preservice teachers need opportunities to sort out which mathematical symbols and forms are conventions and which are amenable to reason; and preservice teachers need opportunities to develop, follow, and critique mathematical arguments.

- *Represent mathematical ideas in a variety of forms: words, diagrams, objects, and symbols.* For example, in our discussion we talked about mental images of the operations; we drew diagrams to express mathematical ideas; and we expressed ideas through language. This leads to the following implications for teacher preparation: When preservice teachers encounter mathematics content, they need to have experience with a variety of forms—not only symbolic representations; mathematics class should be a forum for communicating mathematical ideas in both writing and speech.

- *Appreciate that mathematics, while abstract, is often used to model problems that are based in real-world situations and that one operation may model a variety of situations.* For example, in our discussion we drew upon a range of meanings for division and for fractions, and we examined the connections between those meanings and a variety of problem contexts. This leads to the following implications for teacher preparation: Preservice teachers need to have experiences linking their current conceptions of the operations to problem contexts and vice versa; mathematics course work should include applications or math modeling components.

Finally, I should note these statements are not unusual to those familiar with the National Council of Teachers of Mathematics *Standards*. However, it is important to show the way those ideas are connected to the specific discussions that took place at the conference and to highlight the implications of those ideas for preservice teacher preparation.

CONCLUSION

Although the writing of this report and my attendance at the conference has generated many questions for me, there is one in particular that I would like to highlight. It is clear we cannot expect any undergraduate program to include all of the mathematics content that preservice teachers will need to draw on over the course of their careers. This is especially true if we commit ourselves to providing opportunities for preservice teachers to explore mathematical ideas, develop as mathematical reasoners, and deeply engage with a subset of mathematical ideas to determine the ways children make sense of those ideas over time. Even while I expect that once such ideas about mathematics and its nature are understood, teachers would be in a position to continue to learn mathematics through the process of teaching, I am still left asking, "What is the set of ideas around which the undergraduate experience should be built? What set of mathematical ideas offers the most power to the undergraduate students?" These are questions we should continue to ponder.

REFERENCES

Schifter, D., Bastable, V., & Russell, S. J. (with Yaffee, L., Lester, J. B., & Cohen, S.) (1999). *Developing mathematical ideas, number and operations part 2: Making meaning for operations casebook.* Parsippany, NJ: Dale Seymour.

National Council of Teachers of Mathematics. (1989). *Curriculum and evaluation standards for school mathematics.* Reston, VA: Author.

Remodeling Mathematical Tasks

Olga G. Torres

SESSION GOALS

This session was designed to allow participants to participate in a task of teaching and to focus on the mathematical knowledge needed to do that task. The task of teaching under investigation was remodeling mathematical tasks. The following question was posed:

- *What mathematical knowledge does a teacher need to remodel a mathematical task to make the task simpler, to broaden student access, to add another dimension to the task to move students forward in their thinking, or to use the same concept in a slightly different form to provide another experience with the idea?*

OVERVIEW

The chief activity of the workshop was a variation on a riddle, "Coins in the Purse." As successive clues were posted on the overhead projector, questions were asked so that the group could deduce the value of the coins in a change purse. To capture their mathematical insights and understandings for later discussions, partici-pants recorded their thinking on paper at every stage.

ACTIVITY

First, participants listened to the sounds the coins made when the coin purse was shaken, then the question, "What coins could I have in the coin purse?" was asked. This began a discussion of what coins were possible, given that the coins were U.S. currency.

Clue 1: There are six coins in my purse.

Question 1: What is the most money I could have?

Clue 2: There are only two different values of coins.

Question 2: What coins are possible and what could be some possible maximum amounts?

Some participants felt there was really only one answer to the question of possible maximum amounts, and some thought it possible to have several maximum amounts. Each was asked to explain their perspective. Some felt confusion would arise if statements were not clearly stated, and others stated that the maximum amount was relative to the possible combination of coins the student was considering.

It was interesting to observe how one group articulated that it was in the best interest of students to avoid confusion. But, narrowing the possibilities also narrowed student thinking. And from the other perspective, the broader the language, the more opportunity for students to be flexible with number. One choice was for the convenience of the teacher to be precise and get to the answer quickly, and the other choice was to allow the development of mathematical thinking on the students' part as they work at their solutions.

Clue 3: Only dimes and pennies are in my purse.

Question 3: What are the possibilities?

After time was given for participants to record all the possibilities on paper, the combinations were recorded on the overhead.

Clue 4: There are more dimes than pennies.

This clue eliminated some of the combinations that were generated from the previous clue, leaving two combinations, 5 dimes + 1 penny and 4 dimes + 2 pennies.

Clue 5: There is only one penny.

With this last clue, only one possible answer to the original question remained.

Participants were then asked to reflect individually on the mathematical knowledge they used to process the information given in the activity. After five minutes, they began to discuss their thoughts in small groups. The mathematics they identified included computation, value of coins, proportionality, combinations, inequalities, the logic of compared statements (conjunction), decimals, place value, and linear combinations. The mathematical processes included reasoning, systematic listing, and organization of information.

Using Liping Ma's terminology, participants were actually identifying many knowledge packages—a combination of mathematical understandings used in solving the problem. However, the contents of these packages became very difficult to identify. The packages were not made up of distinct parts, and it was more a case of "unraveling" the contents. The ideas were so intricately woven together that it was hard to identify the underlying mathematics embedded in each. At the same time, some of the mathematical ideas applied in the problem-solving experience by the participants were so well known and seemed so intuitive that the participants did not realize that the mathematics they used was once learned, for example, converting the number of coins into amounts of money. In other cases, it was difficult to break down a knowledge package because this is a new way of thinking. Some of us are so far removed from our initial learning of a concept that it is hard to visualize the essential components of the mathematical concept in the activity. The perception often exists that the ideas taught at the elementary level are simple and that it is easy to teach what students need to learn in these grades. The activity helped to make it apparent that anyone involved in teaching mathematics at the elementary level needs to confront the complexity of the apparently simple mathematical ideas these students need to acquire and develop.

A constant series of questions was

asked as knowledge packages were being identified: What are the essential understandings a learner must have to be able to

- have a sense of place value?
- count money?
- use operations? (addition, subtraction, division, and multiplication)
- represent something symbolically?
- establish equivalency?

Another way of questioning used to get at the underlying mathematics was, "If *the mathematics needed to determine whether two representations are equivalent* is a knowledge package, what are the contents of that package. What are its key pieces?"

It was interesting to note that the papers participants used to record their thinking held tremendous information about the reasoning process of the writer. Some made a table listing all the combinations of 6 coins in an orderly sequence and identified all the possible combinations (see Table 1).

Others randomly listed combinations that worked. And still others used different methods of reasoning. The fact that there were different ways to reason was not always immediately obvious to the participants because many pieces of knowledge were being used. Much discussion about the mathematics in the task occurred as participants became

aware of important "key pieces" contained in such general terms as "place value" or "counting money." Participants also commented on the danger of assuming that these key concepts are present in student/teacher knowledge bases.

Throughout this exercise, I was conscious of how important it is to know about key number concepts, such as inclusion, 1:1 correspondence, and conservation of number, and of how these concepts contribute to acquiring mathematical understandings. At the elementary level, it is critical to know these key concepts, which help provide the foundation for developing number and operation sense.

Participants were asked to remodel the task, identifying the purpose for the remodeled task. The following were among the suggestions:

- Make the task simpler to broaden student access. For example, instead of specifying the number of coins, ask how many ways there are to make $0.51.
- Add another dimension to the task to move students forward in their thinking. For example, specify the number of coins and ask the students to indicate what other information they would need to figure out the amount of money in the purse.
- Use the same concept in slightly different form to provide another experience with the idea. For example, use pattern blocks to find the number of each block.

The discussion of remodeling reinforced the need to recognize how important it was when engaged in remodeling a task to be cognizant of the key pieces that constitute the original "knowledge package." Participants acknowledged that aware-

Table 1. Coin Combinations

Dimes	Pennies
0	6
1	5
2	4
3	3

ness of the key mathematical components of a task helps in remodeling the task to build on or extend students' mathematical experiences and to avoid the possibility of creating a "fun" activity devoid of mathematical content.

DISCUSSION SUMMARY

Points raised in the discussion included the following:

Different ways to present the problem

- The order of clues could be changed.
- The clues could be presented all at once.

Different ways to change the problem

- The number of coins could be changed.
- The problem could use a less abstract form of measurement, such as weight.

Different features of the problem to consider

- The representation is important, including the role of visual and concrete images.
- The problem could be seen as involving sets.
- Language is important.

- The problem can use inverse relations (numbers of dimes and pennies) and involves algebraic reasoning.
- The context can be important because the content underlying the task may depend on context.

General observations about the teacher's knowledge base

- Do all teachers need a rich and varied math background?
- What knowledge do teachers have at the start?
- Belief structures should be considered as part of knowledge.
- Math beliefs are held in the context of some math knowledge.
- Teachers need to understand what knowledge packages there are to unpack.

As I conclude this summary, I'm cognizant of how very complex it is to teach mathematics. One must be informed about human development, knowledgeable of mathematics content, curious about how mathematical knowledge is constructed, patient with the knowledge that understanding is developed over time, and possess a disposition towards learning and teaching that capitalizes on the dynamics of the learning environment—the people, their ideas and experiences, and the physical materials.

Analyzing Student Work

Michaele F. Chappell

SESSION GOAL

The goal of this session centered on the mathematical knowledge, skills, intuitions, and/or dispositions that matter in order to examine and analyze student work. This goal was positioned within a larger context that dealt with understanding the mathematical knowledge elementary teachers need to teach mathematics well. The session focused on these questions:

- *What mathematical knowledge does a teacher need to analyze student work?*
- *What level of mathematical knowledge does a teacher need to respond to varying strategies in ways that will move the entire class forward in their thinking?*

OVERVIEW

Forming the basis for the two group discussions were several student responses to the "Mixing Juice" task, which is to determine the relative concentrations of water and juice concentrate in various mixtures (see Figure 1). The exercise is excerpted from the seventh-grade Connected Mathematics Project text, *Compar-*

ing and Scaling (Lappan, Fey, Fitzgerald, Friel, & Phillips, 1997, p. 27-28).

ACTIVITY

Participants began the session by solving the "Mixing Juice" task. Ensuing dialogue focused on the mathematics entailed in doing the problem. The participants, some individually and some in pairs, critically examined the 12 responses of the student teams (see Figure 2). In the analysis, the participants summarized the responses, noting the strategies used, the differences and similarities between them, and other mathematically related factors that may have contributed to the students' work on the task. At the close of the session, participants recorded their responses to the goal and shared the insights they had related to the focus topic.

DISCUSSION SUMMARY

During both sessions, the discussions focused on three major points: (1) the mathematics embedded in the "Mixing

Figure 1. Mixing Juice

Every year, the seventh-grade students at Langston Hughes School go on an outdoor education camping trip. During the week-long trip, the students study nature and participate in recreational activities. Everyone pitches in to help with the cooking and cleanup.

Arvind and Mariah are in charge of making orange juice for all the campers. They make the juice by mixing water and orange juice concentrate. To find the mix that tastes best, Arvind and Mariah decided to test some recipes on a few of their friends.

Problem
Arvind and Mariah tested four juice mixes

Mix A	Mix B
2 cups concentrate	1 cup concentrate
3 cups cold water	4 cups cold water

Mix C	Mix D
4 cups concentrate	3 cups concentrate
8 cups cold water	5 cups cold water

A. Which recipe will make juice that is the most "orangey"? Explain your answer.
B. Which recipe will make juice that is the least "orangey"? Explain your answer
C. Assume that each camper will get 1/2 cup of juice. For each recipe, how much concentrate and how much water are needed to make juice for 240 campers? Explain your answer.

From *Comparing and Scaling: Ratio, Proportion, and Percent* by Lappan, Fey, Fitzgerald, Friel, & Phillips. © 1997 by Connected Math. Used by permission.

Juice" task; (2) the examination and analysis of the students' work; and (3) the knowledge, skills, and dispositions that matter in analyzing students' mathematics work. An elaboration of each point is provided below.

Mathematics entailed in the task

Participants identified several mathematics content areas embedded in the "Mixing Juice" task. Major topics included the following:

- understanding proportional reasoning;
- comparison of different ratios, percentages, and/or fractions;
- part-to-whole relationships;
- scaling (e.g., how many "recipes" are needed to make the total amount?);
- conversions to different units for comparison (e.g., reducing numerator to 1);
- closeness of the particular numbers—thinking about combining by adding versus multiplying;

Figure 2. Student Work

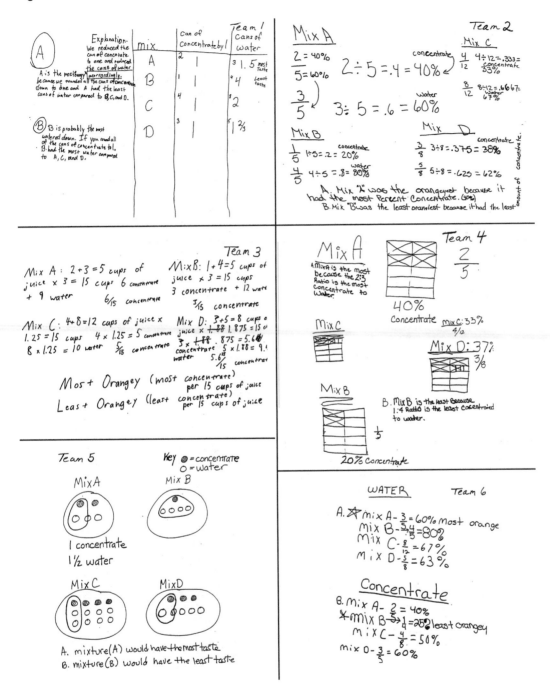

(continued)

Figure 2. Student Work (cont.)

Team 7

A. mix "A" is the most oarngyest because it has the least amouint of water added which is 1½ cups of water.

B. mix "B" is the least fruityest because it has 4 cups of water to 1 cup of concentrate.

Mix A

$$\frac{3}{2} = \frac{1}{1\frac{1}{2}} \begin{array}{l} \text{con.} \\ \text{water} \end{array}$$

Mix B

$$\frac{1}{4} \begin{array}{l} \text{con.} \\ \text{water} \end{array}$$

Mix C

$$\frac{4}{8} = \frac{2}{4} = \frac{1}{2} \begin{array}{l} \text{con.} \\ \text{water} \end{array}$$

Mix D

$$\frac{3}{5} = \frac{1}{1\frac{2}{3}} \begin{array}{l} \text{con.} \\ \text{water} \end{array}$$

Team 8

Mix A—$\frac{3}{5}$ water=60% water
Mix B—$\frac{4}{5}$ water=80% water
Mix C—$\frac{8}{12}$ water=67% water
Mix D—$\frac{5}{8}$ water=63% water

Most orangey—Mix A
Least orangey—Mix B

Team 10

Mix A is most orangy, because...
100% ÷ 5 = 20%   1 cup = 20% of the mixture
20% × 2 cups= 40% concentrate

Mix B is the least orangy because...
100% ÷ 5 = 20%   1cup= 20%
(1÷5)
1 cup × 20% = 20% concentrate

Mix C is neither because...
100% ÷ 12 = 8%   1cup = 8%
(1÷8)
4 cups × 8% = 32% concentrate

Mix D is neither because...
100% ÷ 8 = 12.5%   1cup= 12.5%
3 × 12.5% = 37.5% concentrate

Team 9

Mix A 1st
(most)
$$\frac{2}{5} = \frac{16}{40}$$

Mix B 4th
(least)
$$\frac{1}{5} = \frac{8}{40}$$

Mix C 3rd
$$\frac{4}{12} = \frac{13.3}{40}$$

Mix D 2nd
$$\frac{3}{8} = \frac{15}{40}$$

Team 11

Mix A- $\frac{3}{5}$=60% Water /40% Concentrate
Mix B- $\frac{4}{5}$=80% " /20% "
Mix C- $\frac{8}{12}$=67% " /33% "
Mix D- $\frac{5}{8}$=63% " / 37% "

A.) mix A is the most orangey because it is only 60% water, the least watered down.

B.) mix B is the least orangey because it is 80% water, the most watered down.

Team 12

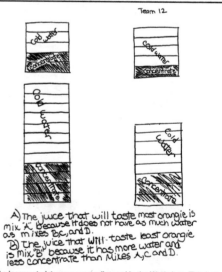

A) The juice that will taste most orangie is mix "A" because it does not have as much water as mixes B,C, and D.
B) The juice that will taste least orangie is mix "B" because it has more water and less concentrate than Mixes A,C, and D.

Note: An incorrect picture was actually used in the Workshop. This is the correct student work.

Student work is used with permission from Traverse City Public Schools via the Connected Mathematics Project.

- closeness of the ratios compared to a 1:1 ratio; and
- distinctions between fractions representing ratios and fractions representing rational numbers.

Other issues surrounding the conversations about the content related to how individual students might think about the task. For instance, one issue pertained to various solution techniques such as "eye-balling" the ratios of concentrate to water versus finding the percentages of concentrate per cup of mixture. A sliding scale or meter analogy was proposed to illustrate how one might think about the "orangeness" situation. The ideas of pictures, tables, and graphs were introduced as possible strategies students may use to find a solution. A second issue dealt with the appropriateness of using one approach over another: how one determines the appropriateness of using ratios versus additive differences, for example. Depending on the user, certain approaches may be more efficient and natural to carry out while others require more work.

Another issue highlighted the potential complexity of the situation. The ratios (and proportions) may be thought about as measures (e.g., concentrate-to-concentrate, water-to-water) *or* as scaling factors. Here, the key idea is keeping track of the *unit*. A closer examination of the concentrate-to-concentrate or the water-to-water measures indicates that one ratio represents the invariant that measures the mixture while the other represents the invariant of the opposite. Although, to some, one of these ratios may seem intrinsically preferable to the other, both will work in finding a solution.

Examining and analyzing the students' responses

Individually, in pairs, or in trios, the participants examined the 12 responses provided by the student teams (Figure 2). Much of this discussion concerned the mathematics involved and the overall focus question, although comments were made either about the students' work or about the analysis process itself. For example, the groups compared several solutions (e.g., see Teams 1, 5, and 7 or Teams 2, 8, and 11) and examined how they were similar in procedure but different in presentation. Participants discussed the likely choices students made about the division and rounding procedures (e.g., see Teams 2 and 3) and about the estimation used in shading parts of wholes (e.g., see Team 4). They observed how certain teams "produced more work" than seemed necessary. They also noted that the explanations provided vary in detail; whereas some teams (e.g., see Team 1) provided thorough explanations, others (e.g., see Team 9) allowed the mathematics to "do the talking." Finally, one team's (Team 12) explanation did not seem to match well with the visual solution that appeared, but it was subsequently learned that an error in transcription might explain the disparity.

Participants recognized the process of analyzing the students' work as quite engaging. They reported how the process allowed them to look through a different lens and examine the various contexts from which fractions and ratios may emerge. They commented that because students' work will likely be analyzed within *frames of reference,* such as teacher expectations or previous lessons, teachers will need to conduct such an activity with open minds. Teachers should recognize their personal values and frames of reference that could lead to certain evaluations of students' work. Participants discussed how the process and the particular task highlight the need for mathematics instruction that builds on students' understandings to construct a meaningful knowledge of ratios. In addition, because problem solvers all have their own individual methods, teachers must be prepared to think differently in order to understand the various methods students may use in solving a problem of this nature.

Identifying what matters

This discussion pertained to the overall focus questions for the session. Participants shared their thoughts on the mathematical knowledge, skills, intuitions, and dispositions that matter in analyzing students' work. Their ideas, which encompass thoughts that are both specific to the "Mixing Juice" task and generic to any mathematical activity, are listed below.

Mathematical knowledge that matters:

- proportional reasoning knowledge package, which, itself, is very complex;
- role of ratio as expressed in various symbols and situations;
- arithmetic associated with manipulating ratios (as opposed to rational numbers);
- flexible understandings of the mathematics (e.g., one could assert that Mix A is the most orange by arguing that the complement of Mix A is the least orange.);
- different visual representations that are transferable to other contexts;
- varied solution strategies and how to compare them for correctness, efficiency, and generalizability; how to rank them by sophistication on a developmental continuum;
- detecting incorrect representations and rationales for such misconceptions

(e.g., knowing which aspects of the concept students misunderstand and how to help students see mistakes in their thinking);
- contextual field (i.e., what mathematics the work supports and where the work fits in the students' broader mathematical experience);
- linkages between concepts (e.g., the meaning of hierarchy);
- constructs well beyond the mathematics involved in the task (e.g., does stating 4 cups to 8 cups call upon a different mathematics than stating 1 to 2?).

Skills involved in the process of learning that matter:

- observe several pieces of data simultaneously;
- consider problems in terms of relationships, rather than specific techniques;
- analyze the mathematical terrain of problems with rich potential for learning;
- recognize valid and invalid concepts (although they may be unfamiliar or have not clearly been expressed);
- determine how to correct invalid ideas.

Dispositions that matter:

- look at problems through a different lens;
- develop interests in and curiosities about students' thinking;
- invite students to communicate their rationale;
- appreciate the varied ways to solve problems *and* recognize that what appears the simplest way for one child may be the least efficient for another;
- assume that students' work contains valuable mathematical thinking;
- evaluate students' work as information about instruction;
- realize that correct answers do not always indicate that students understand the core ideas; likewise, incorrect

answers do not always indicate that students lack such understanding;

- develop a mathematical value system that allows for different choices to be made about reaction to students' work; knowledge of the school mathematics curriculum is important in developing this value system.

Other factors that matter:

- what the teacher does with all of the information obtained from analyzing students' work;
- how the teacher plans for the next day once the information is obtained;
- how to use students' work to generate teacher research questions, such as asking what this child really understands about "*x*";
- the role of the National Council of Teachers of Mathematics (NCTM) *Standards* (NCTM 1989, 2000) in analyzing students' work;
- the balance that should be maintained as teachers sort through the many aspects of students' work, considering the numerous demands upon the teacher and the various subjects to be learned.

The ideas outlined above are not intended to serve as a complete list; at best, they represent an attempt to capture the rich dialogue that transpired during both sessions of the workshop. Presenting them in such a format should not imply that a response to the question of *what matters* can be reduced to a simple "check-off" list of items. Indeed, understanding what matters most when teachers analyze students' mathematical work is a complex phenomenon and undoubtedly will require an integration of several components, some of which have been included here and others yet to be mentioned.

REFERENCES

Lappan, G., Fey, J. T., Fitzgerald, W. M., Friel, S. N., & Phillips, E. D. (1997). *Comparing and scaling: Ratio, proportion, and percent* (Connected Mathematics Series). Palo Alto, CA: Dale Seymour.

National Council of Teachers of Mathematics. (1989). *Curriculum and evaluation standards for school mathematics.* Reston, VA: Author.

National Council of Teachers of Mathematics. (2000). *Principles and standards for school mathematics.* Reston, VA: Author.

Managing Class Discussion

Erick Smith

SESSION GOALS

The session was designed to allow participants the opportunity to participate in a task of teaching and focus on the mathematical knowledge needed to do that task. The task of teaching under investigation was managing class discussion. The questions posed were as follows:

- *What mathematical knowledge does a teacher need to orchestrate productive discussions?*
- *What is the relation between mathematical understanding and teacher questions?*
- *How is what a teacher knows about mathematics reflected in the examples a teacher chooses and the decisions the teacher makes about pursuing discussions about student responses and work?*

OVERVIEW

Tony Brown, a math educator from England, tells of being in a professional session where he had to imagine himself as a fly on the wall and describe what the room would look like. He recalls thinking of tabletops as trapezoids and other shapes and figures that arose from his imaginary setting. He realized that the mathematics he was constructing arose not only from the objects he perceived but from his relationship to those objects. Or as he claimed,

> Any act of mathematics can be seen as an act of construction where I simultaneously construct in language mathematical notions and the world around me. Meaning is produced as I get to know my relationship to these things. (Brown, 1994, p. 156)

For a mathematics teacher, the "world around me" consists primarily of students, the mathematical language and artifacts they produce, the curriculum, and the norms of schooling. Thus, from Brown's perspective, the mathematical meaning a teacher constructs is in relationship to "these things," that is, the mathematical world of students.

If we take this contextual view of mathematical meaning seriously, it naturally leads one to wonder how the mathematics of teaching is related to the content of typical mathematics courses. That is: What do we mean when we say teachers do not have enough content knowledge? Another way to ask this is: How do teachers make mathematical meaning within the context of the norms and goals of schooling as they develop an understanding of their students in general and of the mathematical thoughts of their students in particular?

ACTIVITIES

This session addressed these questions by looking in depth at one classroom example where a problem is posed, sixth-grade students work on the problem in small groups, and the small groups make presentations on the board (see Figure 1).

The focus of the discussion was on what kind of knowledge and understandings a teacher would need to manage a classroom discussion around these presentations. An important goal of this session was to focus on teaching "in the moment," that is, trying to look at what a teacher needs to draw upon in real classroom situations and put less emphasis on general categories of mathematical knowledge.

Participants were given the following instructions:

- Building on what you have just decided, you look at the clock and see you have 15 minutes to the end of class.
- What would be your next step?
- How might you organize a discussion?
- How would you use what the students have presented?
- Where would you like to be at the end of class?
- What would you want the students to learn?
- How might you characterize your goals for the day in terms of the important math content?

DISCUSSION SUMMARY

After some discussion of these issues, the sessions ended on the more general issue:

Now step out of the role as teacher in the moment to be the reflective teacher. What kinds of knowledge and understandings did you call upon to make the decisions you made as the teacher of the moment?

In the discussion, participants identified several areas of content knowledge that a teacher would presumably need in this situation. These included the following:

- A broad understanding of operations including appropriate analogies for the operations and the interplay between addition/multiplication and between subtraction/division.
- An understanding of the role of units, especially in the way units play out in a division problem.
- An ability to translate symbols into actions (and vice versa).
- An understanding of equality and of the mathematical use of the "=" sign.

Participants suggested specific ways in which a teacher might start the discussion, such as focus on solutions that are most problematic (the first and sixth solutions) or focus on a solution that is reasonable (the second solution).

In the discussion, we were able to describe the general mathematical knowledge a teacher might draw upon in this situation, and we were able to describe some specific ways to proceed. What was more difficult was to describe what knowing would be supportive for a teacher "in the moment" and the ways that knowing would be connected to the mathematical worlds of the students. In this particular class, it would be natural

Figure 1. Scenario Presented to Workshop Participants
(Adapted from Schifter, Bastable, & Russell, 1999, pp. 120-122)

The teacher of a sixth-grade classroom posed the following problem to her students.

> You are giving a party for your birthday. From Ben and Jerry's Ice Cream Factory, you order six pints of each variety of ice cream that they make. If you serve 3/4 pint of ice cream to each guest, how many guests can be served from each variety?

Most of the students in the class made a picture similar to the following:

During the initial class discussion, students argued that each person would get three of the little squares, which would equal 3/4 of a pint, and thus they could feed 8 people.

The teacher asked students to spend a few minutes writing a number sentence for this situation, then had several students put their number sentence on the board with a short justification. The presentations of 8 students are given below:

	Equation	Justification
1.	$8 \div \frac{1}{4} = 6$	8 people were served, 6 pints and the picture shows fourths.
2.	$24 \div 3 = 8$	There are 24 pieces, 3 pieces to a serving, 8 people can be served.
3.	$\frac{3}{4} \div 8 = 6$	3/4 pint is the serving, 6 pints of ice cream, so 8 servings.
4.	$24 \div \frac{3}{4} = 8$ or 6	There are 24 pieces altogether and each serving is 3/4 of a pint, so there are 6 pints or 8 servings.
5.	$6 - \frac{3}{4} - \frac{3}{4} - \frac{3}{4} - \frac{3}{4} - \frac{3}{4} - \frac{3}{4} - \frac{3}{4} - \frac{3}{4} = 0$	Take 3/4 pint for each serving. You do this 8 times.
6.	$6 \div \frac{1}{4} = 8$	This was from a student who insisted that they could not accept the previous equation.
7.	$8 \quad \frac{3}{4} = 6$	8 servings of 3/4 of a pint each gives you 6 whole pints.
8.	$\frac{3}{4} + \frac{3}{4} + \frac{3}{4} + \frac{3}{4} + \frac{3}{4} + \frac{3}{4} + \frac{3}{4} + \frac{3}{4} = 6$	3/4 to each of eight people gives 6 whole pints.

From *Developing Mathematical Ideas, Number and Operations, part 2: Making Meaning for Operations Casebook*, by Schifter, Bastable, & Russell. © 1999 by Dale Seymour Publications. Used by permission.

that a group of outsiders would not know the connections and backgrounds that would underlie this connected knowledge. Yet in the group discussion, it was difficult to even decide what it was we were trying to describe.

That this group of experienced professionals did not seem to have language to describe some of the essential kinds of knowledge and ways of knowing that might be important in a particular teaching situation is disquieting. Had there been sufficient time in the sessions, it is likely that more ideas would have been forthcoming and possibly some consensus would have arisen. However, what seems to be a significant conclusion from the session is that we have little readily available language for describing the ways that we want teachers to know subject-matter, that is, language that goes beyond what is typically covered in general mathematics courses.

By focusing on what a teacher needed to know at a particular moment in an actual classroom, this session seemed to highlight a theme that ran through the Workshop sessions. We can make lists of general mathematical topics important to teaching, but understanding how the knowledge of those topics becomes integrated into the actual act of teaching is more difficult. A growing awareness of these issues has led to the development of curricular materials to support teacher learning of mathematics that attempt to connect that learning to the contexts of classrooms by embedding the mathematics into classroom contexts, students' work on mathematics, and teacher interactions about their own classroom mathematizations. As such materials become more widespread, one might expect the development of a language for better describing the mathematical knowledge that supports teaching. As that happens, sessions such as the one described here may offer even stronger insights into the mathematics of teaching.

REFERENCES

Brown, T. (1994). Describing the mathematics you are part of: A post-structuralist account of mathematical learning. In P. Ernst (Ed.), *Mathematics, education and philosophy: An international perspective* (pp. 154-162). London: Falmer Press.

Schifter, D., Bastable, V., & Russell, S. J. (with Yaffee, L., Lester, J. B., & Cohen, S.) (1999). *Developing mathematical ideas, number and operations part 2: Making meaning for operations casebook.* Parsippany, NJ: Dale Seymour.

What Kinds of Mathematical Knowledge Matter in Teaching?

To culminate the Workshop activities that addressed the question, "What mathematical knowledge does a teacher need to teach well?" a panel reflected on their own experiences and how those experiences contributed to their perspectives on the relation between mathematical understanding and teaching.

PANELISTS

Perspectives from a Mathematician
Alan Tucker, State University of New York-Stony Brook

Perspectives from a Mathematics Educator
Deborah Schifter, Education Development Center, Inc.

Perspectives from the Community College
Gladys Whitehead, Prince George's County, Maryland, Public Schools

Perspectives from a Mathematician

Alan Tucker

I am certainly humbled by coming here, and while I think I have some mathematical knowledge, I would never dream of thinking I could come close to teaching in an elementary classroom. So, I find the word *knowledge* a little difficult to process, and I think, perhaps, a lot of the issues are more about reasoning. Moreover, there's too much knowledge. Every single instance we've seen today required a lot of insight and knowledge, and it doesn't seem like a typical preservice teacher in three or six credit hours is going to pick up all this knowledge.

Teaching is as much an art as a science. I think, rightly or wrongly, that being a school teacher is like being a doctor. Doctors have two years of academic training, two more years of quick rotation in different settings, a residency, then two to six or seven or eight years of internship. With only a couple of years in the classroom, teachers are learning as they go along, and they continue to learn.

The mathematical knowledge teachers need is the foundation for their apprenticeship and their lifelong learning. They need critical-thinking skills. I like to think of keeping the principles and the knowledge in mathematics as simple and clean as possible and emphasize building on reasoning skills. As a simple example, if I'm asked a question about division, I'm going to think about division as repeated subtraction. For a lot of the theoretical questions, that gets me a long way. Simplifying the knowledge and beginning from a safe base is one way to get going. From another perspective, I'm running a "math across the curriculum" project, and all the other disciplines seem to have the same problem we have. It's not a matter of facts; it's a matter of what my friends in other disciplines are calling critical-thinking skills. The focus is not mathematical knowledge or mathematical reasoning; I believe there is a more generic way of reasoning in which we're interested here.

Just a quick aside, at the University of Maine, the math department and the English department are in the same building, and one is at the north wing and the other is at the south end, on every floor. This is the critical-thinking skills building. Many of you may know that, before computer science was a well-defined discipline, math majors and English majors were the people that a lot of individuals thought made the best programmers. The point here is that many problems we have transcend mathematics. Critical-thinking skills run across the curriculum.

The reasoning skills teachers need are mind-boggling because there are many situations where we can use mathematics. There are endless numbers of applied situations. Sometimes, examples can't really connect at all, or only marginally, with drills about addition skills and subtraction skills. Sometimes there are natural connections; sometimes these skills seem unconnected.

I find that a common knowledge base can be both an asset and a liability. There are valid conclusions that people build and we use, but then there are lots of false conclusions that have to be broken down. Of course, this is the way the history of mathematics evolved, without a rigorous foundation for much of anything for years and years, until at some point or another, things became so complicated people had to restart. Somehow I think this evolution of our discipline is something we should try to model in the classroom. This approach has its pluses and minuses. Everything we do should have tremendous tension in it—that's they way I look at life—opportunities and things that can go wrong. Students have to be taking chances and welcome the opportunity to do so. The teacher has to be taking chances and try to build on something for which they were not prepared, but that's where the art comes in, as well as the experience. I think that there is also a tension between mathematical reasoning and very applied practical things. At the college level, we talk about teaching service courses in applicable mathematics. We have all sorts of clients telling us what to do and little time to do it. To explore a number pattern the way Deborah did with her class is unthinkable or pushing the envelope a long ways to do such things on a regular basis in calculus.

There are obviously valuable experiences in theory and in applications. I didn't see any really applied things during the workshop today. I didn't see examples of running a store. Many things like that can be done. My dad was a mathematician at Princeton, a very bright guy, and he said at Princeton the most important word in the mathematics department vocabulary was "taste." There are all sorts of examples you can give. There are all sorts of theoretical examples. There are all sorts of applied examples. This is part of the art, to have good taste in the examples that bring things together. I don't know how to teach this to preservice teachers. When you see it, you feel really good about it. The taste in mixing these different approaches, in mixing pure things with applied things, is, I think, where the excitement lies.

Despite widespread concerns about the mathematical education of young people and about the general public's mathematical literacy, I'd like to strike a positive note in my conclusion. When I was in college in the '60s, I can remember headlines in the *New York Times* saying something like "63,255,000 People Employed Last Month." Today we never hear how many people are employed. What we hear now is the increase, the delta. Not only that, the newspapers now talk about the change in the delta. They say that the growth in job creation slowed by 30 percent last month or that the number of new people applying for unemployment insurance dropped last month by 30 percent. Such sophisticated mathematical information was never printed thirty years ago. On *Monday Night Football*, I've heard an announcer say the receiver has practiced hundreds of times running downfield *X* yards and turning around to catch a pass. The idea of fixed yet unknown quantities is becoming part of the vernacular. I don't know what sophistication is going to exist in thirty or forty years when the teachers who are training now are still teaching.

While we lament students' skills, people have, at a common level, a knowledge base right now that is pretty high. One of the exciting challenges for teachers is to build on this knowledge. You can lament what people don't know, or you can take advantage of what they do know. What we saw today at every stage along the way is that young people know a lot, and the opportunities to build on and reinforce that knowledge seems to me very, very exciting.

Perspectives from a Mathematics Educator

Deborah Schifter

Yesterday, Mark got us started making lists of what teachers need to know in order to teach mathematics effectively. In the time I have, I'd like to add a few items to those lists. Some of these items come out of the discussions we've been having; others are my own.

When we looked at Deborah Ball's video this morning, we paid particular attention to how she was helping her students articulate how they figured things out and how she used their own logic to show them the elements of a mathematical argument. This points to a first item that could be added to our list. Teachers need to have a strong sense of what constitutes a mathematical argument, mathematical justification. Furthermore, they must be able to draw out students' ideas to illustrate elements of mathematical justification.

In the last break-out session, we started talking about the importance of teachers being able to recognize valid mathematical argument. This is an issue that is more basic than those we identified in the morning. Many teachers haven't developed the skill of listening to the mathematical justifications or methods that students use to solve problems and determining whether they are mathematically valid. That is, some teachers have no way of assessing mathematical validity if a student presents a method or argument different from the one the teacher learned when he or she was in school. So this is another item to add to our list.

Even when a child presents a right answer, the teacher needs to go further, to look at the mathematical argument and determine whether the argument itself is valid. And when a mathematical argument is invalid (whether the child's answer is correct or not), the teacher must be able to examine the child's logic to determine what aspect of the child's thinking *is* valid. Is it on the order of a careless arithmetic error? Or is there something more substantial—an important idea that the child needs to work on? And if so, just what is that idea?

Another of the issues we touched on this morning is the importance of being attentive when a student offers an idea that broaches an important mathematical domain or "habit of mind." We were thinking about the importance of generalization, and how in the video, Deborah Ball picked up on students' ideas to help the class think about a general claim. The role of generalization is critical in mathematics and teachers themselves need to learn to develop the habit of asking such questions as, "Does this always work?" or "How do you know it will always work?"

I'd like to take this opportunity to point out a dangerous assumption we might make when we listen to students to see if they are getting close to an important mathematical issue. That is, it is easy to attribute too much to what the children are doing. Here is an example that comes from a second-grade teacher: She reported that, early in the year, when her students were working with sums up to 10, they noticed that four plus six equals 10 and that six plus four equals 10. They coined the term "turn-around" to indicate when you add two numbers together, you can reverse the order and they add up to the same sum.

Many of us, listening to the children's conversation, would say that they understand commutativity as a property of addition. But at a certain point in the year, the teacher decided to ask the class explicitly, Do turn-arounds always work? Even though it may have sounded to our ears all year long that the students had been talking about turn-arounds as a property of addition, when the question was posed, they weren't sure. Some of them thought the answer was yes. Many thought the answer was no. They all began to test it out with large numbers. Only after a period of exploration and discussion did several children consider what the operation of addition does in order to develop an explanation for why turn-arounds always work. This tendency of attributing too much understanding as we begin to listen to children's mathematical ideas could be an item on our list.

My discussion group was charged with the task of thinking about intuitions and dispositions, some of the things that might fall under the general umbrella of mathematical knowledge but don't gener-

ally get classified as mathematical content. In our discussions, we started to touch on some things that aren't likely to come up through the analysis of mathematical tasks we were doing in our break-out session. Before I name them, I want to say that, for some of us, these things are almost like the air we breathe. It's hard to see them because they come so naturally to us—but they do need to be stated explicitly.

The list generated by our thinking included: Teachers need to learn that mathematics makes sense and that they should approach mathematics with the expectation that they can make sense of it. It seems to me that many, perhaps most people—teachers among them—graduating from our high schools and colleges are separated very early on from their own mathematical sense-making abilities. It would be good for everyone, but it is particularly important that teachers be reconnected with these abilities. They need to learn that mathematics is about ideas. They need to come to see that they, themselves, have mathematical ideas. Teachers need to have the experience of having mathematical ideas and of making sense of them.

Through the experience of doing mathematics, teachers can become familiar with the pleasure of figuring things out, and seeing how things fall into place. But along with, or most often just prior to, the sense of pleasure come experiences of frustration and confusion. Teachers must learn to work through those uncomfortable feelings to come to the point where the problem they are working on becomes clear. Certainly, if the teachers themselves never have the experience of working through their frustration to this place where it all comes together, they're never going to be able to tolerate their students meeting frustration. And if we want students to develop deeper understandings, they must be allowed to work through their frustrations and confusions.

Another item for the list is that teachers need to become curious about how mathematics works. They might become curious about the number system, for example, learn to formulate their own mathematical questions and learn how to pursue answers to those questions. Teachers have to become mathematical thinkers and questioners in their own right. It feels critical that these items become part of the explicit agenda in teacher education courses.

There's still another item I'd like to address. I have been having a hard time articulating this point, and when I talk to colleagues, they don't always see it as mathematical, but I think it is an important mathematical issue, so I'll try to say it here. Teachers need to learn to look at a classroom scene and discern the mathematics in it, to recognize what is mathematical in what a child is saying. Many of us talk about how, when we show a video, it is difficult to have a group focus on the mathematics. A group of teachers is likely, instead, to talk about whether the children in the class are paying attention, whether the child who speaks feels

confident or not, and similar matters. Often, we attribute such behavior to avoidance and believe the group doesn't want to talk about mathematics. But I am coming to believe it's not a matter of avoidance. Instead, I wonder whether the mathematics in the video simply isn't seen; the mathematics is not recognizable. This then becomes part of the agenda in a course for teachers: to learn to attend to the mathematics in what children say and do.

As I'm talking about some of these very basic issues of what it means to do mathematics, to recognize mathematics, to be a mathematical thinker, I feel the need to mention how important it is for us to take an appropriate stance in our work with teachers. When we talk about what's missing in teachers' mathematical knowledge, about mathematical capacities that are lacking, it is often with a tone of disparagement. But if we want to encourage teachers to venture forward, to make public their mathematical ideas—which are often just baby steps and, in many ways, not so far ahead of the third-grade children we saw on videotape—as we're working to help teachers develop their mathematical capacities, we must act with respect and generosity.

Perspectives from the Community College

Gladys Whitehead

When I was first asked to sit on this panel and received the questions about mathematical content, I said, well, I can write my description of what the content should be on a piece of paper, but I would like to come and learn about the concerns of others. One of the things that impressed me is that you started with the tasks, and from the tasks, you decided to pull out what mathematical content would address those tasks. By the time we finish, we will be addressing another question, about teaching that content.

I've struggled with issues of teacher preparation from two perspectives. I have been at the community college, where we were training elementary education majors and constantly struggling with these concerns: (1) have we given them enough content, and (2) have we given them adequate teaching strategies. As the supervisor of mathematics in Prince George's County, I have the opportunity to go into classrooms and observe teachers. There are two types of observations that are probably the nemesis of a supervisor. One is when you walk into a classroom and clearly there is no content, period; that's the easy one. The tough one is when you walk in and you know the teacher understands the content but is unable to help students get a grasp on the concept.

One question centers on what content we want teachers to have. A tougher question, and one that comes full circle in the question we consider for the next part of the Workshop, is how do we as college professors train our teachers to really teach. In other words, it is not enough to just know the mathematics. How do you give them the skill of pulling out the reasoning, of knowing how to question? We have learned our teaching strategies over the years. We are very experienced and have developed our strategies by trial and error. So, how do we capture all of this experience and hand it to a new teacher?

I watched an excellent new teacher miss what we call a teachable moment. I wondered, how would I have trained her so that she didn't miss that opportunity? After the observation, I shared with her what should occur the next time this happens. The teacher introduced a problem where the students engaged in discussion, wrote in their journals, and shared their reasoning skills. "You have a dozen eggs, and then five of the eggs are broken. Write as a fraction how many are unbroken." A little girl came up, drew a little egg carton and darkened in the broken eggs. She had turned the numbers around. She had come up with a right answer, but it was for a different question. The teacher made her sit down rather than build on why she had turned that problem around in her mind. The teacher sent another student up, who erased the board completely and started over. Teaching teachers how to teach is an abstract concept, but that is really what we are about here. I can make sure that teachers know the content, but if they are going to be teachers, how do I get them to use these questioning, teaching strategies?

At the community college, we decided that, as much as possible, we need to model what we want to happen. Many of us college professors are die-hard, "lecture-type" individuals. We do not always practice group learning. For example, some of us walk in, fill the board with "mathematics," turn around, ask if there are any questions, and we are finished. At the community college, we have been working hard to have labs with our students, hands-on activities, and to practice what it is we want to see happen in the classroom. With elementary education majors, more than that has to happen. You have to convey to them the sense of learning and the sense of being able to help students learn.

After I worked on teacher inservice for so long, I began to build on the advice of the teachers and try to give them some presentation experience in their first two years in our program. I asked my students to present a lesson in their second semester course. They had 10-15 minutes to explain a concept to their classmates. When we finished the exercise, some of my students were astonished to discover that they were really uncomfortable. They did not know how to ask their classmates questions to get at what they wanted. They had envisioned the presentation would be easy. After all, they would be teaching elementary students, and how hard can that be? This is really the question, "How do we get the universities to not only teach the content, the easy part for us, but how do we teach preservice teachers to really be teachers?"

I'm pleased that we are looking at the issue of teacher preparation. I think this implies a bigger question for colleges and for professors. We are the ones that need inservicing now. We need to know how to turn it around. The public schools have always been ahead of us. Prince George's is one of the most progressive community colleges in the state of Maryland. Working with our school system has helped us revamp our training of teachers. Thank you for the chance to share with you.

HOW CAN TEACHERS DEVELOP SUCH MATHEMATICAL KNOWLEDGE?

On the second day, participants took part in sessions that considered various approaches to helping teachers develop mathematical knowledge, skill, and confidence. They then stepped back and analyzed what each approach offered as opportunities to learn mathematics and reflected on how each might support teachers' use of mathematics in their practice. The questions that framed these sessions were

- How might prospective elementary teachers be helped to develop these kinds of mathematical knowledge?
- What are alternative and promising approaches—in the U.S. and internationally—to the mathematics education of beginning teachers?

Investigating Alternative Approaches to Helping Teachers Learn Mathematics

Participants attended two of four concurrent sessions in which they engaged in activities to help them understand how opportunities might be designed to enable preservice teachers to learn the mathematics they will need to teach well.

SESSIONS

Curriculum Materials
Shin-ying Lee, Michigan State University
Marco Ramirez, Tucson Public Schools

Case Materials
Carne Barnett, WestEd

Programs and Practices
Virginia Bastable, SummerMath for Teachers
Jill Lester, Mount Holyoke College
Deborah Schifter, Education Development Center

Video as a Delivery Mechanism
Bradford Findell, Mathematical Sciences Education Board
Deborah Ball, University of Michigan

Student Curriculum Materials: Japanese Teachers' Manuals

Shin-ying Lee

SESSION GOALS

The session, focused on the use of curriculum materials as a way to help teachers learn mathematics, offered participants the opportunity to closely examine the information presented in two sample teachers' manuals and to think carefully about how materials like these may or may not provide resources for teachers or prospective teachers to acquire mathematical knowledge as well as how to teach mathematics. In the first part, participants considered a lesson on weight using a Japanese teacher's manual.

OVERVIEW

There is a strong need for capable, well-trained mathematics teachers if there is to be improvement in the mathematics achievement of American students. Evidence from studies has shown that the mathematical knowledge and teaching skills of typical American school teachers are lower than they should be and lower than that of many of their counterparts in the rest of the world. In addition, teachers' working conditions do not foster the professional growth necessary for effective institutional practices (Lee,

1998). Teachers need to have a conceptual understanding of mathematical knowledge to facilitate the quantitative reasoning ability of their students. It is unlikely that teachers will change their teaching practices unless they have acquired an in-depth understanding of the mathematics they have to teach and have had opportunities to develop the pedagogical strategies necessary for effective teaching (Ball & Cohen, 1996). It is critical to engage in discussion and to suggest practices that could lead to the improvement of American teachers' mathematics knowledge.

This Workshop addressed the nature of the problem and possible solutions by focusing on two questions: What mathematical knowledge do teachers need to have in order to teach well? How do teachers obtain that knowledge? Participants had opportunities to think of new ways to improve teachers' mathematical content knowledge and pedagogical content knowledge at the preservice and inservice level. One possible avenue is to examine the teacher training practices of countries that demonstrate effective instruction in mathematics. Japan is one such country. In comparative studies, Japanese teachers have consistently demonstrated that they teach mathematics in a clear, coherent, and in depth fashion (Stevenson & Lee, 1995). They facilitate students' conceptual understanding of mathematics in an interactive and effective way. The types of instruction observed in these studies illustrate teachers' thorough understanding of the mathematical topics and their knowledge of the elements of effective math lessons. Teachers' manuals for the curriculum provide a significant source of information that may contribute to their knowledge base for teaching mathematics (Gill & McPike, 1995).

Japanese teachers' manuals differ from American curricular materials in several ways. The primary focus is on the fundamentals of mathematics. The mathematics content knowledge and pedagogical knowledge are organized in a systematic and thorough way to facilitate the teaching and learning processes. The Ministry of Monbusho develops curricular guidelines (Course of Study) that comprise the national educational standards in mathematics for each grade level. The Course of Study succinctly outlines the mathematical topics of study as well as the desired structure and sequence of instruction for each year. These guidelines are made widely available and used by local boards of education, schools, teachers, and textbook publishers to develop curricular materials and instructional plans.

Textbooks published by private companies have to be reviewed and approved by the Ministry for conformity to the Course of Study. Companies that publish student textbooks also publish teachers' manuals (*Kyoushiyou Shidousho*). Using the content of students' textbooks as the guideline, the manuals provide a coherent body of subject matter knowledge and offer pedagogical suggestions on how to teach the lessons. The use of the manuals is not mandatory for teachers. However,

the manuals are usually written by expert teachers who have not only demonstrated effective teaching but are also experienced in working with novice teachers. The mathematical knowledge and the suggestions for teaching are practical and realistic, often including content and activities that have been used in research lessons to demonstrate their effectiveness in guiding students to meet the particular lesson goals.

Effective teaching requires that teachers have a thorough understanding of the structure of mathematics at the level at which they are teaching (National Council of Teachers of Mathematics, 1991; Leitzel, 1991). Japanese elementary school teachers can acquire a clear idea of the structure of elementary mathematics through the scope and sequence chart in the teachers' manuals. The scope and sequence Systematic Charts included at the back of every teacher's manual lay out the sequence of all the mathematics concepts students should learn in the four mathematics content areas over the elementary school years. The four strands are identified in the Japanese Course of Study for Elementary School: numbers and operations, quantities and measurement, geometrical figures, and quantitative relations. Each strand is presented in a one-page "Systematic Chart." The same charts are included in the teachers' manuals for all different grade levels. Those charts could serve as the cognitive maps for teachers to understand the structure and connectedness of the entire elementary mathematics system.

Figure 1 shows the systematic chart for numbers and operations. The development of numbers and operations within a particular grade and how it lays the groundwork for concepts in later years are presented in a flowchart format. For

Figure 1. Sequence Chart for Numbers and Operations—Operations

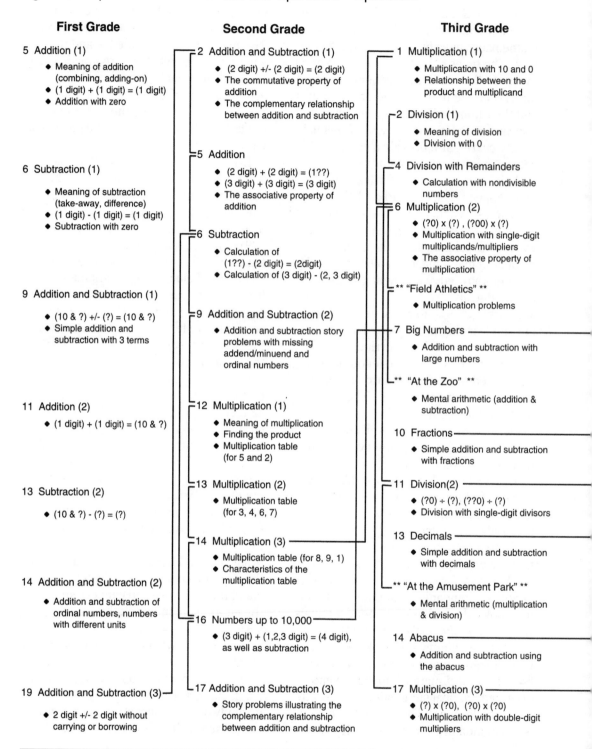

First Grade

5 Addition (1)
- Meaning of addition (combining, adding-on)
- (1 digit) + (1 digit) = (1 digit)
- Addition with zero

6 Subtraction (1)
- Meaning of subtraction (take-away, difference)
- (1 digit) - (1 digit) = (1 digit)
- Subtraction with zero

9 Addition and Subtraction (1)
- (10 & ?) +/- (?) = (10 & ?)
- Simple addition and subtraction with 3 terms

11 Addition (2)
- (1 digit) + (1 digit) = (10 & ?)

13 Subtraction (2)
- (10 & ?) - (?) = (?)

14 Addition and Subtraction (2)
- Addition and subtraction of ordinal numbers, numbers with different units

19 Addition and Subtraction (3)
- 2 digit +/- 2 digit without carrying or borrowing

Second Grade

2 Addition and Subtraction (1)
- (2 digit) +/- (2 digit) = (2 digit)
- The commutative property of addition
- The complementary relationship between addition and subtraction

5 Addition
- (2 digit) + (2 digit) = (1??)
- (3 digit) + (3 digit) = (3 digit)
- The associative property of addition

6 Subtraction
- Calculation of (1??) - (2 digit) = (2digit)
- Calculation of (3 digit) - (2, 3 digit)

9 Addition and Subtraction (2)
- Addition and subtraction story problems with missing addend/minuend and ordinal numbers

12 Multiplication (1)
- Meaning of multiplication
- Finding the product
- Multiplication table (for 5 and 2)

13 Multiplication (2)
- Multiplication table (for 3, 4, 6, 7)

14 Multiplication (3)
- Multiplication table (for 8, 9, 1)
- Characteristics of the multiplication table

16 Numbers up to 10,000
- (3 digit) + (1,2,3 digit) = (4 digit), as well as subtraction

17 Addition and Subtraction (3)
- Story problems illustrating the complementary relationship between addition and subtraction

Third Grade

1 Multiplication (1)
- Multiplication with 10 and 0
- Relationship between the product and multiplicand

2 Division (1)
- Meaning of division
- Division with 0

4 Division with Remainders
- Calculation with nondivisible numbers

6 Multiplication (2)
- (?0) x (?) , (?00) x (?)
- Multiplication with single-digit multiplicands/multipliers
- The associative property of multiplication

** "Field Athletics" **
- Multiplication problems

7 Big Numbers
- Addition and subtraction with large numbers

** "At the Zoo" **
- Mental arithmetic (addition & subtraction)

10 Fractions
- Simple addition and subtraction with fractions

11 Division(2)
- (?0) ÷ (?), (??0) ÷ (?)
- Division with single-digit divisors

13 Decimals
- Simple addition and subtraction with decimals

** "At the Amusement Park" **
- Mental arithmetic (multiplication & division)

14 Abacus
- Addition and subtraction using the abacus

17 Multiplication (3)
- (?) x (?0), (?0) x (?0)
- Multiplication with double-digit multipliers

80

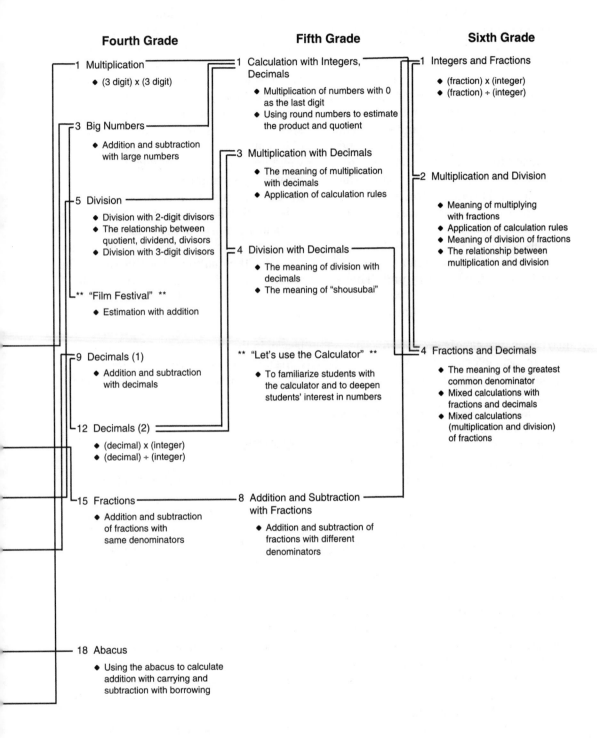

Fourth Grade

1 Multiplication
- ◆ (3 digit) x (3 digit)

3 Big Numbers
- ◆ Addition and subtraction with large numbers

5 Division
- ◆ Division with 2-digit divisors
- ◆ The relationship between quotient, dividend, divisors
- ◆ Division with 3-digit divisors

** "Film Festival" **
- ◆ Estimation with addition

9 Decimals (1)
- ◆ Addition and subtraction with decimals

12 Decimals (2)
- ◆ (decimal) x (integer)
- ◆ (decimal) ÷ (integer)

15 Fractions
- ◆ Addition and subtraction of fractions with same denominators

18 Abacus
- ◆ Using the abacus to calculate addition with carrying and subtraction with borrowing

Fifth Grade

1 Calculation with Integers, Decimals
- ◆ Multiplication of numbers with 0 as the last digit
- ◆ Using round numbers to estimate the product and quotient

3 Multiplication with Decimals
- ◆ The meaning of multiplication with decimals
- ◆ Application of calculation rules

4 Division with Decimals
- ◆ The meaning of division with decimals
- ◆ The meaning of "shousubai"

** "Let's use the Calculator" **
- ◆ To familiarize students with the calculator and to deepen students' interest in numbers

8 Addition and Subtraction with Fractions
- ◆ Addition and subtraction of fractions with different denominators

Sixth Grade

1 Integers and Fractions
- ◆ (fraction) x (integer)
- ◆ (fraction) ÷ (integer)

2 Multiplication and Division
- ◆ Meaning of multiplying with fractions
- ◆ Application of calculation rules
- ◆ Meaning of division of fractions
- ◆ The relationship between multiplication and division

4 Fractions and Decimals
- ◆ The meaning of the greatest common denominator
- ◆ Mixed calculations with fractions and decimals
- ◆ Mixed calculations (multiplication and division) of fractions

example, in the learning of addition and subtraction, the instructional system involves not only gradually increasing the number of digits over time but also takes into consideration the concept of place value. The process of regrouping is systematically introduced in the operations. All the possibilities are laid out in a specific order. Moreover, addition and subtraction are introduced first in separate units and then mixed together in the same unit to facilitate the complementary relationship between addition and subtraction.

Beyond the overall structure of elementary mathematics, Japanese teachers' manuals also lay out coherent information on the mathematical content and pedagogical knowledge for every unit. The overview of the mathematics content and goals, the instructional system, and the instructional plan, as well as key points for instruction, are clearly presented. The mathematical information is always explained in the context of the critical pedagogical issues. Using the unit on weight in the third-grade teachers' manual as an example (see Appendix F), the learning goals of the unit are clearly identified, and a thorough and in-depth treatment of the topic of weight is clearly reflected in these goals. The mathematical components are always presented in the context of teaching. For example, it is pointed out that the concept of weight is more difficult to understand than length or volume because weight is impossible to estimate or judge from the appearance of the objects, therefore making it important to provide students with different manipulative experience. The steps for developing the concepts should go from direct comparison, to indirect comparison, then to measuring by arbitrary unit, and finally to measuring by universal units.

In Japanese teachers' manuals, the common difficulties and mistakes stu-

dents may have are always illustrated for the teachers. Instructional activities are suggested to clarify those misconceptions. For example, it is common for students at this age to believe that an object's weight changes when the physical position or the shape of the object changes. Therefore, it is imperative to engage students in specific activities, such as weighing an object after changing its position and weighing clay after changing its shape to provide opportunities to discuss the misconceptions. In addition, the key points of the discussion address the particular features of the mathematics being taught in the lesson, the developing nature of the mathematical thinking of the students, and the critical mathematical ideas students should learn from the activity. The conceptual basis is illustrated, along with a good lesson script, for every lesson in the curriculum. The connections among mathematical content, students, and teaching are always made explicit.

ACTIVITIES

Participants were first asked to think about the concept of weight for a few minutes. What do they know about the concept and how would they plan their lessons if they were to teach a class of third-grade students the concept of weight? What are the elements that are important for the students to learn? By putting themselves in the role of a classroom teacher and focusing on teaching one specific mathematical topic, the participants were set to evaluate how the Japanese materials may or may not be helpful for American teachers to learn to teach.

Next, the translated materials from the Japanese teachers' manuals for the unit on weight in third-grade mathematics were handed to the participants (Shinpan Sansu 3: Kyoushiyou Shidousho, 1993; refer to Appendix F for the translation). They were given time to read individually and then, in small groups, discuss their assessment of the materials. The participants discussed whether the materials actually expanded their mathematical knowledge about the concept of weight and how the materials may or may not help them to teach the concept.

Finally, the whole group was brought together to discuss whether materials like this would be helpful for teachers—to build their mathematical content knowledge and to help them conduct lessons that would lead to students' understanding of the topic. Questions of how materials of this nature could be used at preservice or inservice training for teachers and what other information would be needed were also raised.

DISCUSSION SUMMARY

The discussion ranged from general concerns about the differences between Japanese and American societies to specific questions about the amount of classroom time devoted to a particular lesson.

Participants asked questions about general Japanese background, the national curriculum, the textbook and curriculum development processes, and preservice and inservice teacher training. Such information was necessary for the participants to place the Japanese teachers' manuals in perspective. An example of one Japanese scope and sequence chart and its English translation were shown to illustrate the sequential and systematic approach to the mathematical concepts throughout the elementary school cur-

riculum (see Figure 1).

There seemed to be a consensus among the participants that materials similar to the Japanese materials would be very helpful. They pointed out that the Japanese materials have more mathematical knowledge and guidance for teaching than most currently available American curriculum materials. The notes in the Japanese teachers' manuals that anticipated how students might respond to questions or activities and the common misconceptions of the students would be particularly helpful for inservice training. Such materials can also be used in preservice training and in the teacher preparation process in the first few years of teaching. Teachers can use the activities suggested in the curriculum to talk with each other about teaching. The diagram of the sequence of concepts within a grade and across different grades clearly shows what mathematical concepts come before and after the current concept. It offers an explicit mathematical knowledge structure that is easy for teachers to follow.

The difficulties American teachers might have using the materials were also addressed. For example, for this unit on weight, Japanese manuals suggest spending 8 hours discussing 14 questions. Given the typical U.S. curriculum and texts, U.S. teachers are accustomed to using many more problems to "fill" time. Japanese lessons tend to use one good leading question with the specific mathematical goal in mind for a discussion of the entire lesson. American teachers may have difficulties with this approach. American teachers need to learn how to ask questions and how to lead a discussion about mathematics ideas in an in-depth approach. They need to have knowledge of mathematical content, and also know how to develop a climate of inquiry. Additional information, such as the diagram in Figure 2, would be helpful for further explicit guidance about how each of the activities in this unit helps facilitate students' thinking and learning about the topics. These kinds of information could provide another piece of mathematical knowledge for thinking about pedagogy.

There were concerns about the different cultural expectations between Japan and the United States. Japanese culture has elements that support teaching and learning. There is an assumption about parent involvement in education that does not necessarily hold true for this country. In the United States, teachers need materials to support communication with parents. There are also issues related specifically to the American context. For example, it is necessary to assist teachers who have students who speak primarily in a language other than English.

Some participants chose to focus the discussion on issues embedded in the American system or their own particular institutions, for example, the lack of good mathematics textbooks at the college level. Therefore, some college teachers choose to write their own teaching

Figure 2. Understanding and Teaching the Concept of Weight

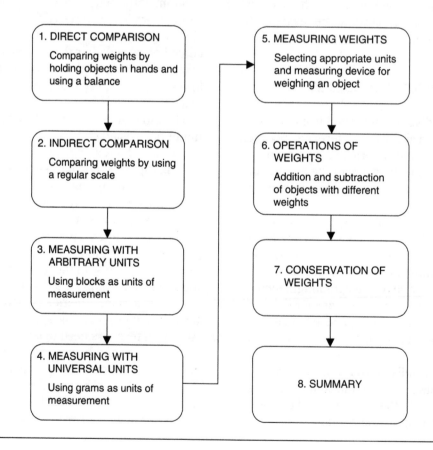

materials and activity books for their classes. Similarly, some elementary curricular materials are not useful for teaching mathematics. There were also concerns about the differences between math content and method courses at the preservice level. Different states require prospective teachers to take different numbers of hours in math courses, and there are also very different expectations of the content of those courses. The college structure of two separate departments—mathematics and mathematics education, both of which are involved in the training of prospective elementary school teachers—may not be the best way to enhance the mathematical knowledge of future teachers. Professors in the mathematics department are not likely to teach content necessary for elementary mathematics nor to understand mathematics in the setting of elementary classroom practices.

During the discussion, most people focused on the materials and carefully examined the content in terms of the mathematical knowledge provided and the issues involved in teaching the concept. Others seemed to focus on questions beyond the materials and beyond the two main questions raised in the workshop.

Those people were more concerned about the specific circumstances with which they themselves have to deal in their own work.

REFERENCES

Ball, D. L., & Cohen, D. K. (1996). Reform by the book: What is—or might be—the role of curriculum materials in teacher learning and instructional reform. *Educational Researcher, 25*(9), 6-8, 14.

Gill, A., & McPike, L. (1995). What we can learn from Japanese teachers' manuals? *American Educator, 19*(1), 14-24.

Lee, S. Y. (1998). School context and mathematics learning. In S. Paris & H. Wellman (Eds.), *Global prospects for education: Development, culture, and schooling* (pp. 45-77). Washington, DC: American Psychological Association.

Leitzel, J. R. C. (Ed.) (1991). *A call for change: Recommendations for mathematical preparation of teachers of mathematics.* Washington, DC: The Mathematical Association of America, Committee on the Mathematical Education of Teachers.

National Council of Teachers of Mathematics. (1991). *Professional standards for teaching mathematics.* Reston, VA: Author.

Shinpan Sansu 3: Kyoushiyou Shidousho. (1993). [*New edition of arithmetic 3: Teachers' guidance*] Tokyo: Kyouiku Shuppan, Inc. (in Japanese).

Stevenson, H. W., & Lee, S. Y. (1995). The East Asian version of whole-class teaching. *Educational Policy, 9*(2), 152-168.

Student Curriculum Materials: Investigations in Number, Data, and Space

Marco Ramirez

SESSION GOALS

The session, focused on the use of curriculum materials as a way to help teachers learn mathematics, offered participants the opportunity to closely examine the information presented in two sample teachers' manuals and to think carefully about how materials like these may or may not provide resources for teachers or prospective teachers to acquire mathematical knowledge as well as how to teach mathematics. In the second part of the session, participants considered a lesson on 3-dimensional geometry from Investigations in Number, Data, and Space, *an elementary mathematics program in the United States.*

OVERVIEW

What kind of mathematical support do curriculum materials provide teachers? Curriculum materials in the United States address teachers' needs in a variety of ways. Traditionally, some teacher-support materials provide just the answers to problems, while others display worked out solutions. As the curriculum has expanded to cover more than arithmetic topics, however, curriculum developers found that teachers needed more and better resources to support their understanding of the underlying mathematical ideas in the new content and in developing approaches to teaching this new content.

In *Investigations in Number, Data, and Space*, a curriculum project funded by the National Science Foundation and developed by TERC, one of the four goals is to communicate mathematics content and pedagogy to teachers. To achieve this goal, the project has extensive teacher-support materials designed to enable teachers to move comfortably through the curriculum even though they may be teaching unfamiliar mathematical ideas (Appendix G). Key mathematical concepts in data, number, and space are outlined for each grade level, so teachers can follow the development of the ideas throughout the grades. The curriculum is presented through a series of teacher books. Each book provides lesson plans; description of the mathematical emphasis of the lesson; the materials preparation needed; reproducible student sheets for activities and games; a family letter; homework suggestions; opportunities for skill and practice; assessment activities; notes to the teacher including vocabulary, notation, and a discussion of the mathematics students are encountering; samples of the unit translated into other languages; dialogue boxes containing teacher-to-teacher discussions from teachers who piloted the project.

ACTIVITIES

Participants worked through a lesson from a fourth-grade unit on three-dimensional geometry, *Seeing Solids and Silhouettes* (Battista & Clements, 1998). The goals of the unit are to have students explore the relationship between three-dimensional objects and their two-dimensional representations and to investigate what objects look like from different perspectives. Students are to use interlocking cubes to construct cube buildings shown in drawings and describe how they mentally see the buildings (see Figure 1). The conceptual development of two- and three-dimensional representations in the program is laid out as follows: noticing shapes in the environment; observing, describing and comparing two-dimensional shapes; developing vocabulary to describe two-dimensional shapes; becoming familiar with the names of two-dimensional shapes; describing characteristics of triangles; grouping shapes according to common characteristics; composing and decomposing shapes; noticing relationships among shapes; using rotation and reflection to arrange shapes; filling a certain region with shapes; visualizing and representing two-dimensional shapes; counting, comparing, and adding quantities; building a pattern by repeating a square unit; seeing how changing the unit affects the whole pattern; constructing, observing, describing, and comparing three-dimensional shapes and objects and their characteris-

tics; creating and using two-dimensional representations of three-dimensional shapes and objects. After working with the cubes, participants read the teacher's materials for that lesson and discussed the role such materials would play in enabling teachers to conduct the lesson meaningfully and in helping teachers understand the mathematics involved.

DISCUSSION SUMMARY

The discussion focused on how such materials would facilitate a teacher's knowledge of mathematics and facilitate the teaching of mathematics. Many of the participants felt a strength of the Japanese materials was the clear presentation of the scope and sequence that would facilitate a teacher's understanding about the mathematical direction of the unit. The participants identified strengths of *Investigations* as: teachers' notes, mathematical emphasis, classroom routines, and translations. Participants considered the degree of support necessary for teachers and spent some time commenting on the reality of teaching from a school perspective, raising issues of teacher preparation in mathematics, credentialing and licensing procedures, time for planning lessons, diverse nature of students' mathematical and cultural backgrounds, home environment and support, and language. If such a reality does in fact exist, participants questioned what type of curriculum-support mechanisms are needed to address the situation in mathematics classrooms. One unresolved issue is the extent to which teacher materials, such as the Japanese or *Investigations* materials, can be used successfully by teachers on an individual basis with little or no leadership support from colleagues.

Figure 1. Fourth-Grade Lesson

Name _____

Make the Buildings

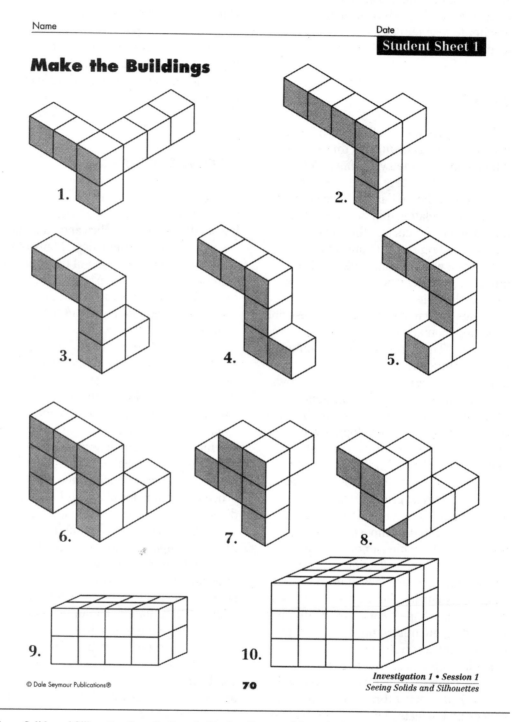

1.

2.

3.

4.

5.

6.

7.

8.

9.

10.

Investigation 1 • Session 1
Seeing Solids and Silhouettes

88

REFERENCE

Battista, M. T., & Clements, D. H. (1998). *Seeing solids and silhouettes: Investigations in number, data, and space.* Reading, MA: Scott Foresman.

Case Materials

Carne Barnett

SESSION GOALS

Participants in this session explored the potential of using narrative case materials, similar to those used in the business, law, and medical professions, as a learning tool for mathematics teachers. The session highlighted the cases and processes developed by the Mathematics Case Methods Project at WestEd as an example for participants to examine and discuss.

On-going studies of the professional development offered by the Mathematics Case Methods Project have shown that involvement in case discussions can have a positive influence on teachers' understanding of mathematics and how they planned their lessons (Barnett, 1998; Gordon & Heller, 1995; Gordon, Heller, & Lee, 1994).

One goal of the presenter was to illustrate how a deliberately facilitated case discussion can help teachers acquire an advanced and flexible knowledge of the mathematics content they teach. Another goal was to demonstrate how deep analysis of the mathematics—in the context of a classroom situation—can prepare teachers to make informed and strategic teaching decisions.

OVERVIEW

The session began with a brief history of the Mathematics Case Methods Project, which started in 1987 as a pilot study in collaboration with Lee Shulman of Stanford University. Shulman's ideas had a strong influence on the project. Most importantly, he pointed out that teachers need a special kind of content knowledge, which he called pedagogical content knowledge. With this in mind, the Mathematics Case Methods Project designed a set of cases to build teachers' understanding of rational numbers that merged with the teaching decisions and learning challenges related to these concepts. Other projects, such as the Developing Mathematical Ideas Project at the Educational Development Center and the budding Science Cases Project at WestEd, are developing similar materials to promote content learning that is grounded in classroom practice.

The Mathematics Case Methods Project is a comprehensive program that includes the development of cases, the creation of videotapes and materials to support the use of cases, and the large-scale dissemination of the case discussion approach. This project primarily serves practicing teachers.

The casebook created by the project— *Fractions, Decimals, Ratios, and Percents* (Barnett, Goldenstein, & Jackson, 1994)— contains teacher-authored narratives that are studied as a collection. The cases describe dilemmas that occurred in lessons on rational number concepts. The accompanying facilitator's guide describes the key mathematical and pedagogical issues that typically arise in each discussion. A second casebook, featuring primary-grade mathematics topics, is in development. During the next part of the session, the presenter modeled how case discussions in the Mathematics Case Methods Project would be introduced to teachers. First, four purposes for discussing cases, related to the mathematics, children's thinking, instruction, and language issues, were presented. (Refer to Appendix H for copies of the overhead transparencies that were used.) Next, participants were invited to take part in a discussion of the case titled "Six-Tenths or Four-Fifths of a Dollar." The presenter modeled a step-by-step process, developed by the Mathematics Case Methods Project, which provides a familiar routine for discussing cases and for focusing the discussion on productive issues. After reading the case but before the discussion, participants worked on a "Starter Problem" related to the case, designed to help them think about what might be difficult or confusing for a child. Then, participants quickly called out factual information from the case. This part of the process helps to keep important pieces of background information from being overlooked. After listing important facts, participants worked in pairs to formulate discussion issues and put them in a question format. Working in pairs helps those who might be intimidated by

the mathematics feel a little more comfortable. As the issues were read to the group, they were recorded on chart paper in the front of the room. Two of the issues brought up in this session, for example, were: "Is it appropriate to use the area model rather than a set model?" and "Were fifths confused with nickels in this lesson?"

These issues are typical for this case and commonly lead to a discussion about the contrasts among various fraction representations and applications. For example, this case elicits examination of the fraction kit used in the case and its limitations for understanding a fraction as a comparison, rather than two separate numbers. It also addresses the limitations of relying on only one representation, such as an area model, and assuming that the students' understandings will transfer to other situations, such as set models or the number line. It also stimulates discussion about whether, when, and how other representations should be introduced.

During the discussion of the issues posed by the group, participants were invited to illustrate their ideas on the chart in the front of the room or with various materials distributed among the tables. By seeing how someone else interprets an idea or solves a problem, each participant's own understanding is enhanced. The public display of these ideas stimulates additional ideas and questions.

During the discussion, the presenter modeled how to invite comments on the issues being discussed, help participants focus on one idea long enough to examine it deeply, and ask questions to elicit justification or evaluation of an idea or to challenge the thinking of the group. These techniques have proven to be helpful in deepening the reflection and inviting careful analysis by members of the group.

Only a short discussion was possible during this session; thus many of the mathematical issues embedded in the case were only touched upon or were not discussed. The section below called "Opportunities Afforded by this Approach" identifies some of the other mathematical ideas that could be discussed in a longer time frame

DISCUSSION SUMMARY

Pitfalls of this approach

The facilitator of a case discussion must be very knowledgeable about the mathematics in the case and have skills to know how to advance the thinking of the group members. Facilitators new to cases should be encouraged to learn from others with more experience.

Participants asked how the process might be used with preservice teachers. They were also concerned about finding the time to cover the content required in prescribed math courses. They were referred to Joanne Lobato at San Diego State University, who has successfully integrated cases into her mathematics course. She designed questions for each rational number case to which students respond in writing and bring to class. This eliminates much of the time needed for discussants to pick out the issues to discuss among themselves. The drawback is that practicing teachers claim that the process of generating the issues themselves is one of the more beneficial parts of the discussion.

There was also concern that many course instructors might integrate a case discussion here and there without realizing that learning from cases can be very different from learning from other materials. The mathematics Case Methods cases, for example, are designed to build

interconnected knowledge about rational numbers and are best discussed as a collection.

Opportunities afforded by this approach

Many participants agreed that cases offer a site for discussing complex mathematical concepts. A mathematician in the group pointed out that mathematics courses are specifically designed for architects and engineers, using problems faced by architects and engineers in their work. The mathematics courses designed for teachers teach the mathematics apart from teaching practice. Case discussions were thought to be a potential candidate for such a course.

It was also pointed out that a single case, such as the one discussed during the session, can offer a platform on which to examine several central ideas of mathematics very closely. For example, there were opportunities to examine the relationship of division to fractions, the difference between discrete and continuous representations, and different models of division. The added benefit of the case discussion approach was that these ideas can be discussed in the context of how they might be taught, learned, or misunderstood by students.

Cases also offer opportunities to examine the role of oral, written, and symbolic language in learning and teaching mathematics. The case discussion in this presentation illustrated that mathematics learning can either be impeded or facilitated by how language is used or interpreted. This is particularly important for teachers who view mathematics as language free and for teachers of limited English speakers.

One advantage of case discussions is that they can be very engaging, as was demonstrated during this session. Participants want to resolve their own confusion and are anxious to have their ideas discussed. Sometimes it is difficult, however, for the facilitator to slow the discussion and allow ample time for reflection and deep examination of others' ideas. The facilitator must focus the discussion and coordinate the ideas offered by the participants to make the discussion useful. As case discussion participants gain experience, they learn the importance of carefully analyzing one idea before moving on to the next.

REFERENCES

Barnett, C. (1998). Mathematics teaching cases as a catalyst for informed strategic inquiry. *Teaching and Teacher Education, 14* (1), 81-93.

Barnett, C., Goldenstein, D., & Jackson, B. (1994). *Fractions, decimals, ratios, and percents: Hard to teach and hard to learn?* Portsmouth, NH: Heinemann.

Gordon, A., & Heller, J. (1995). *Traversing the web: Pedagogical reasoning among the new and continuing case methods participants.* Paper presented at the annual meeting of the American Educational Research Association, San Francisco, CA.

Gordon, A., Heller, J., & Lee, G. (1994*). Mathematics case methods: External longitudinal evaluation.* Unpublished Manuscript.

Programs and Practices

Deborah Schifter, Virginia Bastable, and Jill Bodner Lester

SESSION GOALS

The session centered on excerpts from Developing Mathematical Ideas (DMI), a mathematics inservice program for elementary and middle-grade teachers created by the Center for the Development of Teaching at the Education Development Center, Inc., in Newton, MA. DMI was designed to help preservice and inservice teachers think through the major ideas of K-6 mathematics and examine how children develop those ideas. The goal of the session was to illustrate a model of a program designed to provide teachers with opportunities to learn mathematics.

OVERVIEW

At the heart of the DMI materials are sets of classroom episodes (cases) illustrating student thinking as described by their teachers. In addition to case discussions, the curriculum offers teachers opportunities to explore mathematics in lessons led by facilitators; share and discuss the work of their own students; plan, conduct, and analyze a mathematics interview of one of their own students; view and discuss videotapes of mathematics

classrooms and mathematics interviews; write their own classroom episode; analyze lessons taken from innovative elementary mathematics curricula; and read overviews of related research. When DMI is used with undergraduates, students are assigned to elementary classrooms to complete their assignments.

When completed, the curriculum will comprise a series of five seminars, each designed for 24 hours of class time and organized around a particular mathematical theme. Two seminars have been developed so far: Number and Operations: Building a System of Tens, and Number and Operations: Making Meaning for Operations. Three seminars under development are Examining Features of Shape; Measuring Space in One, Two, and Three Dimensions; and Working with Data.

BUILDING A SYSTEM OF TENS

This seminar begins with cases from second- and sixth-grade classrooms focusing on the methods children use for adding and subtracting two-digit numbers when, building on their knowledge of the number system, they construct their own procedures. What are the various ways children naturally tend to think about separating and combining numbers? And what must they understand in order to work with numbers in these ways? These questions motivate the rest of the module. The focus of the last half of the seminar is how these basic concepts are applied and extended in the middle-grade years through multidigit multiplication and division and work with decimal fractions.

As seminar participants investigate children's thinking, they also engage in the mathematics for themselves, practicing mental arithmetic, and sharing their strategies for adding, subtracting, multiplying, and dividing multidigit numbers. In our experience, many who come to the seminar believe that the algorithms they teach offer the only valid methods of computation. And those who invent their own strategies often feel sheepish, as if they are "cheating" by using "less sophisticated" methods. At first, then, teachers need to loosen their hold on these beliefs. As they more fluently maneuver in our number system, they also begin thinking about properties of the operations. In particular, they develop models for multiplication and division and work through how the distributive property is involved when multiplying or dividing multidigit numbers. Toward the end of the module, seminar participants consider representations of, and operations with, decimal fractions and examine how ideas of place value, which they have been studying since the beginning of the course, play out when applied to the right of the decimal point.

MAKING MEANING FOR OPERATIONS

This module, which examines the actions and situations modeled by the four basic operations, begins with a view of young children's counting strategies as they address problems they would later solve by either adding, subtracting, multiplying, or dividing. It then looks at different situations modeled by whole-number addition/subtraction and multiplication/division. The latter part of the module revisits the operations in the context of rational numbers. Which ideas, issues, and generalizations need to be refined or revised once the domain under consideration is extended to include rational numbers? For example, how does one make sense of multiplication and division when the numbers being operated on—fractions—already have an implied division?

As in the first seminar, while teachers work through the cases to learn how children confront these mathematical issues, they also work through the mathematics for themselves. Since most teachers are products of an education that emphasizes rote memorization of math facts, they, too, need to think through the variety of situations modeled by addition and subtraction, and they, too, need to examine various representations of multiplication and division. Especially challenging for teachers is the work on operations with fractions.

WORKSHOP ACTIVITIES: THE BREAK-OUT SESSION

In the teacher preparation workshop, we drew mainly on material from Building a System of Tens, showing examples of videotape, print cases, mathematical explorations, and seminar participants' writing assignments to illustrate the flow of ideas and demonstrate how the various strategies provide different windows on the same or related ideas. Having talked the group through the issues that arose in the sessions on the base-10 structure of number and addition/subtraction multidigit computation, we stopped to work together on the session devoted to multidigit multiplication. Specifically, we showed video cases of two children who explain their methods for solving 12×29 and 17×36, respectively, and of one child, Thomas, who presents a strategy for 17×36 that does not work. This is what Thomas did to multiply 17×36,

$$
\begin{array}{cccc}
17 & 36 & 20 & 800 \\
+\ 3 & +\ 4 & \times 40 & -\ 4 \\
\hline
20 & 40 & 800 & 796 \\
 & & & -\ 3 \\
 & & & \hline
 & & & 793
\end{array}
$$

Our purpose for including the latter case in our curriculum is that, though mistaken, this child's strategy has strong elements of logic. By taking apart Thomas's solution methods and identifying what is solid in his thinking—it would be an effective strategy for adding $17 + 36$—and where his logic has gone awry, and comparing elements of strategies to those of his classmates, teachers can practice important pedagogical skills while working out for themselves concepts of multidigit multiplication. This case illustrates how teachers can transform student error into a learning opportunity for their classes.

DISCUSSION SUMMARY

In Sunday's DMI break-out session, some participants became involved in sorting out for themselves the issues that the Thomas video case presented and could see its value for teacher learning. But other members were unwilling to

accept the premise that a child's incorrect method is worth examining. Instead, they argued that Thomas's teacher should have been teaching in such a way that none of her pupils would make such an error.

This impulse to "fix" child or teacher whenever a mistake is made is prevalent in the culture of mathematics education. In fact, teachers and teacher educators often believe that successful teaching means an absence of error. But mathematicians will say that doing mathematics entails making mistakes and learning from them. One aspect of our work with teachers is to help them explore error as a vehicle for further learning. Therefore, we believe the impulse to "fix" must be checked if classrooms are to become contexts for the development of mathematical habits and for building from an analysis of common error.

Other participants' comments that emerged from the session included the following:

- Pedagogical strategies—manipulative use, for example—don't need to be taught separately; they can arise naturally in the contexts of the cases and mathematical explorations.
- In teacher education courses, different strategies should be used complementarily. For example, print and video cases each have their respective advantages. Also, after examining children's thinking in the written cases, it is important that teachers check out similar ideas with "live" children in their classes.
- When undergraduates have only one mathematics course to prepare them for teaching, dedicating so much time to one theme only is difficult. For example, in the DMI course materials, prime and composite numbers are not specifically addressed.

- When inquiry is the style of the class, participants' thinking is validated, appreciated, and valued (as opposed to settings in which all ideas come from the instructor). And with specific reference to preservice courses, undergraduates have the opportunity to ask questions related to their fears about teaching.

Video as a Delivery Mechanism

Bradford Findell, Deborah Loewenberg Ball

SESSION GOALS

The session "Video as a Delivery Mechanism" focused on using video as an alternative approach to help teachers learn mathematics. The goal of the session was to consider how video can be used to provide opportunities for learning mathematics. The session was organized around two video clips. The first video excerpt was a 5-minute teacher-directed class discussion of student solutions to a mathematical problem. The second excerpt was the beginning of a 30-minute lecture prepared as part of a video course on arithmetic for prospective elementary teachers.

For each video, participants were asked to identify and discuss opportunities and pitfalls presented by the video. In particular, what opportunities for learning mathematics are afforded by the video and how might they be exploited? What potential pitfalls does the video bring and how might they be mitigated? The intent was to think about characteristics of a video that make it productive for engaging in discussions of the mathematical problems of teaching.

A VIDEO CASE: CINDY

The first video came from the VideoCases for Mathematics Professional Development project, directed by Nanette Seago.[1] In their work, they found that it was important to ask participants to engage in the mathematics before viewing the video. To that end, the participants were asked to solve the problem in Figure 1, trying to anticipate also how a middle-school student might approach the problem.

Some participants used a table to arrive at a solution, others used general algebraic approaches, and most arrived at a formula such as $P = T + 2$, where P is the perimeter and T is the number of triangles. Some participants were concerned about what units of length might be used to measure the perimeter. In the problem statement, there is no mention of the length of a side of a triangle. The simplest approach is to assume the length is one unit. But this assumption doesn't completely resolve the problem because the resulting formula obscures a neces-

---

[1]Judith Mumme and Nicholas Branca are Principal Investigators for the project.

Figure 1. Polygons All in a Row

If equilateral triangles are placed in a row, as shown below, how does the perimeter vary with the number of triangles? What would the perimeter be if 100 triangles were placed in such a row?

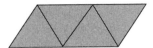

Can you come up with a general method and express it algebraically? Explain your reasoning.

sary unit conversion: T is a number of triangles, whereas P is a length.

The emphasis in the discussion was that different approaches yield solutions that look different but are algebraically equivalent. Some participants wondered whether the solutions would have been different if they had been asked to think about how preservice or inservice teachers would approach the task. Which approach, they wondered, would provide more direct access to the mathematics? And for whom would such an approach work?

Participants then watched a video segment from an eighth-grade class engaged in the same triangle problem. Participants were asked to look in particular for the mathematics in the video in order to focus the subsequent discussion toward the mathematical opportunities and pitfalls.

SUMMARY OF CINDY VIDEO

In this excerpt, Cindy, the teacher, brings the class together to discuss their solutions to the triangle problem. She points out that the class has noticed two rules: a "plus one" rule that describes how the perimeter changes with each

additional triangle, and a "plus two" rule that describes the relationship between the number of triangles and the perimeter. She illustrates these rules in a table (see Figure 2).

To describe the "plus two" rule, a student suggests the equation $T + 2 =$ perimeter, where $T =$ the number of triangles. Cindy points out that every new triangle adds three edges and asks why the rule should be "+2" and not "+3". One student shows that when a triangle is added, some of the edges get "closed up." Another student suggests that the triangles account for the top and bottom edges, and the "+2" comes from the two ends. Then Lindsay asks, since there are two ends with two edges each, "shouldn't it be +4?" In response to Lindsay's question, one student proposes what it might be like with squares. Cindy puts Lindsay's

Figure 2. Cindy's Table

Triangle		unit Perimeter	
1	+2	3	>1
2	+2	4	>1
3	+2	5	>1
4		6	

question on hold and poses versions of the problem that replace the triangles with squares, regular pentagons, and regular hexagons.

DISCUSSION SUMMARY

Participants identified opportunities and pitfalls of using the video as listed in Table 1. Several of these provoked extended discussion. In particular, participants noted that the video case could be used with many different audiences for many different purposes, but that a facilitator would probably be required, especially if the goal was to learn some mathematics.

Participants were concerned about the mathematical focus of the lesson. Was the purpose to look for patterns or to analyze perimeter? Was this a lesson in geometry or in patterns and algebra? The lesson was supposed be part of a unit on functions, where the specific purpose is to use the context to get data from which a rule can be generated. Some participants viewed the vagueness of the goal as a potential pitfall; others suggested that the vagueness might present an opportunity to discuss the importance of setting clear goals for lessons and keeping the goal in focus during the lesson.

There was some sentiment that the purpose and the mathematics were somewhat confused in this episode, and that the confusion was compounded by the several ideas that seemed to contribute to "rules." The "plus one" and "plus two" rules could be used to highlight the vertical and horizontal relationships in the table, providing opportunities for distinguishing between recursive and "closed form" representations of functions. The "plus 3" and "plus 4" ideas, on the other hand, were tied more to the geometry of

the situation. With so many ideas in such a short time, unless the teacher is able to lead the class toward a synthesis of the ideas, it will be difficult for students to form clear understandings that will support deeper learning about function. Also, unless the teacher has a clear understanding of the mathematics, it will be difficult for her to lead the class toward such a synthesis. The teacher needs to explore the mathematical territory of the problem prior to teaching it.

The Cindy video can be used to discuss teacher decision making: Why, for example, did Cindy choose to postpone responding to Lindsay's question? And how are teachers' decisions influenced by what they see as the goal of the lesson?

A VIDEO LECTURE: HERB GROSS

The second video excerpt was a portion of "Gateways to Arithmetic, Lecture #7: Subtracting Whole Numbers" from a 51-lecture collection on mathematics content. In each 30-minute videotape, Herb Gross lectures for a video audience, sometimes speaking directly to the camera. He writes notes and solutions as he proceeds through the content.

SUMMARY OF VIDEO LECTURE

This lecture begins with a short discussion of some pointers on how to use the video. The professor announces, "I have made the decision to jam the tape full of information. You can always rewind the tape and watch it again" whenever the verbal description is too fast. He explains that whether a fill-in-the-blank question is easy or hard depends on where the blank is. In Figure 3a, for example, the second question is easier because one associates

Table 1. Opportunities and Pitfalls of the Cindy Video

Opportunities	Potential Pitfalls
Using the Video • The video can be used with many audiences and with many purposes. • The video shows the "messiness" of real classrooms and teaching, which may serve as a source of motivation. • Teachers or facilitators may stop the video and proceed at whatever pace is desired.	**Using the Video** • The video cannot be used without a facilitator. • The goal of the lesson seems unclear. • This video case may focus more on pedagogy than on mathematics. Teachers might avoid or fail to recognize the mathematics. • If the goal is to learn mathematics, this video might not be an efficient use of time.
Mathematics • The video is mathematically rich, showing multiple ways to connect with particular mathematical goals. • Participants can explore the relationship between the recursive and closed formulas and then look at how it plays out with students. • Participants can examine the equivalence of alternative approaches given by students. • The video can be used to talk about the importance of mathematical justification. • Participants can discuss the role of language. How might the teacher respond, for example, to students who interpret the word "row" differently? • The video shows connections between pedagogy and mathematics. It can be used to talk about the mathematics of teaching.	**Mathematics** • What are the important mathematical ideas? It is hard to tell from the linearity of the tape. • Teachers may not know the math well enough to engage. Can they learn it from this tape? • The language of the teacher may lead to misunderstandings. For example, the idea of a "row" is difficult with pentagons.
Teacher Decisions • The video can be used to talk about teacher decision making. How does a teacher decide how to answer questions and which student ideas to pursue? • The video can be use to explore missed opportunities provided by student statements.	
Students • The video provides a window into student thinking	

Figure 3. Comparing Fill-in-the-Blank Questions

_____ is the capital of California. $3 + 2 = $ ___
Sacramento is the capital of _____ . $3 + $ __ $= 5$

(a)   (b)

Sacramento with California even if one does not know that it is the capital. In the first question, on the other hand, one might associate California with many cities. Similarly, in Figure 3b, the first question is easier because one can get the answer by association or by pressing keys on a calculator. The second question, however, requires some understanding.

Gross doesn't like the "take-away" concept and instead emphasizes the connection between addition and subtraction, pointing out that, in technical terms, subtraction is called "inverse addition." He shows (Figure 4a) how one might give change from a $500 bill for a $279 purchase. So 500 – 279 means the number we have to add to 279 to get 500. He shows connections to more traditional written procedures for subtraction (Figure 4c) by showing how one might trade a $100 bill for ten $10 bills and then trade one of those for ten $1 bills (see

Figure 4b). Borrowing is to subtraction, what carrying is to addition.

DISCUSSION SUMMARY

Again, the participants identified opportunities and pitfalls (see Table 2), several of which provoked extended discussion. In particular, several participants voiced their perspectives that presenting a lecture as a means of instructing preservice teachers is in conflict with what they feel teachers should be prepared to do in their classrooms. But because the video can be paused and viewed again, and because there is no interaction, viewing the video is not the same as sitting in a lecture.

Although some participants suggested that the video could be used without a facilitator, others wondered what a viewer has to know about subtraction and place-

Figure 4. Methods for Computing 500 – 279

	$100	$10	$1
	5	0	0
	4	10	0
	4	9	10
−	2	7	9
	2	2	1

(a):
279
+ 1
280
+ 20
300
+ 200
500

(c):
$\overset{4}{\cancel{5}}\overset{9}{\cancel{0}}\overset{1}{0}$
− 279
221

(a)   (b)   (c)

Table 2. Opportunities and Pitfalls of the Herb Gross Video

Opportunities	Potential Pitfalls
Use	**Use**
• The facilitator or the teacher can stop or rewind the tape to review the lecture or to investigate or reflect on the mathematics. • The video can be used without a facilitator. • Facilitators can ask teachers, "Can you make sense of this video?"	• Teachers may not know the math well enough to engage. Can they learn it from this tape? What does one need to know about place value in order to learn from the tape? • The video may allow passive engagement in the mathematics content.
Mathematics	**Mathematics**
• Videos like this can provide a useful synthesis or summary of the mathematical topics. • The video is mathematically rich, showing multiple ways to connect with particular mathematical goals. For example, the statement "Numbers in the same column modify the same noun" may be used as a source for discussion of place value. • Participants might explore why it is important to view subtraction as inverse addition. • A facilitator might use mathematical ideas in the lecture and make them simpler for students.	• The important mathematical ideas may be hard to tell from the linearity of the tape. • The video omits some conceptual difficulties in subtraction. • The procedural focus may ingrain the standard subtraction algorithm more deeply. • The lecture may perpetuate the belief that if you repeat something enough, people will understand.

value for the video to make sense. Although the video provides a useful synthesis of some mathematical ideas, some conceptual difficulties are omitted. Some participants suggested that the lecture might be used as a source of mathematical questions for deeper consideration and reflection.

CONCLUSION

In keeping with the guiding principles of the second day of the Workshop, we looked at these videos as sources for mathematical questions. The perspective was to ask how video can serve as a tool in the mathematics learning process. We were able to shed some light on two very different uses of video with preservice teachers, perhaps leading to consideration of different types of video to serve different learning goals for teachers. Furthermore, by exploring both opportunities and pitfalls in each of the videos, participants were able to move beyond quick conclusions about the quality of the video to ask questions about the potential for mathematics learning.

Promising Approaches for Helping Prospective Elementary Teachers Learn Mathematics for Teaching

The closing panel offered a broad array of perspectives—from mathematics to teaching to policy—on how teachers come to learn the mathematics they need to know to teach well. The moderator concluded the session by presenting an argument for why sites of teaching practice might provide opportunities for teacher learning and broadened the list of sites of practices beyond those considered in the Workshop.

PANELISTS

Looking at Textbooks
  Richard Askey, University of Wisconsin-Madison

The Professional Growth of a Classroom Teacher
  Carol Midgett, Southport Elementary School

The Importance of Mathematical Content
  Alice Gill, American Federation of Teachers

NSF and Teacher Preparation Programs
  James Lightbourne, National Science Foundation

Where Are We? Moderator's Summary
  Joan Ferrini-Mundy, Mathematical Sciences Education Board

Looking at Textbooks

Richard Askey

INTRODUCTION

When considering what knowledge elementary school teachers need, the first book to read is the recent one by Liping Ma (1999). The answers given by many of the Chinese teachers she interviewed start to illustrate what teachers should know. There are even some suggestions about what we can do to help teachers develop this knowledge. One of the suggestions surprised me very much. Ma claimed that one of the main ways in which the Chinese teachers she interviewed developed their deep understanding of elementary mathematics was by serious study of their texts.

Here is an example of a problem that appears in a Chinese fifth-grade book and also in a Japanese elementary school text. The curves in Figure 1 are halves of

---

Figure 1. Comparing Circles

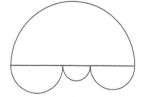

---

circles. The question is whether the length of the large half-circle is longer (along the circumference), shorter, or equal to the sum of the lengths of the three smaller half-circles.

This is a very nice problem, since it helps students to understand how the fact that the circumference of half of a circle is proportional to the diameter is important and not just a fact they have memorized and then used to compute the circumferences of different circles with different diameters. Having good multi-step problems seems to be a characteristic of a mathematics program that works. It is probably a necessary condition for a good mathematics program. Of course, as Ma says, much of the study comes from looking seriously at problems that do not need as much insight as this one does and developing different ways of solving them.

There seems to be a general feeling that long ago our textbooks only had procedures for students to follow, and reasoning was only introduced in high school geometry. A casual glance at old arithmetic books can give this impression, but a more careful reading of some of them shows this is false. Here are two illustrations from an arithmetic book by White (1870). More details will be given here than were possible in my presentation, since the details are important and the relevant texts are not widely available. One can occasionally find old texts at used bookstores, especially those in small towns and in the country.

DIVISION OF FRACTIONS

One of the problems used by Deborah Ball (1990) and again by Liping Ma (1999) in their work on the mathematical knowledge of elementary school teachers was to divide $1\frac{3}{4}$ by $\frac{1}{2}$, and make up a story problem with this division being the operation leading to a solution. The topic of division of fractions is treated very well by White. The same general format is used for two special cases and the general case. In each case, a few word problems are given, some more complicated calculations are done with numbers, and then this is summarized by principles and/or rules. Then the text contains other problems for the student to do. A few examples of each from White's text will be given here.

Case I. Fractions divided by integers.
2. A man divided 8/9 of his farm equally between 4 sons; what part of the farm did each receive?
4. If 10 oranges cost 5/8 of a dollar, what will 1 orange cost?
10. Divide 12/25 by 6.

This is worked out two ways, by dividing the numerator by 6 and by multiplying the denominator by 6. This is followed by nine problems for students to do, ending with dividing $6\frac{2}{3}$ by 10. The word problems give a good illustration of what is happening, and the calculation problems strengthen arithmetic skills. Then a general result is stated.

98. Principle. A fraction is divided by dividing its numerator or multiplying its denominator.

Case II. Integers divided by fractions.
20. How many times is 2/5 of a cent contained in 4 cents? Solution. In four cents there are 20 fifths of a cent, and 2 fifths of a cent is contained in 20 fifths of a cent 10 times.

   [I doubt if fractions of cents were used in 1870, but following the introduction of state sales taxes in the 1930s, a number of states used mills for sales taxes. In Missouri, where I grew up, there were one mill and five mill tokens, a mill being a tenth of a cent.]

22. If 5/8 of a yard of silk will make a vest, how many vests will 5 yards make? 7 yards? 10 yards?
26. Show that $\dfrac{8}{(3/5)} = \dfrac{8 \times 5}{3}$
33. What is the quotient of 125/(21/50)?
100. Rules. To divide an integer by a fraction,
   1. Multiply the integer by the denominator of the fraction and divide the product by the numerator. Or,
   2. Divide the integer by the numerator and multiply the quotient by the denominator.

Case III. Fractions divided by fractions.
37. How many times is 2/5 of an inch contained in 4/5 of an inch?
40. How many times is 1/3 contained in 3/4? 1/4 in 2/3? Suggestion: Change the fractions to twelfths.
46. What is the quotient of (12/13)/(8/11)?
57. If a family uses 4/9 of a barrel of flour in a month, how long will 2 1/3 barrels last?
60. If a man walks 3 3/10 miles in an hour, in how many hours will he walk 20 1/4 miles?
101. Principles.
   1. The quotient of two fractions having a common denominator equals the quotient of their numerators.
   2. The multiplying of both dividend and divisor by the same number does not change the value of the quotient.
102. Rules. To divide a fraction by a fraction.
   1. Reduce the fractions to a common denominator and divide the numerator of the dividend by the numerator of the divisor. Or,

2. Invert the terms of the divisor and then multiply the numerators together and also the denominators. Or,
3. Multiply both the dividend and the divisor by the least common multiple of the denominators of the fractions and divide the resulting dividend by the resulting divisor.

Notes.
1. The third rule depends on the second principle; and since multiplying two fractions by their least common multiple changes them to integers, the new dividend and divisor are always integral.
2. It is not necessary that the pupil be made equally familiar with these three methods of dividing one fraction by another. He should thoroughly master one of them.

There is a lot of good mathematics contained in a few pages. I think this material could be used as Ma says the Chinese teachers she interviewed used their texts, to develop a deeper understanding of the mathematics they teach.

SQUARE ROOTS

An even more impressive treatment is given for square roots. Section 14 is titled "Involution and Evolution." "Involution" is defined to be the process of finding powers of numbers, and "evolution" is the process of finding roots of numbers. In a note after the definition of "evolution," it says that "Evolution is the inverse of involution."

The chapter starts with powers. The first, second, third, and fourth powers of 4 are illustrated, with the last written as $4 \times 4 \times 4 \times 4 = 256$. This section ends with "etc.," so the student is to infer the general rule from this example. Many problems are given for the students to calculate, including fractions and decimals with numerical work expected to be done up to the fifth power.

Powers are then defined. The second power of a number is the product obtained by taking the number twice as a factor. An illustration of a 3 by 3 square is given, and the following comment is made. "It is also called the Square of the number, since the area of a geometrical square is represented by the product obtained by taking the number of linear units in one of its sides twice as a factor." Similar comments are made about third powers, or cubes, including an illustration of a 3 by 3 by 3 cube.

Rule. To raise a number to a given power, multiply the number by itself as many times LESS ONE as there are units in the exponent of the given power. The last product will be the required power.

The next subsection gives a second way to find a square and a cube.

32. What is the square of 53?

$$53 = 50 + 3, \text{ and } 53^2 = (50 + 3)^2$$

$$
\begin{array}{ll}
50 \ + \ 3 & \\
50 \ + \ 3 & \\
(50 \ \ 3) + 3^2 & = (50 + 3) \ \ 3 \\
50^2 + \ (50 \ \ 3) & = (50 + 3) \ \ 50 \\
\hline
50^2 + 2(50 \ \ 3) + 3^2 & = (50 + 3)^2
\end{array}
$$

Parts Added
$$
\begin{array}{rl}
50^2 = & 2500 \\
2(50 \ \ 3) = & 300 \\
3^2 = & 9 \\
\hline
= & \mathbf{2809}
\end{array}
$$

In like manner, it may be shown that the square of any number, composed of tens and units, is equal to the square of the tens, plus twice the product of the tens by the units, plus the square of the units.

Problems are given, including squares of three digit numbers. Then cubes are introduced, starting with 53 again.

The cube of 53 = $(50 + 3)^3 = 50^3 + 3(50^2 \times 3)$ + $3(50 \times 3^2) + 3^3$, as can be shown by multiplying $50^2 + 2(50 \times 3) + 3^2$ by $50 + 3$.

This is used as background material for taking square roots and cube roots. The section on square roots starts by listing the squares of 1, 10, 100, and 1,000 and the squares of 9, 99, 999, and 9,999.

Then this section continues with:

A comparison of the above numbers with their squares shows that the square of a number contains twice as many orders as the number or twice as many orders less one.

This is followed with:

406. Hence, if a number be separated into periods of two orders each, beginning at the right, there will be as many orders in its square root as there are periods in the number.

The first problems deal with how many "periods" there are in the square root of 2809, then 36864, and larger numbers up to 14440000.

The procedure for evaluating a square root starts with marking off pairs of numbers, and taking the largest square root of the pair or single digit on the left hand side of the number. For 2809, the pairs can be denoted by 28'09, although a dot above the right member of each pair is used in the book. The leftmost pair is 28, and $5^2 = 25$ is the largest square less than or equal to 28. This 5 appears in the second spot, or the tens place, since the square root of a four digit number has two digits if it can be found exactly, and so is greater than or equal to 10 and is less than 100. It is still in this range if the square root cannot be found exactly. The next term is found by using the procedure for forming a square. This is done with numbers in White's book, but it is easier to use letters. The rule above for squar-

ing can be written as

$$(10a + b)^2 = 100a^2 + 20ab + b^2 = 100a^2 + (20a + b)b.$$

The 5 found above is really 50, and the partial square root is $50^2 = 2500$. The difference of 2809 and 2500 is 309. Multiply 50 by 2 to get 100, and see how many times this divides into 309. 3 is a possibility as the next digit, but that is not sure since you need to calculate $(20a + b) \times b = (2 \times 50 + 3) \times 3 = 300 + 9$.

If the number whose square root is wanted were 2808, then 53 would be too large, the partial quotient of 3 would be too large, and 2 would have to be used instead. To continue, one just adds a decimal point, a bunch of zeros depending on how much accuracy is wanted, and continue. One problem asked was to find the square root of 586.7 to three decimal places.

As usual, Principles and Rules are then stated. These seem dogmatic, and if one has not read the text and worked the problems, these look like rules given to memorize without any reason why they hold. I hope the reader is convinced that this is not necessarily what happened, since the text contains much more than just rules to memorize. However, there is still more.

The next section, 411, is titled "Geometrical Explanation." The method of taking powers and of using this to take square roots is illustrated by a series of pictures (see Figure 2).

The same is then done for cube roots. Here are the pictures that help explain how this method works (see Figure 3).

These explanations are excellent. Current books do not have explanations for this square root algorithm, since square root algorithms are no longer taught. If all that were taught was an algorithm without any reasons why it

Figure 2. Geometrical Explanation

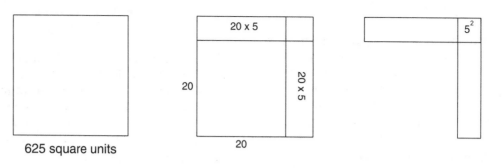

625 square units   20 x 5   20 x 5 5^2

Figure 3. Geometrical Explanation of the Process of Extracting the Cube Root

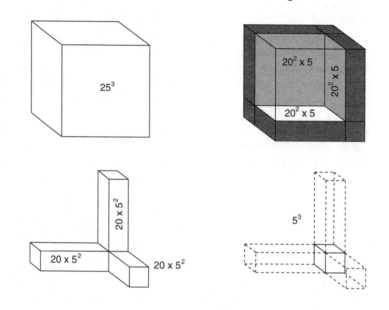

Figure 4. Geometric Picture for $(a + b)(c + d)$

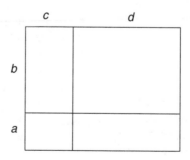

works, then there would be no reason for teaching it. There are other ways to do an algorithm one does not understand, such as punch a button on a calculator. However, if important mathematics can be taught while learning an algorithm, that changes the picture.

What I would like is the method outlined above, with one picture added to it (Figure 4), to give a geometric picture for why $(a + b)(c + d) = ac + ad + bc + bd$.

I would also like a second method of taking square roots via the old Babylonian method that we now say comes from Newton's method. There is also a very nice pictorial way of explaining this method, which is usually not given.

Draw a square with area N, and mark off a length a which is approximately the square root of N. Let e denote the error made. Then

$$N = (a + e)^2 = a^2 + 2ae + e^2.$$

We cannot solve this equation without taking a square root, which is what we are trying to learn to do. However, e is small, so e^2 is smaller. Drop it and solve the resulting linear equation for e. The resulting approximation is the old Babylonian method for extracting square roots. To see that you understand this method, work out the corresponding formula for cube roots.

What we get are algebra tiles, which seem to me to be a very restricted way of doing things that might hamper a more general picture one wants students to develop. My feeling about these tiles has been confirmed in discussions with a number of very good teachers who have had students who used algebra tiles in other programs and then had more trouble with symbolic manipulation than they should have. Drawing pictures is flexible. Algebra tiles also have the unfortunate tendency of reinforcing the mistaken view which many students have that x^2 is greater than x.

AREAS OF TRIANGLES AND PARALLELOGRAMS

Let me contrast one topic as it is done in our textbooks and in a set from Singapore (Primary Mathematics Project Team, 1993-1995). This is the area of a triangle. In many of our textbooks, this is done in the following manner. First, the formula for the area of a rectangle is motivated in reasonable ways. Second, a formula for the area of a parallelogram is found by the construction shown in Figure 5.

There is one problem with this argument. It does not deal with the general case, since the parallelogram can look like

Figure 5. Finding the Area of a Parallelogram

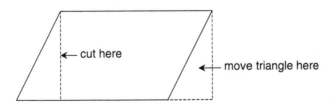

Figure 6. Another Parallelogram

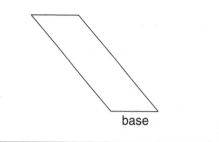

base

Figure 6. There are ways of dealing with this case, but in most of our textbooks this gap in the argument is not mentioned.

To find the area of a triangle, a parallelogram is cut in half by a line connecting opposite vertices. If the general case of a parallelogram has not been done, the general case of a triangle will also not have been done.

In a Singapore series of elementary school math books, area is introduced in the second half of third grade (Primary Mathematics Project Team, 1993-1995, 3B). Here, unit squares are used to build up more complicated figures, and halves of squares and half of a two by one rectangle are also used. They are combined into figures that are not too complicated. In the first half of fourth grade (Primary Mathematics Project Team, 1993-1995, 4A), areas and perimeters are considered again. One problem in a workbook has students compute areas and perimeters of five rectangles. They are asked to find two rectangles with the same area and two rectangles with the same perimeter. The teacher's manual (Primary Mathematics Project Team, 1994-1996, 4A) specifically points out that a figure that has a bigger area need not have a longer perimeter. More complicated figures are introduced, including a picture of a ship that was constructed with 4 by 3 postage stamps as

the pieces and a couple of diagonal cuts made so that fractions of the rectangles have to be considered. It is only in the first half of fifth grade where a formula is introduced for the area of a triangle. Up to this point, all of the areas of triangles have been based on at most half integer multiples of the unit square. In fifth grade (Primary Mathematics Project Team, 1993-1995, 5A), this restriction is removed, and the general case of a triangle is considered.

First, there is an early section on areas of specific types of polygons. These are relatively simple ones whose vertices lie on the grid points so that the figure can be decomposed into subpieces each of which is made up of rectangles or halves of rectangles. For example, there is a triangle with vertices at the points (2,0), (0,3) and (4,4) on a 4 by 4 grid. (The points are not labeled with numbers but are here for ease of reference.) The student is asked to find the area of the 4 by 4 square with vertices (0,0), (4,0), (0,4) and (4,4) and of the three triangles that are in this square and outside of the given triangle. In the workbook, students are asked to find such areas without hints. A formula for the area of a triangle is not given in this section.

Later in the same book, there is a section on areas of triangles. It starts with three illustrations of triangles and associated rectangles. For all three triangles, the base is taken to be the horizontal segment. The first is a right triangle with vertices at (0,0), (6,0), and (0,5). The second triangle has vertices at (0,0), (6,0), and (4,6), and so is completely contained in the associated rectangle, which has the vertices on the edges of the rectangle and the base as one side. The third triangle has vertices (0,0), (4,0), and (7,6), and so lies outside of the rectangle with base 4 and height 6. Students are asked to find the area of each shaded triangle and its related rectangle. They did harder problems earlier, so these problems should cause no difficulty. On the next page, arguments are given to show that the area of the triangle is half that of the related rectangle. For the right triangle, the same picture is repeated, since this argument works for all right triangles, not just those whose vertices lie on grid points. In the other two cases, new arguments are given (see Figure 7). In both cases, the triangle is decomposed into subparts that are moved to make a rectangle with the same base and half the height. These triangles are pictured with coordinates on the grid points, so it might seem that the general case is not considered. However, the arguments are completely general.

Four pages of problems follow in the text, and these are the type of problem Ma mentioned. Serious study of them can lead to alternative ways of solution and other insights. For example, the picture in Figure 8a suggests that another way of finding the area of a triangle is to decompose the triangle into two right triangles. Another figure (Figure 8b) suggests a way of doing this when an obtuse angle occurs, and the perpendicular from a vertex to the opposite side does not hit the base.

Will the students pick up on this and learn more than a formula? Some will, and many more will if the teachers know what to look for and what questions to ask. The teacher's guide (Primary Mathematics Project Team, 1994-1996,

Figure 7. Areas of Triangles

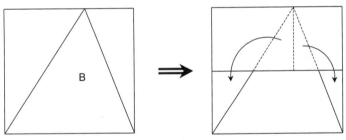

Area of related rectangle = 6 x 6 = 36 square units
Area of triangle B = __ square units

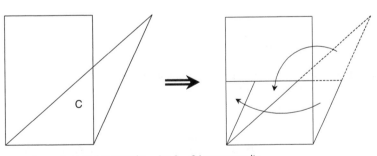

Area of related rectangle = 4 x 6 = 24 square units
Area of triangle C = __ square units

Figure 8. Decomposing Triangles into Right Triangles

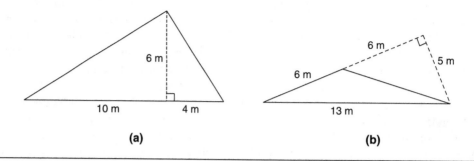

(a)   (b)

5A) has a number of useful suggestions about how to structure the 12 lessons suggested for this topic. At the start, the students are to cut out triangles, then cut them apart and reassemble them into related rectangles. The last suggestion is

Draw different triangles in different orientation with given base and height on the board. Get the student to find the area of each triangle using the formula. Bring to the pupils' attention that each side of the triangle can be regarded as a base. The base of a triangle need not be drawn horizontally all the time.

Figure 9. Areas of Triangles and Parallelograms (Lappan et al., 1998, p.67)

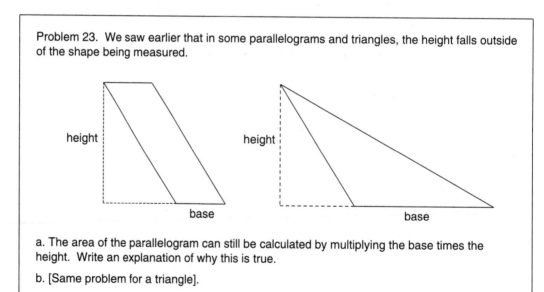

Problem 23. We saw earlier that in some parallelograms and triangles, the height falls outside of the shape being measured.

a. The area of the parallelogram can still be calculated by multiplying the base times the height. Write an explanation of why this is true.

b. [Same problem for a triangle].

From *Covering and Surrounding: Two-Dimensional Measurement Teacher's Edition* by Lappan, Fey, Fitzgerald, Friel & Phillips. © 1998 by Connected Math. Used by Permission.

The last point is important, since students frequently only see pictures of triangles with the base horizontal.

Most U.S. books do not treat the general case. Here is the treatment from one book which at least mentioned the general case. The book (Lappan, Fey, Fitzgerald, Friel, & Phillips, 1998) is one of the sixth-grade volumes in the Connected Mathematics Program. The area of a parallelogram is done in the usual way, as outlined above. The remaining case is mentioned as shown in Figure 9.

Here is what the *Teacher's Guide* says about this problem.

23a. Answers will vary. This is particularly difficult because it is hard to see that the parallelogram can be cut into three pieces and reassembled to form a rectangle with the given base and height as side lengths. Some students may rename the base the height and then describe why the formula works for the new base and height.

That is all that is said. I cannot make sense of it. I do not know what three pieces the authors had in mind, nor do I know what parallelogram they had in mind when they wrote to rename the "height" as the base. What they probably meant in the last case was not renaming the "height" but one of the two sides not parallel to the one used as the base. Some students will do this, but they need to be told that is not acceptable, since either of the two nonparallel sides could be the base and there needs to be a demonstration that the formula works in both cases.

There are reasonable ways to show that the area formula continues to hold in the case when the easy argument fails. One is to cut the parallelogram by lines parallel to the base to form smaller parallelograms where the simple argument works and then add up the areas. This requires the distributive law, which students should

know and be able to use. Another way is to complete the picture drawn above by drawing another triangle to form a rectangle. Then move the two triangles together to form a rectangle with the same height. Its base is the length of the side of one of the triangles where the side is the one on the same line as the base. The remaining part of the original rectangle is a rectangle whose area is the same as the area of the given parallelogram, and the height and base of this rectangle are the same as the height and base of the parallelogram. To help teachers, these arguments would have been useful in the *Teacher's Guide*.

If we had teachers with mathematical knowledge shown by most of the Chinese teachers interviewed by Liping Ma, then we would not have to worry too much about what is in our manuals for teachers. However, we do not have many teachers with this knowledge base, so we have to provide for them.

REFERENCES

Ball, D. (1990). The mathematical understandings that prospective teachers bring to teacher education. *The Elementary School Journal, 90*(4), 449-466.

Lappan, G., Fey, J. T., Fitzgerald, W. M., Friel, S. N., & Phillips, E. D. (1998). *Covering and surrounding, teacher's edition* (Connected Mathematics Series). White Plains, NY: Dale Seymour.

Ma, L. (1999). *Knowing and teaching elementary mathematics: Teachers' understanding of fundamental mathematics in China and the United States.* Mahwah, NJ: Lawrence Erlbaum.

Primary Mathematics Project Team. (1993-1995). *Primary mathematics, 1A to 6B and associated workbooks* (2nd ed.). Singapore: Federal Publications.

Primary Mathematics Project Team. (1994-1996). *Primary mathematics teacher's guide, 1A to 6B* (2nd ed.). Singapore: Federal Publications.

White, E. E. (1870). *A complete arithmetic.* Cincinnati, OH: Van Antwerp, Bragg and Co.

The Professional Growth of a Classroom Teacher

Carol Midgett

My comments about productive ways of helping prospective elementary mathematics teachers learn about mathematics content and the nature and practice of mathematics are framed in this way. First, I shall synthesize some promising approaches in which I have engaged. Second, I will note the promising approaches discussed this weekend.

Integrating the 1989 National Council of Teachers of Mathematics (NCTM) *Curriculum and Evaluation Standards* into practice had a profound influence on my teaching. The *Standards* deepened my personal knowledge of mathematics and enabled me to recognize and understand many more connections within the discipline of mathematics. For example, I came to more fully understand the connections between patterns and algebra. Although I had taught my students to recognize, create patterns using multiple media, extend and correct patterns, I failed to see the pervasive value of patterns in all strands of mathematics and their multiple foundations in algebra. The *Standards* also gave me a view of the development of mathematical ideas across the K-12 continuum and where my grade level contributed to that continuum. The 1989 NCTM *Standards* extended my

understanding of the role of discourse in learning mathematics, both for myself and for my students. I came to realize that talking about mathematics enables one to examine and clarify conceptions and misconceptions and to benefit from the collective wisdom of the group. Discussion allows young children the same opportunities for stating ideas, examining conjectures, clarifying hypothesis, and understanding the "what and why" of mathematics.

One far-reaching impact of the '89 *Standards* on my instructional practice and development as a teacher leader came from my participating in the NCTM project to implement the geometry standards. Based upon my high school experience, my view of geometry was entirely from an Euclidean perspective. My experiences in the geometry project gave me a picture of the role of geometry in the field of mathematics as related to measurement and number. I began to see geometry as a way of viewing the world. With the rich experiences of the geometry project as the impetus, I established a math support group for K-8 teachers that began in 1991. This group of more than 70 teachers continues to meet monthly to discuss issues related to mathematics instruction and to support each other's growth and understanding of mathematics. We have moved from generating activities to discussing the nature of significant mathematical tasks and how they should be taught to help students make sense of mathematics.

A second significant event in my personal journey came in 1989 when North Carolina implemented the first- and second-grade assessment. The contributions the K-2 assessment has made to my professional practice are documenting student learning to inform practice, informing students of their growth and development, and informing parents and administrators of what mathematical learning is occurring and needs to occur. Nine years ago, we began conducting student-led conferences. The preparation for, and presentation of, the conferences have led to children assuming responsibility for their own learning. They have helped parents understand the content of the state curriculum and how students need to understand mathematics as well as the procedures for applying that mathematically meaningfully. This vision of making sense of mathematics helps parents recognize the absolute need for mathematics instruction and products to look different from their own experience. The three-way student-led conferences have created a perfect triangle that includes cooperation and collaboration among student, teacher, and parent. Now the parents of my students are actively engaged in setting goals for their child's learning and readily accept their responsibilities to achieve them.

The third milestone in my growth and development is my involvement in the professional development system at the regional university, the University of North Carolina at Wilmington. To serve student interns, I was required to take two graduate-level courses. One helped me to understand the theory of learning-centered supervision and cognitive coaching. The second course engaged me in the practice of coaching for learning. Serving as a partnership teacher provides an excellent, ongoing opportunity for me to be involved in another learning community with preservice teachers and university faculty. The transfer of coaching practices extends to my young students. The art of reflection is no longer a dream but a reality for me and for my first-graders. It is a natural consequence of each instructional event. Reflective practice has increased the quality and quantity of learning among the members of our classroom community.

Another milestone came in 1995-96, when I participated in the National Board for Professional Teaching Standards (NBPTS) process leading to certification. It synthesized all that had gone before. The tasks required that I analyze my instructional practice and its impact on student learning. I had to provide evidence, as well as artifacts, proving that I thoughtfully planned, intentionally taught to a learning objective, and reflected upon the impact of my practice on student achievement. It was also necessary for me to articulate (in writing) this analysis to present a picture of my practice to a critical reviewer. Meeting National Board Standards has been both an affirmation and a challenge. It affirms that integrating curriculum, instruction, and assessment is valued as essential. It challenges me because I am no longer content to teach and move on! I must analyze my practice against the learning target and plan for re-teaching, re-directing, or extending the knowledge and skills of my students.

The most recent milestone in my professional development, which is really just beginning, is the initiation of performance-based licensure in North Carolina. This too, is based on standards and provides an opportunity for me to nurture novice teachers and support their growth and development. This engagement in analyzing and reflecting on instruction creates an ever-spiraling learning curve. It also forces me to articulate what I am doing, why I am doing it, and its impact on learning. Working with novice teachers continues the experiences with university student interns. It enables me to make a value contribution to my profession. It helps me to guide others to routinely engage in reflective practice as an essential practice not an "if I have the time" activity. It allows me to help generate and perpetuate a community of learners.

The second aspect of my presentation today addresses the positive and promising approaches resulting from this Teacher Preparation Conference. As a practicing classroom teacher, I sometimes feel that top-down management has no view of the reality of the classroom. Therefore, it is most significant that we are gathered as a community of learners. The participants represent all the levels of educational practice from the classroom to the national policy level. It is a beautiful experience to know that a classroom teacher's words have similar or equal value to other members of the community assembled here. A second thing is the affirmation of knowing that we all grapple with essentially the same issues. We talk about the fundamentals of mathematics. It is as difficult for us to define and describe them here as it is for me at home in my classroom. We're also examining ways to structure and restructure tasks

for the maximum mathematical learning potential. We are grappling with the complexities of teaching. We are struggling with how to communicate those complexities to preservice teachers and instruct them to become effective teachers. We are examining designs for preservice education that will give education majors an experience that parallels what we expect them to do when they assume responsibility for classroom instruction.

Everything that we've done has focused on learning and developing the knowledge and skills to teach for learning. We talk about the changes that each of us must make if we are to reform teacher preparation and the learning of mathematics in American classrooms pre-K-16. Just think, as teachers—and all of us are—we have unlimited possibilities and we have unending challenges. Whether we are assisting

- six-year-olds in understanding mathematics,
- preservice teachers to recognize the inadequacies of their own mathematics instruction,
- planning professional development to extend the learning of veteran teachers,
- structuring university classes to retool professors,

we are identifying the common practices that lead to learning and the structures that support their teaching. How exciting for a first-grade teacher to be part of a journey that has started us on the investigation of some promising possibilities! I am ready to accept the challenge to change and to lead that process with others.

The Importance of Mathematical Content

Alice Gill

My work has primarily been with teachers who are already in service, but they're much like preservice teachers when it comes to professional development, except for two things. First, they have experience in real classrooms, under real conditions. Second, the kind of teaching for which they were prepared, and through which they learned, has been part of their daily practice for a long time, making it more entrenched. So, it's more difficult for these teachers to change, I think, than it might be to give preservice teachers a good foundation.

I cannot reflect on what we've done today without going back to yesterday and the conversation about mathematical content. As we go through all of the skills and processes teachers need to know, it's important that we keep in mind the mathematics behind it all. The big ideas about definitions, about understanding what a mathematical claim is and how it can be justified are critical in classrooms today. Teachers are picking up the language of the standards, but many really don't understand what it all means mathematically. Generalizations and language are highly important. You have to be very careful, not only when you pose problems but when you explain things to

students. For example, when we talk to elementary teachers, just the definition of a "row" can lead to a discussion, because row has non-mathematical conceptions of a grid with rows and columns. Many teachers have never thought about that and, therefore, have not thought about the importance of connecting to the mathematics of coordinate geometry and teaching that in mathematics rows are horizontal and columns are vertical.

Many teachers don't understand (and this is because we haven't taught them) how to develop a concept, as opposed to just throwing something out for students to learn as "the way it is." We know there are teachers who really don't even have a good grasp of the procedures and algorithms for mathematics in grades above the ones they expect to teach in elementary school. The sad thing is that the way our licensure system works and the way teachers in school districts are assigned, teachers may think they're going to teach first or second grade and end up in sixth or seventh because they hold a K-8 license. We can't let them be unprepared for whatever class they eventually may have to teach. So, teachers really need to know the mathematics and know it well. When Liping Ma said, "know the fundamental math deeply, profoundly," that's exactly what teachers need.

A number of the processes and vehicles that we looked at today, I think, are very powerful, as long as you keep in mind where teachers are and what additional supports you may need to provide. Video is a wonderful tool to help teachers reflect, to step back and see what's going on in a classroom—what effect, for example, one question has, as opposed to another one. I've used the Third International Mathematics and Science Study's (TIMSS) eighth-grade geometry videos with elementary teachers to show the difference in the kinds of answers different kinds of questions provoke. Is it a question that has substance and requires students to think and articulate or begin to see a basic mathematical idea or does the question prompt students to just parrot something back that they don't understand? Is it just filling in a blank? Hopefully, we can move teachers to begin to first view videos of others, and then to video their own classrooms—perhaps privately at first—and examine their own practice from such perspectives. Later, they can share their own videos or exchange classroom visits with peers and talk about teaching and lessons without feeling personally threatened.

Analyzing student work is very important, but you can't analyze it until you know the math behind the work. Who are the people who facilitate groups when teachers get together? I always worry about that. You need a leader who really knows the math that they see on the students' papers in front of them, what the math could be, as well as what the math is.

Analyzing tasks is an important ability teachers should have, and I look at this from two perspectives: (1) what math is contained in this task, what can a teacher get to, and (2) how can we help teachers

distinguish intellectual difficulty from "this is hard for kids" because we haven't taught it to them. When the mathematicians studied the TIMSS videos to analyze the lesson content, one of their conclusions was that U.S. lessons didn't have many intellectually difficult tasks, and they often don't. As researcher William Schmidt has observed, our curriculum does not really spiral, that is, increase the complexity of a topic as it appears in the curriculum over time, it just goes around in a circle. As teachers, we need to know how to move students from a simple problem or task to a more complex one so we are deepening their understanding and not just continuing at the same level.

According to the TIMSS study, there was little reasoning in U.S. lessons. Yet mathematical reasoning is at the heart of the discipline. This needs to be addressed in preservice programs. Teachers need to understand reasoning as it applies to lower grades, as well as the reasoning of formal proof. Some of the activities showcased here can be powerful tools for developing an understanding of how to focus on reasoning in the classroom. The work of Deborah Ball and Hyman Bass in this area holds great promise. Video provides opportunities to follow student thinking about a problem or procedure. The questions a teacher uses to draw out the student's thinking, uncover missing steps, or lead a student to see or articulate a fundamental mathematical idea can be made visible as it plays out in real time. Cases are also very useful for analysis. Why didn't these kids know a particular concept? What else could the teacher have done to help them understand? A case study can offer an opportunity to reflect on how to build a concept that the students missed. Navigating a mathematical discussion is certainly important because such discussions are going to go on in classrooms. Teachers have to know what to take and run with, and what not to, and what kinds of questions to ask to move student thinking. All of that, of course, depends on knowing the mathematics behind what it is a teacher is doing.

One topic related to how teachers learn and know the mathematics they teach has not been mentioned in my sessions so far at this conference. There is a very urgent need in schools today for teachers to understand how to look at math standards. There are state standards, district standards, NCTM *Standards*, textbooks, and curriculum frameworks. There are many other resources that the teachers can use, and teachers have to figure out how to put all of these together. They're often doing that without being able to say, "Oh well, it's stated differently here, but that's really the same concept as (or maybe a subskill of) the statement over there." They need to be able to look at mathematics from a larger perspective and from different viewpoints so that they don't think there are a thousand things to teach as little separate ideas. This is not a task for the general education people who talk about instructional planning. This is very specific to the discipline of mathematics. If teachers can't put the information all

together and if they can't understand how one thing connects to another, they have a tough time, their students have a tough time, and they may well leave teaching very soon.

Carol Midgett talked about having been given a conceptual framework so that she could see where what she taught fit into the whole picture. It's very important to know, for example, that the concept of division is the same whether you're using whole numbers or fractions. This strategy came up in one of the workshops. We need to help teachers think about intervention with students who don't understand by making a connection to a basic concept that they already know. Many teachers wouldn't think of going back to whole number division because they haven't been prepared with an adequate conception of either division or fractions to know how to make the connection.

The development of excellent math teachers is a complex process. No single idea or tool will accomplish what is needed, including requiring deeper knowledge of mathematical content. However, that knowledge is the necessary foundation that makes powerful tools work. We have a big job, but it has to be done.

NSF and Teacher Preparation Programs

James Lightbourne

Improvement in the preparation of future teachers in both content knowledge and educational practice is a critical factor in improving mathematics education. The experiences in which we have engaged at this Workshop have highlighted the significance of preparing teachers in ways that enable them to gain a fundamental understanding of mathematics. Programs described by the speakers here provide promising avenues through which future teachers can gain this understanding of mathematics.

One observation about the activities at this Workshop is that they are all designed to promote student understanding of mathematics. Skills are important, but I think these students are best served for their roles as future teachers if they come to think about mathematics in the ways that a mathematician thinks about mathematics. As teachers, they will then have the understanding necessary to go beyond teaching mathematics as a bag of manipulations and tricks, routine drills that will not surprisingly be quickly forgotten. Rather, they will be able to provide their students with experiences to gain the insights and confidence necessary to learn and use mathematics.

The NSF Collaboratives for Excellence in Teacher Preparation (CETP) program has been one effort at NSF to promote achievement of significant and systemic improvement in the science, mathematics, and technology preparation of prospective kindergarten through grade 12 teachers. The program has particularly emphasized the importance of involving science and mathematics faculty and their departments in K-12 teacher preparation. Twenty-four projects have been awarded through the CETP program from 1992 through 1999 at funding levels of $500,000 to $1 million per year for up to five years. Information about the projects can be found at: http://www.her.nsf.gov/HER/DUE/awards/cetp/cetplist.htm.

The following brief descriptions from CETP project reports illustrate aspects of the projects and findings in evaluating the impact of the projects.

The Arizona Collaborative (ACEPT) developed a classroom observation instrument for evaluating reformed teaching K-20 classrooms across all science and mathematics disciplines. Findings indicate a strong correlation between the use of reformed teaching strategies and students' achievement pre/post test gains. An instrument for assessing the effectiveness of ACEPT reforms on student views about mathematics was administered to over 4,000 mathematics students at Arizona State University. Findings indicate shifts in elementary preservice students' mathematical methods toward increased perseverance and use of general problem solving approaches, for example, as well as changes in beliefs (e.g., difficult problems require multiple attempts). Success rates have remained high (at around 90%) in two mathematics preservice courses (*Theory of Mathematics for Preservice Elementary Teachers* and *Methods of Teaching Secondary Mathematics)* that have adopted a more rigorous and conceptually focused curriculum.

Evaluation of ACEPT reform in chemistry courses indicates that: 95% of students attend class compared with 60-70% prior to ACEPT. The dropout rate in reformed sections is 3-4% compared with 20-30% in non-reformed sections. Student performance on identical questions improved by 17% in reformed sections with comparable student characteristics (GPA, SAT, age). A physics concept test administered to students in the Fundamentals of Physical Science course at Arizona State University indicated that inquiry-oriented teaching leads to substantially improved understanding of physics concepts among non-science majors (including elementary education majors).

In addition to increasing the mathematics requirements for future teachers at the Collaborative institutions, the Virginia Collaborative (VCEPT) was instrumental in influencing changes in state policy regarding certification of elementary and middle schools teachers. Whereas previously the state did not require prospective elementary teachers to study any science or mathematics, new licensure requirements include 12 hours of mathematics and 12 hours of science for a K-6 license and 21 hours of mathematics for a middle school license to teach mathematics. Previously any teacher was certified to teach all subjects in middle school when certified to teach in any two of four areas: social studies, language arts, science, or mathematics. Students enrolled in a VCEPT course were asked to indicate the importance of various course characteristics in helping them to learn in the course. The three characteristics most often cited as being very important were active student learning, interesting and intellectually involving concepts, and assessment of student performance in different ways.

The Maryland Collaborative (MCTP) has developed an instrument to examine preservice students' attitudes and beliefs about the teaching of mathematics and science. MCTP undergraduate classes are taught by faculty in mathematics, science, and education who make efforts to focus on "developing understanding of a few central concepts and to make connections between the sciences and between mathematics and science." The MCTP Research Group investigated whether prospective teachers enrolled in MCTP adopt more positive attitudes over time towards mathematics and science, and towards the teaching of these subjects over time as they participate in the MCTP program. In particular, the study considered whether preservice students' beliefs about the best ways to teach mathematics and science are compatible with the project's goals; use of constructivist instructional strategies, emphasis on connections between mathematics and science, and appropriate use of technology when teaching mathematics and science, and encouragement of students from diverse backgrounds to participate in challenging and meaningful learning. Findings indicate that MCTP teacher candidates' beliefs about the nature of the two disciplines, and about how one ought to teach science and mathematics, are becoming more in line with beliefs advocated by current reform efforts in mathematics and science education. The significance of this result is particularly interesting since, during most of the three-year period when MCTP teacher candidates were surveyed, the majority of them were completing the MCTP-revised mathematics and science content courses, and had not yet begun to take the MCTP-revised pedagogy courses or student teaching.

The *College Algebra in Context* course at the Colorado CETP (Colorado State University) is a reform course that replaces breadth with depth, covering a few topics considered central to mathematics in great depth and maximizing the use of student-centered activities to encourage students to construct knowledge, explore the meaning behind mathematical concepts, employ multiple strategies in problem solving, and communicate mathematical ideas. A comparison of students in the reform college algebra class with students in a traditionally taught class indicated the students in the reform class scored significantly higher than traditionally taught students in three dimensions: conceptual understanding, ability to employ multiple approaches, and communication skills.

At San Francisco State University, one of the San Francisco Bay Area CETP institutions, Mathematics 301, a course required for future mathematics teachers, was revised to increase the hours and revise the materials and processes used during the class. Student achievement increased as measured by the increase in

B's (from 27% to 48%) and decrease in C's (from 40% to 24%). Also at San Francisco State University, two capstone courses for secondary mathematics teachers involved problem solving, cooperative learning, the use of technology, and a variety of assessment techniques were introduced. Enrollment doubled in the revised courses.

In conclusion, effective preparation of future teachers requires a comprehensive effort on the part of colleges and universities and their faculty. The challenges cover a range of areas, including, for example:

- faculty improving their courses and how they are taught;
- institutions providing resources and incentives for faculty;
- students having research experiences and early teaching experiences;
- mathematics, education, and K-12 faculty communicating and working together;
- teachers being supported in their novice years, and provided continued professional development.

Many effective practices have developed. However, their implementation remains perhaps the greatest challenge, requiring institutional and faculty commitment and priority for the preparation of their students as future teachers.

ACKNOWLEDGMENT

Appreciation is expressed to Dr. Joan Prival, NSF Division of Undergraduate Education, for providing the information about the CETP projects for this article.

Where Are We?
Moderator's Summary

Joan Ferrini-Mundy

The sessions in this part of the Workshop focused on helping teachers learn the content they need to teach well by considering sites of actual teaching practice as the vehicle for instruction. An earlier speaker pointed out that video provides the opportunity to actually focus on questions and answers as they arise, which can lead to additional opportunities to learn. Another speaker indicated that teachers are being charged to look at standards, national standards and state standards, to develop frameworks for their own teaching. This means teachers have to navigate and align these different standards across their own work trying to make a consistent message for their own classrooms. Other conversations suggested other promising sites of practice, and it seemed that a reasonable way to focus our discussion was to begin to make a list about tasks of teaching that serve as places where teachers have an opportunity to learn some mathematics. Such a list might include the following potential sites of practice:

- Learning to use and adapt student curriculum materials and teachers' guides

- Critiquing and reviewing instructional materials
- Studying cases of mathematics teaching
- Analyzing cases of student thinking
- Analyzing videotapes of teaching, including an analysis of questions and answers
- Analyzing student work
- Remodeling mathematical tasks and analyzing the nature of tasks
- Managing classroom discussion
- Implementing assessments
- Looking at standards

As we think about this perspective on developing teacher knowledge, we might make some conjectures about why sites of practice seem promising as contexts through which teachers can learn mathematics, in particular the mathematics it takes to teach well. The discussion has highlighted different possibilities and reasons, conjectures that are still emerging in my own thinking as reasons why these sites of practice might be productive. One reason might be that such sites could be motivational for a prospective teacher. The opportunity to begin working with curriculum material that teachers might envision themselves using six months later in a classroom could be a natural incentive. Likewise, viewing a real classroom on tape could be motivational and useful as a way to think about issues of practice and their relation to the content knowledge needed to effectively function as the teacher in the videotaped classroom.

Another factor is that sites of practice are instances of actual application. I think this connects back to something Hy Bass said yesterday, the notion that we teach a calculus course and include in that course applications that an engineer might find realistic. In the same way, sites of practice such as we have discussed offer the possibility for devising applications and problems of teaching that teachers might find productive as places to think more about mathematical questions.

Sites of practice might also be thought of as generative. As an individual, they cause me to think about, or to focus on, areas of mathematics that might not have seemed as productive or important in other settings. The complexity of a set of student answers can draw you into other kinds of mathematics that you might not have been choosing as a focus at the beginning.

Finally, sites of practice serve in an activating role. They cause you to think about mathematics you might not have thought of before and to draw on mathematics that you might have known but that might not have come to the surface without this sort of spark.

These reasons sites of practice might be promising are just a beginning that poses a tentative set of suggestions. It would seem feasible that the next steps are to add to, refine, and explicate the list, making the conjectures more robust. As next steps then, in an interactive mode, we should begin to propose arguments for why these might be reasonable conjectures, and we should begin to actually design experiences to help further the argument. One way to go forward is to actually try out certain kinds of ideas to get a better understanding about which elements of this list might be most useful in terms of making the case. We need to begin in a disciplined way, using what we know about doing research, the task of studying outcome as we build coherence and language, and grounded arguments about using sites of practice to help preservice students come to know the mathematics they will need to teach well.

Concluding Remarks

Deborah Loewenberg Ball

Over the last two days we analyzed teacher practice for the mathematics entailed by that practice and opportunities teachers had to learn mathematics from the actual work of teaching. This consideration of what teachers need to know to teach well and how they come to learn what they need to know raises many issues. Much of what teachers need to know is under-specified. What kind of knowledge do teachers need beyond what students need? On one hand, we have been talking about the "packages" of knowledge that organize mathematics that is important for teaching. On the other, we have also seen the importance of being able to "unpack" mathematical knowledge in order to listen to students, choose tasks, and otherwise use mathematics in teaching. How can we design opportunities for learning that enable teachers to understand the nature of learning mathematics, to appreciate their students' struggle to learn, and to recognize the mathematics in what their students are saying? How can we provide opportunities for teachers to learn that will give teachers a sense of the mathematics they choose to pursue and an understanding of why they made those choices? How can we as a community of mathematics educators frame a structure for teacher development that will begin to address these issues?

The Workshop was not structured to provide answers, but rather to set the stage for the next steps. What can we take from this Workshop? The experience was designed to be an intellectual resource for your own thinking shaped by the notion from Ma's work of a profound understanding of fundamental mathematics—that teachers need to know what they are teaching in a deep and substantial way. The artifacts presented to stimulate your thinking were based on using mathematics in practice, centered around some of the core tasks of teaching. Opportunities to learn mathematics can be found by using sites of practice or outside of practice. In the first instance, it is easy to get lost in the doing and not pay attention to the actual mathematics involved. In the second, it is necessary to mediate among course materials, texts, what knowledge is actually needed and learned in the process, and the actual use of that knowledge in the classroom. The bridge between these ways of coming to know raises new questions: What is understanding of mathematics for teaching? How can we develop this understanding in the professional education of teachers?

As mathematics educators, we need to pursue the important questions and begin to develop the ideas. In your own work, try out some activity or approach centered around the kind of thinking that framed the Workshop. Document what happens and probe the effects to see what underlying factors may be present. Think carefully about the nature of the evidence you present. Write about your experiences and present your ideas to your colleagues in a variety of forums. As a community, we can begin to collect these experiences and evidence, testing our theory against the reality of teachers and students, and begin to move forward in a real analysis of what mathematics teachers need to teach well and how they come to learn the mathematics they need to know.

DISCUSSION GROUP REPORTS

Discussion groups were an integral part of the Workshop, providing the opportunity to take advantage of the experience and expertise of the participants and to engage all of those present in analyzing and discussing the Workshop activities. The participants were assigned to one of ten working groups. Each group was asked to prepare a response to one of five questions critical to considering the mathematics elementary teachers have to know and how to help them learn that mathematics. Throughout the Workshop, the groups met three times to consider their task—interspersed with presentations, activities, and informal discussion, using the Workshop experiences as a way to provoke their thinking. The goal was to collectively develop ideas about the mathematics content preparation of teachers. The following papers provide the responses of two groups to each question and illustrate the beginning of some core ideas about the nature of developing teacher content knowledge in preservice programs.

Question #1. Often teaching is seen as presenting material to students. But of course teaching includes many more small and large tasks—figuring out what students know, composing good questions, assessing and revising textbook lessons, and so on. What are some of these recurrent tasks of teaching that require the use of mathematics?

Question #2. Not everything is a question of knowledge. From what we have done together, what are some mathematical instincts, sensibilities, dispositions that seem crucial to teaching mathematics? What mathematics beyond what is taught in class must a teacher know to do a good job teaching mathematics in that class?

Question #3. There is so much to know of mathematics. Creating longer and longer lists of what teachers should know does not seem promising. What are some of the big ideas in mathematics that would seem to have a lot of leverage in practice? How do teachers need to understand these ideas—for example, what does it mean to be able to "unpack" ideas, as well as to connect them?

Question #4. What are some promising ways to help teachers learn mathematics that also help them develop mathematically? What are the key features of what makes an approach promising?

Question#5. What are some promising ways to help teachers not only develop mathematical understanding but learn to *use* mathematical insight and knowledge in the context of practice? What are the key features of what makes an approach promising? Are there ways to engage preservice teachers in learning mathematics through the tasks they will actually do in practice?

Question #1

Often teaching is seen as presenting material to students. But of course teaching includes many more small and large tasks—figuring out what students know, composing good questions, assessing and revising textbook lessons, and so on. What are some of these recurrent tasks of teaching that require the use of mathematics?

Leader: *Mercedes McGowan;* Members: *Dan Burch, Michael Hynes, Shirley Smith, Jane Swafford, and Alan Tucker*

ASSUMPTIONS MADE IN FRAMING THE DISCUSSION

We made the assumption that recurrent tasks of teaching implied examining and thinking about classroom practices that apply to the teaching of mathematics generally and that we were not to focus our discussion on unpacking our thinking about the tasks associated with the teaching of a particular topic or grade level.

SUMMARY OF THE MAIN POINTS OF DISCUSSION

Recurrent tasks of teaching that require the use of mathematics identified by our group included

- uncovering students' current base of knowledge and the common base of knowledge shared by the class;
- assessing the "generality of knowledge," i.e., knowing where a mathematical concept fits into a sizeable, interrelated body of knowledge;
- selecting worthwhile tasks designed to provide experiences with fundamental

concepts and techniques, active student participation, and abundant opportunities for students to make discoveries.

As we began unpacking our own knowledge of recurrent tasks of teaching, we addressed the question, "What is a worthwhile task?" There was a common understanding that worthwhile mathematical tasks enable students to build particular organizations and classification schemas that can be utilized to explain subsequent, more abstract ideas. Characteristics of worthwhile mathematical tasks were identified and included tasks that

- are open-ended—meaning that the solution should not be readily available;
- contain significant mathematics and have multiple pathways to the solution;
- develop understanding of
  (a) the meaning of operations,
  (b) the algebraic properties of numbers,
  (c) relationships among quantities that change,
  (d) the ambiguity of mathematical notation,
  (e) the degrees/levels of complexity in a given context domain;

131

- model and guide the construction of acceptable mathematical arguments and justifications;
- are accessible and challenging;
- promote flexible thinking;
- include time to reflect.

During the two days, we continued to struggle to unpack our thinking about recurrent tasks of teaching that require the use of mathematics while avoiding discussion of a particular topic or content area. As we came back together after attending various breakout sessions, we synthesized the ideas and discussions of those various breakout sessions into our small-group discussions. We began to discuss "the mathematics of teaching"—how our knowledge of mathematics influences the ways in which we assess our students, evaluate programs, assign grades, use a rubric, choose textbooks, envision a course, design a lesson, and select mathematical tasks for investigation.

Our discussions also unpacked some of our personal underlying assumptions and beliefs about the nature of mathematics, how students learn, the role of the teacher, the role of technology, and the means of achieving skill competencies. Given the diverse backgrounds of the group members, it was not surprising that there was no consensus on these issues.

ISSUES

The issue of what mathematical knowledge a preservice teacher needs to know was a recurrent topic of discussion throughout the conference. One general consensus was there is no way to provide preservice teachers with all the mathematics content knowledge we would like them to know. Rather, we need to think more deeply about how to provide preservice teachers with "sufficient" mathematical knowledge and desire for life-long learning so they continue to grow in their understanding of mathematics and of teaching on the job. We identified the need to develop a coherent vision of the course(s) as an essential component of a teacher's planning for instruction if one is to break away from the "cake-layer" mentality of disconnected courses and Skill 1 today, Skill 2 tomorrow, etc.

We left the conference with the following questions unanswered:

1. How do teachers' beliefs and attitudes constrain their ability to envision the course as a coherent entity?
2. What might help teachers who lack a coherent vision about the courses as a whole avoid being caught up in the bits and pieces of curriculum?
3. What is "mathematical instinct" and how is it nurtured?
4. Where do we learn to ask questions that build on students' prior knowledge?

Question #1

Often teaching is seen as presenting material to students. But of course teaching includes many more small and large tasks—figuring out what students know, composing good questions, assessing and revising textbook lessons, and so on. What are some of these recurrent tasks of teaching that require the use of mathematics?

Leader: *Deann Huinker;* Members: *Carne Barnett, Helen Gerretson, Kay Sammons, Mark Saul, Betty Siano, and Gladys Whitehead*

ASSUMPTIONS MADE IN FRAMING THE DISCUSSION

We agreed that teachers engage in numerous recurrent tasks as they plan for the teaching of mathematics and facilitate student learning of mathematics. The tasks involve both short-term and long-term planning and reflection, as well as on-the-spot decision making. Many of the on-the-spot decisions made by teachers are unconscious.

We brainstormed and listed many recurrent tasks and discussed which required the use of mathematics. From the lists, six categories of recurrent tasks that required the use of mathematics emerged. The categories included (1) managing class discussions, (2) establishing a classroom culture for mathematical reasoning, (3) designing and selecting tasks, (4) analyzing student thinking and work, (5) planning instruction, and (6) assessing student learning. Table 1 provides a list of tasks for each category. We realize that some tasks may fit into more than one category; however, we placed each task within the one category we felt made the best fit.

SUMMARY OF THE MAIN POINTS OF DISCUSSION

Several questions were raised concerning the relationship of recurrent tasks to teachers' mathematical knowledge. Do any of these recurrent tasks require the use of mathematics? Does the mathematical content knowledge of teachers impact their decision making as they engage in these tasks? What mathematical content knowledge is needed to make good decisions? What day-to-day tasks and decisions are difficult for teachers to make when they lack specific mathematical knowledge?

Three assertions emerged from our discussions regarding the recurrent tasks of teaching that require use of mathematics. These involved the level of teachers' mathematical knowledge, the impact of this content knowledge on recurrent tasks of teaching, and the preparation of teachers.

Teachers need to develop a deep, interconnected understanding of the mathematical content knowledge they are expected to teach. Teachers need to know more mathematics than their students. However, it is even more important that

Table 1. Recurrent Tasks of Teaching

Category	Tasks
Managing Class Discussion	• When to probe for deeper understanding? How to probe? What links to make? • Selecting the language/terminology to use to explain an idea or procedure, to pose a task, or to relate to students' explanations and observations. For example, the teacher needs to decide whether to use formal or informal language. • Anticipating misconceptions. • Deciding when to give feedback and what type of feedback to give to students. • Deciding when to acknowledge "good" mathematical thinking or an explanation and when to remain nonjudgmental. • Deciding how to build on what students say. • Deciding which student solutions or strategies to focus on in whole-group discussions. • Assisting students by providing hints to move them along in their thinking (scaffolding). For example, the teacher needs to decide whether to repeat what the student said, ask a question, pose a related problem, or pose a counter-example.
Establishing a Classroom Culture for Mathematical Reasoning	• Sharing or developing criteria with students for their work. • Developing definitions as a group. • Examining and critiquing student ideas and work as small groups or a whole class. • Discussing expectations with students for their mathematical explanations.
Designing and Selecting Tasks	• Selecting the language to use to describe a task. • Making tasks accessible to a range of learners. • Selecting a context for a task. • Evaluating mathematical tasks. For example, the teacher should look at tasks through a child's eyes to determine the "hard" parts of the task. • Sequencing the use of mathematical tasks. • Remodeling mathematical tasks. • Selecting mathematical tasks that will yield the best results for student learning.
Analyzing Student Thinking and Work	• Interpreting student explanations and making sense of what they are saying. • Determining the mathematical validity of a student strategy, solution, or conjecture. • Determining a student's prior knowledge of a mathematical idea. • Figuring out what students know and do not know, as well as what conceptual knowledge connections are missing or are fragile. • Examining student strategies and solutions to determine which are more elegant and sophisticated requiring that teachers have a sense of the range of potential strategies and solutions.
Planning Instruction	• Deciding what mathematical topics to teach. • Composing good questions. • Making long-range and short-range plans. • Assessing and revising textbook or resource book lessons. • Designing lessons. • Selecting mathematical models and manipulatives to use. • Making decisions regarding the amount of time to spend on a topic, lesson, or activity.
Assessing Student Learning	• Designing formal and informal assessments. • Setting criteria to make judgments about student work. • Analyzing and using information from assessments to guide student learning.

teachers understand the interconnectedness of mathematical ideas and develop knowledge packages (Ma, 1999) for key mathematical topics. This will allow teachers to more clearly identify students' current understandings and the direction in which to further that understanding.

The power of mathematical knowledge for teachers becomes apparent in their decision making as they interact with students. We posit that a strong relationship exists between teachers' mathematical knowledge packages and their ability to make "good" decisions that push student learning. Teachers make numerous on-the-spot decisions as they interact with students. Deciding what questions to ask students, when to provide an example, what diagram or model to use, and when to let them struggle are all examples of decisions that can be impacted by the depth of teachers' mathematical knowledge. It is also likely that a teacher's mathematical content knowledge plays a major role in deciding how much time to spend on a topic or what to emphasize regarding that topic. For example, teachers that lack an understanding of geometry are probably more likely to skip the topic or teach it at a low level of reasoning with an emphasis on memorizing definitions and formulas.

The preparation of teachers needs to explicitly connect mathematical knowledge to the recurrent tasks of teaching. Taking more mathematics content courses is not sufficient preparation for teaching. Prospective teachers need to examine the recurrent tasks of teaching in relation to mathematical knowledge. For example, rather than examining assessment strategies in general, discussions could focus on how to design assessment strategies to target specific aspects of mathematical knowledge. Then after using the assessments, discussions could focus on what

next steps could be taken to further students' mathematical understanding based on the results.

Methods courses and field experiences, as well as content courses, should be examined to determine whether there is a better way to help prospective teachers make a connection between their mathematical knowledge and the recurrent tasks of teaching such as we explored during the sessions. For example, mathematics methods courses are often organized by mathematical topics. Methods courses could be organized by the recurrent tasks of teaching. Even though the tasks of teaching are interconnected and support each other, the organization by specific tasks could provide a framework for teacher learning. If methods courses remain organized by mathematical topics, then greater attention to the tasks of teaching need to be addressed within each area. These courses could make use of written and video cases to analyze student work, student thinking, and teacher decision making. The specific cases should be selected to bring out a discussion of mathematical content, not just pedagogical issues. Discussions could then center on why teachers made decisions in relation to the mathematical knowledge students demonstrated.

ISSUES

In examining the recurrent tasks of teaching that require use of mathematics, we were forced to look at the work of teachers rather than just examining their mathematical content knowledge. We struggled but came to understand that mathematical knowledge is connected to the day-to-day work and decision-making of teachers. However, we also found it difficult to articulate the connections between the recurrent tasks of teaching and mathematical knowledge. The challenge we leave for others to consider and explore is to reveal and make explicit the connections between mathematical knowledge and the tasks of teaching.

REFERENCE

Ma, L. (1999). *Knowing and teaching elementary mathematics: Teachers' understanding of fundamental mathematics in China and the United States.* Mahwah, NJ: Lawrence Erlbaum.

Question #2

Not everything is a question of knowledge. From what we have done together, what are some mathematical instincts, sensibilities, dispositions that seem crucial to teaching mathematics? What mathematics beyond what is taught in class must a teacher know to do a good job teaching mathematics in that class?

Leader: *Carol LaCampagne;* Members: *Don Balka, Irene Bloom, Carey Bolster, Blanche Brownley, Judy Kasabian, Cathy Liebars, Deborah Schifter*

ASSUMPTIONS MADE IN FRAMING THE DISCUSSION

Group 2 had some trouble distinguishing between necessary teacher knowledge of mathematics (Question 1) and mathematical instincts, sensibilities, dispositions that seem crucial to teaching mathematics (our Question 2). We believe that mathematical knowledge and these instincts, sensibilities, and dispositions are often inseparable. Surely both are needed in order for a teacher to have a profound understanding of elementary mathematics and its teaching. Thus we often intertwined knowledge and "habits of mind" in our discussion.

SUMMARY OF THE MAIN POINTS OF DISCUSSION

Group 2 identified five major instincts, sensibilities, and dispositions that we felt were crucial for the good teacher of mathematics to possess: mathematical habits of mind; ability to create a classroom community of mathematical discourse; view of mathematics as fluid, dynamic, and connected; ability to solve mathematical problems; and the ability to make wise classroom decisions.

The good teacher of mathematics possesses mathematical habits of mind. These mathematical habits of mind include the ability to reason mathematically; to construct a valid mathematical argument, to judge the validity of the mathematical arguments of others, and to understand the nature of proof. People with these habits of mind have authority over their own mathematical learning. They do not view mathematics as either black or white. People with mathematical habits of mind become confident in their own mathematical knowledge and ability. They develop a positive attitude toward mathematics. Such people are curious about mathematics and learn mathematics beyond what is taught to them in school or college. Such people become lifelong mathematical learners. These habits of mind were exemplified in the video segment presented by Ball and Bass.

The good teacher of mathematics creates a classroom community of mathematical discourse. Such teachers understand and assess the mathematical thinking of their students. This teacher moves students from learned helplessness about mathematics to independent mathematical thinkers. The good teacher is flexible and may change the lesson plan because of student discourse but ultimately keeps an eye on the "big mathematical picture." This teacher chooses the appropriate language of mathematics for the discourse and encourages students to use common ways to talk about mathematics and common ways to judge the mathematical truth of an argument. The good teacher listens to student ideas. The video clip of Dr. Ball's class exemplified the creation of a classroom community of mathematical discourse

The good teacher of mathematics views mathematics as fluid, dynamic, connected, as a powerful group of ideas to be explored, not as a collection of disjoint facts to be memorized. Such a teacher views mathematics as a growing body of knowledge, not as a static body of knowledge set forth hundreds or thousands of years ago, recognizing the connection between mathematics and the sciences (both physical and social) and between everyday lives and the lives of the students.

The good teacher of mathematics is a problem solver and possesses the tools to solve mathematical problems. This teacher has the ability to tolerate frustration in working through a problem to a satisfactory solution, enjoying mathematical problem solving, and seeing mathematical problems in everyday life experiences. Such a teacher is mathematically curious. The pre-Workshop task and the accompanying chapters from Liping Ma's book motivated us to think of the teacher as problem solver and of the ability to use problem solving strategies to encourage students to also become good problem solvers.

The good teacher of mathematics pos- *sesses the ability to make wise classroom mathematical decisions—both in the planning of lessons and in on-the-spot classroom situations.* This teacher has the ability to identify the big ideas in the mathematical curriculum and emphasizes them. The teacher can choose appropriate mathematical problems with multiple entry points that elicit a variety of student responses. A good teacher possesses the internal flexibility to manage the resulting classroom discussion, to question, to probe, and to elicit mathematical knowledge from students. Such a teacher probes student explanations and looks for counter-examples. The good teacher reflects on her/his teaching and the mathematical learning of the students and uses students' mathematical ideas as a way to advance knowledge. The good teacher takes a variety of student solutions to problems and makes sense of them. The teacher detects the mathematical errors of students, helping them to understand and correct these errors.

ISSUES

These attitudes and skills are those that Group 2 would like to see built into the undergraduate preparation of teachers of mathematics. We acknowledge several roadblocks to building them into the undergraduate program. First, we feel that the undergraduate mathematics faculty would need much preparation themselves to conduct their classes in a way to encourage the development of such attitudes and skills into their students. Second, we acknowledge the need for students to have considerable practice as they develop these skills. We feel that some experience in teaching in the context of their own undergraduate classrooms via short presentations as well as early entry into the middle school classroom to observe and to begin teaching under supervision is needed. A greater collaboration between college and schools is also needed to ensure that beginning teachers receive the support and nurturing from both school and college to develop their teaching abilities. Nowhere was the honing in on teaching skills more apparent than in the presentation by Liping Ma concerning Chinese teachers.

Question #2

DISCUSSION GROUP #9

Not everything is a question of knowledge. From what we have done together, what are some mathematical instincts, sensibilities, dispositions that seem crucial to teaching mathematics? What mathematics beyond what is taught in class must a teacher know to do a good job teaching mathematics in that class?

Leader: *Judy Sowder;* Members: *Benjamin Ford, Jim Lewis, Olga Torres, Rosamond Welchman*

ASSUMPTIONS MADE IN FRAMING THE DISCUSSION

The use of the adjective "mathematical" in this question led to discussion of how to distinguish mathematical instincts, sensibilities and dispositions from pedagogical ones, such as the disposition to listen carefully to and reflect on students' responses. It was often difficult to make this distinction because good pedagogy is combined with mathematical instincts, sensibilities, and dispositions when good mathematics is being taught. We all agreed that the following points attend to the mathematical focus of the question.

SUMMARY OF THE MAIN POINTS OF DISCUSSION

Teachers must be inclined and able to take the work of their students and explain or illustrate this work mathematically in different ways. A teacher should be able to follow the logic of a student's argument, whether correct or incorrect, to narrow in on an important mathematical idea of the argument and expand on it through questions that lead students to more fully understand the idea, or by representing the idea in a different way that will prevent overgeneralizing or undergeneralizing the idea. For example, many students will say that 34.5 is smaller than 34.42 because there are only three digits in the first number but four digits in the second number. These students have a weak understanding of place value and have overgeneralized a property of whole numbers. A teacher who recognizes this overgeneralization might illustrate the meaning of 0.5 and 0.42 using base 10 blocks. As another example, a student may divide to solve the problem "A certain kind of cheese costs $1.89 per pound. How much will a package weighing 0.79 pounds cost?" because he knows that the answer must be smaller than 1.89, and "knows" that "division makes smaller." The teacher who recognizes this misconception as an overgeneralization of whole number arithmetic will be able to provide illustrations to show this student that "multiplication makes bigger and division makes smaller" do not always hold when rational numbers are involved.

This mathematical instinct to approach

problems from many points of view is clearly required to adequately analyze student work on open-ended tasks. The breakout session analyzed student work involved in an orange-juice mixture problem that was approached by students in many different ways. The teacher who is unable to switch freely among the approaches of the students will be unable to adequately respond to their thinking. In another session, Hyman Bass pointed out that when mathematical reasoning is part of the classroom culture, the mathematical reasoning of third-graders can be consonant with the mathematical reasoning of professional mathematicians. Thus, the reasoning of third-graders needs to be respected and understood by the teacher.

A teacher must be able to break down a mathematical idea into its fundamental components. This ability implies that the teacher has a deep understanding of an idea's underlying mathematics. Some teachers, for example, know the algorithm for dividing fractions and explain it using division and multiplication as inverse operations. But a teacher with deep understanding knows there are several components that must be in place before division of fractions can be understood. She will know there are two underlying notions for division; partitive (e.g., 12 cookies shared by 3 children, how many cookies each?) and quotitive (e.g., 12 cookies, 3 to each child, how many children?). This teacher also has a deep understanding of fractions, including the fact that fractions are used to represent part-whole situations, division, measurement, ratios, and probabilities. The teacher will be able to present situations involving multiplication and division of fractions and understand the role of referent units and the confusion they cause for children. For example, suppose Jan is making candy that calls for $\frac{1}{2}$ cup of

corn syrup. She has $\frac{3}{4}$ cup of corn syrup on hand. How many recipes can she make? How many $\frac{1}{2}$ cups of corn syrup does she have? (Notice that this problem uses the quotitive model for division.) The problem would be represented as $\frac{3}{4} \times \frac{1}{2} = 1\frac{1}{2}$. What does the $\frac{1}{2}$ stand for? That is, what is the referent unit for $\frac{1}{2}$? It is one cup (of corn syrup). What does the $\frac{3}{4}$ stand for? The referent unit for $\frac{3}{4}$ is also one cup. And what is the referent unit for the quotient, $1\frac{1}{2}$? $1\frac{1}{2}$ *what*? The quotient refers to the number of $\frac{1}{2}$ cups, not to the number of cups. The teacher must ascertain whether or not children can interpret the quotient correctly in such a problem. She can lead students to understand why this problem calls for division and then, through several problems, lead them to a deeper understanding of the division of fractions algorithm. For example, suppose the teacher speaks about the problem $3 \div \frac{1}{2}$ in the following way: for each whole, there are 2 halves, so when I divide 3 by $\frac{1}{2}$, I can say there are 2 halves in each of the 3 wholes. This reasoning can eventually be extended to show why $\frac{3}{4} \div \frac{1}{2} = \frac{3}{4} \times 2$.

The inclination to break a problem into smaller pieces is required when analyzing student work. In addition, remodeling tasks on the fly, as was examined in another of Saturday's breakout sessions, requires the ability to quickly discern those aspects of a problem that are causing it to be unsuccessful in getting at the desired concept.

A teacher must be disposed towards focusing on the major ideas of mathematics and know how they are developed. There are several fundamental or "big" ideas in the mathematics taught in K-8 classrooms, ideas such as place value, proportion, symmetry, and rate of change. When a teacher has a good grasp of these ideas, she can guide the instruction toward them, particularly at times when questions are asked that might at first seem to be unconnected to the progress of the lesson. A teacher with this disposition and with understanding of the content can find order when chaos seems to exist. She will not be afraid of dealing with a variety of student responses.

The teacher with this disposition is also likely to pick up on a student's comments that contain a hint of a connection to other mathematics. The teacher would recognize this connection, weigh the value of pursuing it, then be able to ask questions that would draw out the connection. Knowledge of the mathematics that comes before and after the class being taught will help this teacher make decisions on whether ideas are worth pursuing at the time they occur.

Liping Ma's work (1999), discussed in the opening plenary session of the meeting, emphasizes the importance of "fundamental mathematics." The teacher with the disposition we are describing here has a deep understanding of fundamental mathematics and can quickly identify the core ideas in any topic.

Teachers should expect conceptual understanding of mathematics for themselves and for their students. A person who believes that mathematics makes sense is far more likely to seek out that sense and to be successful in mathematics. Teachers who believe that they are capable of understanding the mathematics of elementary schools will seek this understanding. This process begins when the teacher recognizes that understanding is not present. Although this point might sound trivial, many teachers believe they understand elementary school mathematics when they know how to carry out algorithmic procedures and can teach children these algorithms. In such cases, there is not so much an unwillingness on their

part to understand as much as there is a lack of knowing that their content knowledge is incomplete. When teachers have opportunities to explore the mathematics that underlies procedures, this opportunity opens doors for them. They now know what it means to understand mathematics, which is the first step toward seeking further understanding. They have a "profound understanding of fundamental mathematics," as discussed by Ma. Teachers who understand mathematical ideas can then judge whether or not their students are ready for these ideas and might delay instruction on certain topics until they know that the students can understand the mathematics involved.

A teacher should be disposed to enjoy mathematics and to have an interest in learning new mathematical ideas. The teacher who enjoys mathematics has enthusiasm and curiosity that can be infectious in the classroom. This disposition develops out of doing hard thinking about mathematical ideas in ways that lead to success and confidence. Teacher preparation courses and inservice programs must provide opportunities for teachers to tackle the mathematical ideas they are expected to teach in an atmosphere that allows these teachers room and time to grow and to succeed.

Enjoyment should not be confused with "fun." Teachers sometimes want mathematics to be fun for students and seek out activities they think students will enjoy. Too often, the students enjoy the activity or game and not the mathematics, which gets lost along the way. But enjoying mathematics implies a willingness to undertake the hard work that can lead to wonderful mathematical discoveries and a strong sense of satisfaction. Building a classroom culture, such as that described in Ball's session, is a first step toward establishing a community in which mathematics can be enjoyed.

ISSUES

What opportunities do teachers have to develop the "mathematical instincts, sensibilities, and dispositions" that seem crucial to teaching mathematics? In many places, teachers have support for a few days of inservice work, but this amount of time is not sufficient to undertake the development spoken of here. The work described by Schifter, Bastable, and Lester in their session on alternative approaches to helping teachers learn mathematics is one promising approach to teacher development, but there are few such opportunities available to teachers.

Where do teachers find the time to plan classes that will lead to the teaching of mathematics as described throughout this workshop? In China, according to Ma, teachers spend a good part of their day in preparation for teaching, whereas elementary teachers in this country are usually teaching all day, and prepare on their own time. There is not an easy solution to this problem, but it is one that must be solved if we want teachers to be successful in understanding the mathematics themselves and leading their students to understand, appreciate, and enjoy mathematics.

Question #3

There is so much to know of mathematics. Creating longer and longer lists of what teachers should know does not seem promising. What are some of the big ideas in mathematics that would seem to have a lot of leverage in practice? How do teachers need to understand these ideas—for example, what does it mean to be able to "unpack" ideas, as well as to connect them?

Leader: *Nadine Bezuk;* Members: *Dick Askey, David Dennis, Shelly Ferguson, Jill Bodner Lester, Leigh Peake, Erick Smith*

ASSUMPTIONS MADE IN FRAMING THE DISCUSSION

In an effort to address this question, we discussed what it means to be a "big idea" in mathematics, and how "big ideas" differ from "average ideas." We also discussed the meaning of "unpacking ideas." We often had to remind each other that our task was to focus on the big ideas and not to make another list. During our discussion, group members would often say to each other, "Yes, that's an important concept, but is it a *big idea*?" Our working definition of a "big idea" was a concept or topic that is foundational to many other topics. This is compared to an important idea, which, though significant, is a topic on which relatively fewer other topics are dependent. Throughout our discussion, we attempted to keep this distinction in mind.

We found the topic of teacher development to be intertwined with our group's question. Group members shared their experiences in working with teachers, which seemed to help them think about the notion of "unpacking ideas." This also highlights the importance of teacher development in improving mathematics learning.

SUMMARY OF THE MAIN POINTS OF DISCUSSION

We addressed our group's question in several ways. We began our discussion by identifying what we believed are the "big ideas" of mathematics that instruction needs to include. We also discussed other points we felt important for teachers to understand, recognize, or address in their teaching, and what teachers should be able to do and understand to be able to "unpack ideas."

Several workshop sessions spurred our thinking. Liping Ma's work (1999), and particularly her notion of profound understanding of fundamental mathematics, made a significant contribution to our discussions. Ma's work highlighted for us the importance of a few fundamental concepts, or "big ideas," to further understanding of mathematics.

Dick Askey also intrigued us with

alternative models and formats by sharing information about and examples of mathematics textbooks used in other countries.

Deborah Ball's session on the use of classroom videos again highlighted for us the interconnection of "big ideas" and teacher development, as well as the large number of decisions teachers must make during every mathematics lesson.

The big ideas of mathematics. Our group identified the following topics as "big ideas" of mathematics:

- multiplicative structures, including multiplication, division, fractions, decimals, percents, ratio and proportion, connection between rational numbers and repeating decimals;
- structure of the number system, number sense, decomposition/place value, using benchmarks to estimate numbers;
- systems of operations, operation sense, structure of operations, properties of operation systems (i.e., operations as an interconnected system rather than experiencing operations individually or in isolation);
- similarity, scaling with respect to dimension;
- geometric measure, including area, finding area by dissection of figures, comparison of polygonal areas, perimeter, volume;
- uses and concepts of variables;
- the notion of proof.

Other points. Our group also discussed other points that we felt are important for teachers to understand, recognize, or address in their teaching. They include the following:

- Teachers need to recognize the importance of generality.

- Teachers need to recognize and take advantage of opportunities for making connections in the curriculum, to help children understand interrelationships between concepts.
- Teachers need to decide what to pursue (and what *not* to pursue) and seize opportunities.
- Teachers need to know what concepts students will be encountering in a certain school year and in the next few years. This will help teachers shape students' strategies to highlight those that will lead to important concepts and de-emphasize strategies that will not be widely used in mathematics in upper grades.
- Teachers need a rich understanding of concepts and related topics and of the linkages between topics.
- Teachers need to understand the order of difficulty of concepts and how problem contexts may make problems easier or harder.
- Teachers need to recognize that powerful mathematical ideas evolve through connecting multiple representations.
- Teachers need to recognize that powerful mathematical ideas can be expressed with precision and clarity.
- Teachers need to develop flexibility about ideas, recognizing what is important and how it connects with other topics.
- Instruction for teachers and prospective teachers needs to start by identifying the mathematics that we want children to understand. Instruction should start with those topics, so that prospective teachers really understand those concepts and then understand where those topics are usually taught and what comes next.

In order to "unpack ideas," teachers should be able to:

- effectively judge the validity of any strategy offered by a child (e.g., so that teachers are not telling students who are using less familiar strategies that they are wrong);
- recognize parts of students' understandings that are valid and can be built upon, even if answers or processes are incorrect;

- use language correctly, recognize limitations in students' incorrect language, and make connections between everyday, less formal language and formal mathematical language;
- switch flexibly between different interpretations of concepts.

Question #3

There is so much to know of mathematics. Creating longer and longer lists of what teachers should know does not seem promising. What are some of the big ideas in mathematics that would seem to have a lot of leverage in practice? How do teachers need to understand these ideas—for example, what does it mean to be able to "unpack" ideas, as well as to connect them?

Leader: *Ruhama Even;* Members: *Rachel Collopy, Alice Gill, Genevieve Knight, Neil Portnoy, Marty Simon*

ASSUMPTIONS MADE IN FRAMING THE DISCUSSION

The initial response of the group to the above question was to state important topics that elementary school teachers need to know and understand well to teach mathematics. As listing topics did not seem useful, the group decided to choose two different mathematical constructs and try to unpack what it means for teachers to understand them, anchoring the analysis in specific concrete situations. The two constructs chosen were proportional reasoning and generalization, as both are central in mathematics but of different natures. Time did not allow for significant progress on both topics. Later, the group expanded the discussion of the question and focused on the nature of teacher content knowledge and its relation to teaching.

SUMMARY OF THE MAIN POINTS OF DISCUSSION

The first topic mentioned as an important topic that elementary school teachers need to know and understand well in order to teach mathematics was *proportional reasoning.* Instantly, it became clear that such a title is only the tip of an iceberg. Struggling with the question, What are teachers' understandings of proportional reasoning, group members emphasized the ability to distinguish between additive and multiplicative reasoning, mentioned the need for conceptual knowledge of the four basic operations, and suggested different examples of ratio as measurement (mixture, slope, fractions).

At the first plenary panel discussion, Mark Saul presented a list regarding teachers' understanding of fundamental mathematics. Proportional reasoning was *not* included in this list. This omission puzzled group members, as proportional reasoning was the first topic mentioned in our group, and it occupied a great deal of the first day discussion.

The proportional reasoning discussion

147

led to more general questions, such as these: What understandings can we reasonably expect teachers to have? What is important to know about mathematics? What kinds of understandings are needed? Examination of these questions gave rise to and highlighted the importance of processes, such as abstraction and generalization in mathematics. For example, group members emphasized that teachers should know what is generalizable and know important generalizations that cut across different topic areas.

The rather long, still quite in its initial stages, examination of what understanding teachers should have about proportional reasoning, convinced the group that mentioning more topics would not advance the group work. It was clear that a thorough analysis of what it means for teachers to know mathematical topics, concepts, and processes is needed.

In addition to an initial unpacking of teacher understanding of specific mathematical topics, concepts, and processes, the group discussed the *nature* of teacher content knowledge. Group members debated the idea that it comprises two kinds. One kind is of the same nature as K-12 students' knowledge of mathematics. The other kind goes beyond students' knowledge and has to do with the specific act of teaching, an anticipatory level of mathematical knowledge (e.g., knowing the difference between partitive and quantitative division). The group also felt that teacher content knowledge should be viewed in a broad sense to include understandings, conceptions, subject-matter related beliefs, knowledge about the nature of the discipline, and so forth.

Teacher knowledge in relation to teaching was considered in two ways, although briefly, because of time constraints. It was emphasized that one's thinking about teacher knowledge of

mathematics is connected to one's vision of good teaching of mathematics, and therefore advancement in the first requires more articulation of the latter. Another idea which the group planned to work on was to analyze teacher content knowledge in a *specific teaching situation*. The group felt that analysis of teacher content knowledge in the context of teaching has the potential to provide insight into and advance understanding of this issue. We intended to analyze the video excerpt from Ball's third-grade class where students were asked to write number sentences equal to 10. The group was intrigued by the teacher's decision to introduce algebraic symbols in the third-grade discussion. Group members felt, for example, that such a teacher decision requires teachers to know, not only that letters can be used to generalize a pattern observed in a series of number sentences but also that letters in algebra are used in different ways (e.g., generalized number, unknown, variable, parameter).

ISSUES

In conclusion, the group felt that to advance in its response to the question presented, it is important to further examine the following:

- teacher content knowledge of specific mathematical topics, concepts, and processes;
- different parts of teacher knowledge of mathematics: The knowledge expected from students, specific-teacher knowledge, teacher knowledge of mathematics in the context of teaching.
- vision and models of good teaching of mathematics and connections to teachers' knowledge of mathematics.

Question #4

DISCUSSION GROUP #4

What are some promising ways to help teachers learn mathematics that also help them develop mathematically? What are the key features of what makes an approach promising?

Leader: *Dwayne Channell;* Members: *Hy Bass, Michaele F. Chappell, Ed Esty, Don Gilmore, Margaret Jensen, Lena Khisty, Marie Sheckels*

ASSUMPTIONS MADE IN FRAMING THE DISCUSSION

The group focused discussion on ways that tasks in *mathematics content courses* could be designed to improve the mathematical understandings of preservice teachers. While admitting that many suggestions could be implemented in either a methods or a content course, the group believes that all suggestions are appropriate for inclusion in content courses. It is also recognized that successful implementation of some suggestions will necessitate cooperative efforts among the faculty who teach mathematics content and those who teach mathematics methods.

SUMMARY OF THE MAIN POINTS OF DISCUSSION

Current shortcomings in the teaching of mathematics content. The discussion group identified two overriding problems that need to be addressed:

- Preservice teachers (PSTs) typically possess a superficial understanding

rather than deep understanding of elementary mathematics.
- PSTs typically have not experienced making sense of mathematics and do not believe that sense making is a necessary component of understanding mathematics.

Participants suggested that fault for these shortcomings might be attributed to instruction that values speed and efficiency in arriving at "the" answer without regard for the need to reason and develop understanding.

Discussion focused on methods of situating mathematics instruction to require PSTs to examine their mathematical beliefs and understandings and encourage them to shed their reliance upon procedures without meaning.

The group believes that an important goal in the mathematics education of PSTs is to help them develop as teachers who value sense making and reasoning as necessary components of mathematical understanding and who instill those values in their own students. Consequently, instructional and assessment experiences need to be designed to permit PSTs to identify their own "conceptual images" of mathematics and foster a change in those images so they are more conducive to meaningful learning. Mathematical experiences designed for PSTs should often reflect the ways in which they will use their mathematical knowledge in classroom teaching, for example, designing assessments, evaluating the written work of others, interpreting and assessing the validity of verbal arguments, and modifying mathematical tasks. Many of these "core teaching tasks" were identified in the conference plenary sessions and were echoed in breakout group discussions.

Promising approaches for teaching and situating content. In many, if not most, universities, the mathematics content preparation for PSTs is centered around the content in commercially published textbooks that, by the nature of the market, cover an immense amount of subject matter but do not always engage students in ways that promote a broad, thorough, and deep understanding of mathematics as discussed at this conference. It was suggested that students may better develop mathematically if faced with fewer topics investigated in much greater depth. In doing so, instruction could be based around several big ideas or underlying structures in mathematics. PSTs could be immersed in rich problem settings that require them to approach a task or problem situation from multiple perspectives, draw connections among those perspectives, and strengthen their flexibility and fluency as mathematical thinkers and communicators. As was frequently mentioned at this conference, such experiences would permit PSTs to develop "knowledge packages." The group realizes that determining core essential content knowledge would be a very political process with more than one feasible solution. We also recognize the

need to involve stakeholders from several factions in the process. However, the difficulties inherent in such a task do not lessen its importance.

Several alternatives for situating mathematical learning experiences for PSTs were suggested. Each suggestion offers the possibility of deepening the PSTs mathematical knowledge and perhaps strengthens their abilities to recognize the relationship of this knowledge to their future classrooms.

Some of the suggestions center around modifying traditional mathematical tasks from a focus that is strictly on the development of content knowledge to tasks that also emphasize the development of pedagogical content knowledge. Examples include:

- Present PSTs with a mathematical task and require them to create new, related questions that remodel the task.
- Have PSTs analyze the mathematics a student would need to know to investigate a task and delineate the mathematics they would learn by working through the investigation.
- Provide PSTs with a situation and have them create a variety of questions that could be asked about the situation (continue with the previous suggestion by having them make an analysis of the needed mathematics and the learned mathematics from each question generated).
- Provide PSTs with several correct approaches to solving a given task including, as appropriate, pictorial mental reasoning strategies, traditional procedural algorithms, and alternate sense-making algorithms. Have them discuss and critique the advantages and disadvantages of each, including any implications for promoting student understanding.

Other suggestions focus on injecting explicit connections of mathematical knowledge to the teaching of K-8 students. Examples include the following:

- Present PSTs with examples of K-8 student work that reflects invalid or incomplete reasoning or alternatives to traditional methods of solution. Engage PSTs in an analysis and critique of the work. Why do they think a student might reason in a particular incorrect way? Why do the students not understand or what are the origins of their confusion? Presentation of the student work could be made available in the form of individual written work or in videotapes of actual classroom episodes involving the interaction of a teacher with several students.
- Require PSTs to design an assessment instrument for testing knowledge of content they have recently discussed. Develop a key (rubric) for assessing student performance on the instrument. Administer the instrument to other class members and evaluate their performance.

- Present PSTs with some traditional mathematics for which they possess a memorized algorithm that could be used to solve the problem. Require the PSTs to abandon reliance upon the algorithm and use sense-making strategies to explain a solution that could be understood by elementary/middle school students who do not possess knowledge of the algorithm.

Key features of suggested approaches. Each of the alternatives suggested here situates mathematics in tasks that are motivating and relevant to future elementary/middle school mathematics teachers while maintaining an emphasis on critical thinking and mathematical understanding. While the advantages of such tasks over more traditional approaches may seem apparent to some, widespread acceptance of such suggestions is unlikely unless each is given a realistic evaluation in mathematics classes with preservice teachers.

Question #4

What are some promising ways to help teachers learn mathematics that also help them develop mathematically? What are the key features of what makes an approach promising?

Leader: *Nancy Edwards;* Members: *Ava Belisle-Chatterjee, Robert Howard, Shin-ying Lee, Carol Midgett, Joyce Miller, Pat O'Connell Ross, Al Otto*

ASSUMPTIONS MADE IN FRAMING THE DISCUSSION

Liping Ma's treatise on *Knowing and Teaching Elementary Mathematics* (1999) informed our discussion by enabling us to think systemically about a framework for content preparation of elementary teachers in mathematics.

Ma's insightful analysis of U.S. teachers' emphasis on procedure that results in a telling of rules and an accounting of step-by-step processes led the group to discuss ways to break from this approach. The group felt most content instructors and methods teachers have focused on an enormous number of concepts to teach prospective teachers, resulting in a "piece by piece" arrangement of the knowledge needed to teach students. The group found the thought structure of the Chinese teachers who emphasized the grouping of knowledge into packages as a revolutionary way of thinking that holds great potential for teacher content and methods preparation. These packages underlie what our group referred to as "core tasks" that must be present if prospective teachers are to understand the meaning behind that which they

teach. The group also discussed the nature of mathematical problems that would give conceptual support to the core tasks, such as the subtraction problem described in Ma's work.

A discussion of Ma's research caused the group to see research as a key to change the approaches of content instructors and methods teachers. The group concluded that some of the most promising ways to help prospective teachers learn mathematics and develop mathematically are to evaluate research findings that indicate the core tasks and mathematical problems prospective teachers need to know and do to accomplish their work.

SUMMARY OF THE MAIN POINTS OF THE DISCUSSION

Ball's presentation on Teaching Mathematics for Understanding, Schifter's Learning Mathematics for Teaching, Torres' Remodeling Mathematical Tasks, and Bastable's Analyzing Student Thinking, all formed the basis for the summary list of characteristics needed for maximum effectiveness in identifying and using core tasks and mathematical problems:

- The best core tasks should aid prospective teachers to experience doing mathematics in the same way that mathematicians do it—i.e., in a way that makes sense to them. This involves investigating, conjecturing, and justifying the nature and uses of mathematics. The content should be taught in such a way that students struggle and engage in dialogue as mathematicians do. This leads to new mathematical understandings. The dialogue should foster responsibility among prospective teachers as a community of learners.
- The best core tasks should build upon "real world" applications (contextualized in reality), with prospective teachers able to foster a seamless transition between concrete and abstract mathematical thought. Attitudinal change can come when prospective teachers see uses for mathematics in real-world models.
- The best core tasks need to be taught the way we want teachers to teach, making lessons very explicit to the goals to be accomplished.
- The best core tasks should lead to experiences where the parts are learned very well with depth, coherence, and reasonableness, as opposed to the study of too many topics superficially learned and quickly forgotten. Prospective teachers need experience in learning some aspect of mathematics very well and to reflect on the structure or schema that enabled them to reach that level of interest. They should then be encouraged to apply that aspect to solve problems in diverse mathematical contexts. This should lead to a sense of how to learn mathematics on one's own, with an awareness of the need for continued study after completing mathematics courses.

Instructors need to research what misconceptions elementary teachers have and design tasks that get at those problems. Promising ways include the following:

- The use of problem sets and case studies.
- The use of standard problems suggested by research mathematicians as well as mathematics educators. Some "classic" (i.e., standard) problems have started to appear in the literature as problems actually researched with varying populations to see if those problems really do lead to greater mathematical understanding among prospective teachers as well as students. It would seem advantageous to use proven problems rather than trying to have individual instructors invent new ones that may or may not help rectify the misconceptions that elementary teachers have.
- The inclusion of more examples of children's mathematical thinking through videos and work samples studied in the content courses (not just in the methods courses). This sends a powerful message that children's mathematical thinking is worthy of indepth responses from the mathematical community.
- The remodeling of tasks to get at the problem areas, challenging the prospective teachers to remodel tasks as assignments to see early on if they understand and use the structure of mathematics in this remodeling.
- The use of multiple representations moving beyond using concrete models for the sake of using them. Such models can have the same fallacies as symbolic representations if not done for the right reasons.
- Completing only 35 problems a semester. (The thinking was that a three-credit

course probably could handle no more than two in-depth problems per week in a 16-week semester with the possibility of an introduction problem and one presented as a midterm and final exam question.) Some problems will last over a period of days, fostering quality over quantity in learning.

The plenary session on the Promising Approaches for Helping Prospective Teachers Learn Mathematics for Teaching aided the group by identifying ways to affect change in the teacher preparation content, including the following:

• The establishment of a network to share what misconceptions elementary teachers have and design tasks that get at those problems, combining best practice and the research.

• The support of a Master Teacher-in-Residence Program at the college level—to team teach and keep content instructors realistically aware of the needs that will be faced in the elementary classroom. Such a program could foster mutual respect among the content mathematician, the mathematics educator, and the master classroom teacher. Prospective teachers in such programs witness collegial networks with potential for on-going support in their own future classrooms. This sends a powerful message of the importance of mathematics on all levels of development—from the very young child to the adult.

Question #5

What are some promising ways to help teachers not only develop mathematical understanding but learn to *use* mathematical insight and knowledge in the context of practice? What are the key features of what makes an approach promising? Are there ways to engage preservice teachers in learning mathematics through the tasks they will actually do in practice?

Leader: *Mark Klespis;* Members: *Tom Carpenter, Liping Ma, Patricia Reisdorf, Skip Fennell, Paul Kuerbis, Judy Merlau, Ginger Warfield*

ASSUMPTIONS MADE IN FRAMING THE DISCUSSION

We interpreted this question to mean we needed to examine ways in which preservice teachers can synthesize the content knowledge they receive and then apply this knowledge in practice. Prospective teachers must come to appreciate how basic mathematical ideas are introduced, developed, and retained by students. The interplay among a teacher's content knowledge, understanding of that content, and awareness of strategies for presenting it in practice is a complex endeavor. At each level—preservice, student teaching, and inservice—there is a need for teachers to talk with others so they can tap into the shared knowledge of all practitioners in the field.

SUMMARY OF THE MAIN POINTS OF DISCUSSION

Preservice teachers can synthesize mathematical content and pedagogical content knowledge through core conversa- *tions with other members of the mathematics education community.* Teachers share their mathematical knowledge in conversations with their students. At the same time, students share their knowledge with their peers. The group agreed it was essential that students and their instructors actively converse about mathematics. This idea gave rise to the phrase "core conversations" to describe instances where students and teachers engaged in an in-depth discussion of one or more aspects of a piece of mathematical knowledge. In content and methods classes, these core conversations can be enhanced in many ways. One way is to have students view video clips of elementary school students learning mathematics with a goal of analyzing the mathematical knowledge needed to teach effectively. A second suggestion was to have students participate in a mathematics forum where different solution paths to a problem could be discussed.

One emphasis at this Workshop was to ask people to think of a list of core mathematical ideas that preservice teachers should know. Such a list is necessary, but we need to ascertain the core conversations surrounding preservice teacher issues as well.

Several questions arose: Do we practice what we preach here? How often do we meet with colleagues as we have done at this Workshop to discuss issues related to teaching at our own campus or school? If we believe these conversations have value for our students, we need to have them ourselves. Core conversations help all of us refine and improve our teaching practices. The group felt strongly that these conversations need to begin early. This led to our second central assertion.

The mathematics education community's resources must be available to preservice teachers now—starting in their college classroom. Prospective teachers need to be aware of the multiplicity of mathematics education resources early in their preparation—resources beyond their college instructors. One immediate suggestion was to make sure students know at least one good mathematics Web site. Another suggestion in a similar vein was the development of a virtual online community. A key feature of this community would be to facilitate communication among all the groups involved in mathematics teacher preparation.

Some examples of mathematics education networks include the following:

- Texas Statewide Systemic Initiative
- ToToM (Teachers of Teachers of Mathematics)
- Mathematics Forum at Swarthmore
- Operation Pipeline
- National Science Foundation's best practices—a report on curriculum reform projects
- America Counts
- The Eisenhower National Clearinghouse Web site

Liping Ma described at length the working conditions of Chinese teachers. A great deal of their day is spent discussing the next day's lesson with other teachers on their team. This team can consist of teachers working at the same grade level, but it can have teachers from the grades immediately above or below the grade levels being taught. This structure is not common in current U.S. schools. The team approach to teaching, however, is an excellent program to adapt to preservice programs, especially in light of the group's discussion of core conversations about mathematical content and pedagogy. A cohort of students could discuss fundamental mathematical concepts throughout the semester in a mathematics content class and then attempt to incorporate the mathematical insight in the context of teaching practice—in either a content or methods course.

Early apprenticeships in mathematics teaching must be required in the teacher preparation program. One way to make sure preservice teachers feel connected to the larger mathematics education community is to require field experiences early in their college careers—experiences that go beyond the level of classroom observation and that engage prospective teachers in some actual acts of teaching. Such experiences will help students see themselves as teachers-in-training rather than simply college students. It is also important for students to see the issues with which inservice teachers need to deal daily.

Field experiences must flow continuously from the preservice level, to "internship," to master teacher level. As one grows in mathematical and pedagogical knowledge, a person's core conversations move outward. That is, talking begins within groups in a preservice mathematics classroom, expands to mentor teachers during the first year of teaching, and then to colleagues at all levels as one enters the profession.

There must be an agreement on the fundamental mathematics needed for teaching. There must be a consensus on what core mathematics is essential for teaching. Such a consensus was not reached in our group. However, if the U.S. curriculum is a "mile wide and an inch deep," as the Third International Mathematics and Science Study researchers suggest, what implications does this have for our preservice curriculum? The Texas Statewide Systemic Initiative's *Guidelines for the Mathematical Preparation of Prospective Elementary Teachers* (Molina, Hull, & Schielack, 1997) is one attempt to provide guidance to colleges and universities in this area.

ISSUES/COMMENTS

It is easy to say we need to stress the what and how of mathematics. But how do we do this in practice? Multiple representations of concepts? Using student work to develop understanding?

Group members saw evidence during the Workshop that an in-depth exploration of a small domain of mathematical knowledge allowed us to unpack the layers of mathematics needed to fully understand (and teach!) a concept. As important as it is to discuss the core knowledge of mathematics needed to teach, we realized it was equally important for students to be aware of core conversations that arise from these experiences. Then students and instructors can lay bare their understandings of mathematics so that each group can continue to grow professionally. The challenge we face is to get students to "unpack" their knowledge and, most importantly, induce them to look to the larger mathematics education community for help.

REFERENCE

Molina, D. D., Hull, S. H., & Schielack, J. F. (1997). *Guidelines for the mathematical preparation of prospective elementary teachers.* Austin, TX: Texas Statewide Systemic Initiative for Science and Mathematics Education.

Question #5

What are some promising ways to help teachers not only develop mathematical understanding but learn to *use* mathematical insight and knowledge in the context of practice? What are the key features of what makes an approach promising? Are there ways to engage preservice teachers in learning mathematics through the tasks they will actually do in practice?

Leader: *Dale Oliver;* Members: *Virginia Bastable, Marilyn Hala, Marco Ramirez, Gerry Rossi, Jack Schiller, Terry Woodin*

ASSUMPTIONS MADE IN FRAMING THE DISCUSSION

The phrase, "learn to *use* mathematical insight and knowledge in the context of practice," was the focal point of the group discussion. What is the nature of content knowledge that makes a difference in the classroom, that allows teachers to recognize and act on teachable moments in mathematics? How can mathematics teacher educators facilitate the transition from content knowledge to the practice of teaching?

SUMMARY OF THE MAIN POINTS OF DISCUSSION

The following summary is a reflection of the general consensus that emerged in the group through the four small group meetings within the conference. The summary begins with a brief description of two qualities of mathematical knowledge that are particularly important for teachers to effectively apply that knowledge to the practice of teaching. Follow-

ing the description are three assertions about promising practices in teacher preparation that support the development of these qualities.

Teachers who use mathematical insight and knowledge in the context of practice draw from a coherent view of the development of mathematical ideas in elementary school children. One aspect of a deep and profound understanding of mathematics in the elementary curriculum is the understanding of how these ideas grow over time. At a minimum, a teacher needs a coherent view of this process within the one-year curriculum of the level at which they teach. This understanding of how mathematical ideas grow over time includes knowledge of effective strategies for working with children and a sense of meaningful assessment.

Ideally, teachers have a coherent view of the development of mathematical ideas encompassing the entire K-8 mathematics curriculum. In a sense, the teacher who is most ready to apply mathematical knowledge of a content area to the practice of teaching mathematics knows the K-8 mathematics curriculum of that content area as a whole. While this is a lofty and perhaps unachievable goal during undergraduate teacher preparation, such a goal is not out of reach for a specific content package (place value, for example) that can then be extended to other content packages as teachers continue to extend their mathematical understanding in the context of practice.

Teachers who use mathematical insight and knowledge in the context of practice value the process of mathematical inquiry for themselves and for their students. One piece of evidence that a teacher is making a useful transition from content knowledge to the practice of teaching is when the teacher takes advantage of "teachable moments" in the classroom. (A teachable moment is that time when a student or a group of students asks a question or makes a conjecture from their own thinking and is poised to expand their understanding of the mathematics from that thinking.) The mindset (beliefs) of a teacher toward mathematics has great influence over the use of mathematical insight and knowledge in teaching mathematics. Teachers who believe that mathematics is no more than a set of rules, a collection of techniques, or a list of vocabulary terms are less likely to see mathematical inquiry as relevant to the teaching process and, therefore, less likely to take advantage of teachable moments that fall outside of these definitions. However, if the process of inquiry (exploration, conjecture, and proof) is part of what a teacher believes is mathematically relevant and important, then such a teacher is more willing to wrestle with mathematics ideas on their own and thus better prepared to build on student insights for fostering student learning. Moreover, such a teacher will view their own development of mathematical knowledge as an ongoing process that can be

achieved in various ways, including through their work in the classroom.

Consider the topic area of place value. This phrase encapsulates many mathematical ideas. A teacher who practices active inquiry into mathematics is more willing to ask questions like "What ideas are here? How are they articulated? How can these ideas be unraveled to reveal possible pathways for leading student inquiry?" This teacher is also more likely to view such questions as being important.

Studying elementary mathematics from an advanced viewpoint demands intellectual intensity. Teaching elementary mathematics is an intellectually intense and challenging endeavor. To do so well requires that teachers acquire a deep understanding of elementary mathematics, in itself a substantial intellectual challenge (Ma, 1999). Hence, prospective teachers need intensive and focused opportunities in which they can acquire a deep understanding of, appreciation for, and confidence in elementary mathematics. On one hand, it is not enough for departments of mathematics to offer survey courses in elementary mathematics that do not reflect the required intensity or depth of inquiry that is required. On the other hand, departments of mathematics are urged to recognize that such intense intellectual activity focused on elementary curriculum or on elementary mathematics is valuable and worthy of undergraduate mathematics credit.

There are two important forms that mathematics department offerings can take: those that are curriculum-centered (and thus address a coherent view of the development of mathematical ideas in K-8 curriculum), and those that are foundational (and thus address the nature of mathematics as an inquiry-based discipline). In either case, the pedagogical aspects of teaching mathematical content cannot be ignored. In fact, pedagogic and content issues are intertwined in the pursuit of a deep understanding of elementary mathematics, and thus education departments must also guard against offering methods courses without the requisite intellectual intensity or connection to content issues.

Explicit connections between mathematics and classroom practice strengthen content and pedagogical knowledge. For the most part, teachers have a hard time unraveling packages of mathematical ideas into component parts and supporting ideas that inform their teaching. An approach that seems promising for improving a teacher's facility with mathematics is to design opportunities for learning mathematics including explicit connections to the elementary curriculum. For example, if it is important that elementary teachers learn about calculus, then explicit connections between the concepts of calculus and the content in the K-8 curriculum need to be a substantial part of the experience of learning calculus. Mathematics teacher educators are encouraged to study and articulate the connections that are most helpful for teachers.

Alternatively, any new opportunities for learning about the teaching of mathematics at the elementary level need to highlight the process of mathematical inquiry and connect to significant mathematical ideas. Mathematics teacher educators are encouraged to design experiences for prospective teachers and teachers to study and analyze "teachable moments" in the classroom (some where teachers capitalize on such moments and others where teachers miss teachable moments). There are two means for studying classroom application in this way that seem promising: the study of written cases of an episode or string of episodes in the classroom and the analysis of classroom videotapes.

The combination of connections, from mathematical ideas to curriculum and from teaching practice in the classroom to mathematical ideas, works together to establish a professional habit of mind that includes asking questions such as, "Why would I ask a student to do this mathematical task? What is the mathematical purpose of the task? What other mathematical or related areas connect to this mathematical activity?" Such questions can play an important role in the intellectual development of prospective teachers.

Teaching is an intellectual activity that requires time and an expectation of inquiry. How are teachers motivated to study the connections mentioned under the previous assertion? How can overburdened and undersupported teachers find time to look at even the next page of the mathematics text and ask themselves, "Why am I having my students do this? What is the purpose?" If teachers are to make real gains in the application of mathematical knowledge to the practice of teaching, then the culture of teaching must begin to change. The new culture must support time and the expectation that a significant use of that time will be to study mathematics and the elementary mathematics curriculum.

The process of changing the culture can start in the undergraduate preparation of teachers by including coursework in the use of resources (print and electronic materials, professional organizations and conferences, mentors, and peers) to pursue questions that arise in classroom contexts. This kind of inquiry into mathematics and the related pedagogical issues can be an integral part of being an elementary educator if the process is modeled carefully and consistently in teacher preparation programs.

ISSUES

Throughout our discussion, the issues that surfaced most often were connected to a common belief in the broader educational community that teaching elementary mathematics is elementary. How can mathematics and education faculty be engaged in reexamining the intellectual challenges in knowing elementary mathematics deeply? How can such faculty be motivated to rethink the connection between knowing mathematics and teaching mathematics? How will mathematics departments be motivated to offer curriculum-based courses for teachers? How will teachers and the school districts in which they work be motivated to value learning more about the mathematics that they teach?

The Workshop was a good start toward establishing the intellectual intensity of mathematics teacher education: that knowing and teaching elementary mathematics is anything but elementary. There is much work left to do.

APPENDICES

Appendix A: Pre-Workshop Reading

Participants were given the following documents to read before they attended the Workshop.

Ball, D. L. (1991). Teaching mathematics for understanding: What do teachers need to know about subject matter? In M. Kennedy (Ed.), *Teaching academic subjects to diverse learners* (pp. 63-83). New York: Teachers College Press.

Ball, D. L. (1990). Prospective elementary and secondary teachers' understanding of division. *Journal for Research in Mathematics Education, 21*(2), 132-144.

Clemens, H. (1991). What do math teachers need to be? In M. Kennedy (Ed.), *Teaching academic subjects to diverse learners* (pp. 84-96). New York: Teachers College Press.

Darling-Hammond, L. (1997). *Doing what matters most: Investing in quality teaching.* Prepared for the National Commission on Teaching and America's Future, New York.

Lampert, M. (1989). Choosing and using mathematical tools in classroom discourse. In J. Brophy (Ed.), *Advances in Research on Teaching, vol. 1* (pp.223-264). Greenwich, CT: JAI Press.

Ma, L. (1999). *Knowing and teaching elementary mathematics: Teachers' understanding of fundamental mathematics in China and the United States.* Mahwah, NJ: Lawrence Erlbaum. [Chapters 1 and 4.]

National Research Council. Mathematical Sciences Education Board. (1996). *The preparation of teachers of mathematics: Considerations and challenges.* Washington, DC: Author.

Schifter, D. (1998). Learning mathematics for teaching: From a teachers' seminar to the classroom. *Journal of Mathematics Teacher Education, 1*(1), 55-87.

Simon, M. A., & Blume, G. W. (1994). Building and understanding multiplicative relationships: A study of prospective elementary teachers. *Journal for Research in Mathematics Education, 25*(5), 472-494.

Wu, H. (1999). Professional development of mathematics teachers. *Notices of the American Mathematical Society, 46*(5), 535-542.

Wu, H. (1999). Preservice professional development of mathematics teachers. Unpublished manuscript. Available at http://math.berkley.edu/~wu/.

Appendix B:
Workshop Agenda

Mathematics Teacher Preparation Content Workshop
National Academy of Sciences
2101 Constitution Ave., NW
Washington, DC 20418
19-21 March 1999

Friday, March 19

6:00 p.m.-7:00 p.m.	**Reception**	NAS Great Hall
7:00 p.m.-7:15 p.m.	**Welcome and Overview**	NAS Great Hall

Rodger Bybee, Executive Director, Center for Science, Mathematics, and Engineering Education, National Research Council

Deborah Ball, Chair of Workshop Steering Committee, University of Michigan

7:15 p.m.-7:45 p.m.	**Discussion Groups**	NAS Great Hall
7:45 p.m.-8:30 p.m.	**Panel Discussion**	NAS Members Room

Teachers' Understanding of Fundamental Mathematics

Panel: Liping Ma, Stanford University
Mark Saul, Bronxville High School
Genevieve Knight, Coppin State College
Reactor: Joan Ferrini-Mundy,
Center for Science, Mathematics, and
Engineering Education

Saturday, March 20

Reconsidering the Mathematics That Teachers Need to Know

8:00 a.m.	**Continental Breakfast**	NAS Lecture Room Annex
8:30 a.m.-10:30 a.m.	**Plenary Activity**	NAS Lecture Room

Investigating Teaching Practice: What Mathematical Knowledge Is Entailed in Teaching Children to Reason Mathematically?

Hyman Bass, Columbia University
Deborah Ball, University of Michigan
Reactor: James Lewis, University of Nebraska-Lincoln

10:30 a.m.-10:45 a.m. **Break**

10:45 a.m.-12:45 p.m. **Concurrent Sessions**

Investigating Teaching Practice: What Mathematical Knowledge, Skill, and Sensibilities Does It Take?

Analyzing Student Thinking	NAS Lecture Room

Virginia Bastable, SummerMath for Teachers

Remodeling Mathematical Tasks	NAS 150

Olga Torres, Tucson Public Schools

Analyzing Student Work	NAS 180

Michaele F. Chappell, University of South Florida

Managing Class Discussion	NAS 250

Erick Smith, University of Illinois-Chicago

12:45 p.m.-1:45 p.m.	**Lunch with Discussion Group**	NAS Great Hall
1:45 p.m.-3:45 p.m.	**Repeat morning concurrent sessions**	
3:45 p.m.-4:00 p.m.	**Break**	
4:00 p.m.–4:45 p.m.	**Discussion Groups**	NAS Great Hall
4:45 p.m.- 5:30 p.m.	**Plenary to Synthesize Saturday's Work:**	NAS Lecture Room

What Kinds of Mathematical Knowledge Matter in Teaching?
Panel: Alan Tucker, State University of New York, Stony Brook
              Deborah Schifter, Education Development Center
              Gladys Whitehead, Prince George's County Public Schools
Moderator: Gail Burrill, MSEB, National Research Council

Sunday, March 21

Helping Teachers Learn Mathematics

8:00 a.m.	**Continental Breakfast**	NAS Lecture Room Annex
8:30 a.m.-8:45 a.m.	**Orientation for Goals and Activities**	NAS Lecture Room
	Deborah Ball, University of Michigan	

8:45 a.m.-10:15 a.m. **Concurrent Sessions**
Investigating Alternative Approaches to Helping Teachers Learn Mathematics

Student Curriculum Materials   NAS Lecture Room
Shin-ying Lee, University of Michigan
Marco Ramirez, Tucson Public Schools

Case Materials   NAS 150
Carne Barnett, WestEd

Programs and Practices   NAS 180
Virginia Bastable, SummerMath for Teachers
Jill Lester, Mount Holyoke College
Deborah Schifter, Education Development Center

Video as a Delivery Mechanism   NAS 250
Deborah Ball, University of Michigan
Bradford Findell, MSEB, National Research Council

10:15 a.m.-10:30 a.m.	**Break**	
10:30 a.m.-12:00 p.m.	**Repeat morning concurrent sessions**	
12:00 p.m.-1:00 p.m.	**Lunch**	NAS Great Hall
1:00 p.m.-2:30 p.m.	**Discussion Groups**	
2:30 p.m. -3:15 p.m.	**Plenary to Synthesize Sunday's Work:**	NAS Lecture Room

Promising Approaches for Helping Prospective Elementary Teachers Learn Mathematics for Teaching
Panel: Richard Askey, University of Wisconsin-Madison
             Carol Midgett, South Port Elementary School
             Alice Gill, American Federation of Teachers
             James Lightbourne, National Science Foundation
Moderator: Joan Ferrini-Mundy,
                     MSEB, National Research Council

3:15 p.m.-3:30 p.m. **Adjourn, closing summary comments**
Deborah Ball, University of Michigan

Appendix C:
Homework Problems

The following "homework" problems were assigned at the end of the first evening and at the end of the next full day. Note that the problems are slightly different: The first is a task of teaching, the second a task of teacher preparation.

Day 1 Homework
A Task of Teaching: Preparing to Teach a Mathematics Problem

Several digits "8" are written, and some "+" signs are inserted to get the sum 1000. Figure out how it is done.

TASK: Prepare to teach this problem to a class. Do whatever you think you need to do to be ready to teach it to a specific class you have in mind.

Stand back and reflect: What mathematics did you use to do this task of preparing to teach? What sorts of mathematical understanding and sense did you draw on? How did you use what you did?

Day 2 Homework
A Task in Teacher Preparation: Comparing Two Versions of a Mathematics Problem

A. Several digits "8" are written, and some "+" signs are inserted to get the sum 1000. Figure out how it is done.

B. Write down as many 8's and + signs as you want in a row so that you write a statement that equals 1000. Find all the possible solutions to this problem.

TASK: A teacher took the original 8's problem and revised it for her class. How does problem B compare with the version in A?

Stand back and reflect: What opportunities for learning mathematics could be drawn from teachers' engagement with this task?

REFERENCE

Gelfand, I. M., & Shen, A. (1993). *Algebra.* Boston, MA: Birkhäuser.

Appendix D:
Workshop Participant List

Don Balka
St. Mary's College
Notre Dame, IN

Carne Barnett
WestEd
Oakland, CA

Virginia Bastable
Mount Holyoke College
South Hadley, MA

Dan Berch
U.S. Department of Education
Washington, DC

Nadine Bezuk
San Diego State University
San Diego, CA

Sally Blake
University of Texas at El Paso
El Paso, TX

Irene Bloom
Arizona State University
Tempe, AZ

Carey Bolster
Public Broadcasting System
Annapolis, MD

John Bradley
National Science Foundation
Arlington, VA

Carole Brooks
Tucson Public Schools
Tucson, AZ

Blanche Brownley
Washington, DC, Public Schools
Washington, DC

Tom Carpenter
University of Wisconsin-Madison
Madison, WI

Dwayne Channell
Western Michigan University
Kalamazoo, MI

Michaele F. Chappell
University of South Florida
Temple Terrace, FL

Rachel Collopy
University of Michigan
Ann Arbor, MI

Linda Davenport
Education Development Center
Newton, MA

David Dennis
University of Texas at El Paso
El Paso, TX

Nancy Edwards
Missouri Western State College
St. Joseph, MO

Ed Esty
U.S. Department of Education
Chevy Chase, MD

Joyce Evans
National Science Foundation
Arlington, VA

Ruhama Even
Weizmann Institute of Science
Israel

Francis Fennell
National Science Foundation
Arlington, VA

Shelley Ferguson
National Council of Teachers of
    Mathematics
Reston, VA

Benjamin Ford
Sonoma State University
Rohnert Park, CA

Helen Gerretson
University of Northern Colorado
Greeley, CO

Alice Gill
American Federation of Teachers
Washington, DC

Don Gilmore
Metropolitan State College of Denver
Denver, CO

Marilyn Hala
National Council of Teachers of
    Mathematics
Reston, VA

Robert Howard
University of Tulsa
Tulsa, OK

DeAnn Huinker
University of Wisconsin-Milwaukee
Milwaukee, WI

Michael Hynes
University of Central Florida
Orlando, FL

Margaret Jensen
Huegel Elementary School
Madison, WI

Martin Johnson
University of Maryland
College Park, MD

Judy Kasabian
El Camino College
Torrance, CA

Lena Khisty
University of Illinois-Chicago
Chicago, IL

Mark Klespis
Sam Houston State University
Huntsville, TX

Paul Kuerbis
Colorado College
Colorado Springs, CO

Carole LaCampagne
U.S. Department of Education
Washington, DC

Shin-ying Lee
University of Michigan
Ann Arbor, MI

Jill Lester
Mount Holyoke College
South Hadley, MA

James Lewis
University of Nebraska
Lincoln, NE

Cathy Liebars
The College of New Jersey
Ewing, NJ

James Lightbourne
National Science Foundation
Arlington, VA

Liping Ma
Stanford University
Stanford, CA

Miriam Masullo
National Action Council for Minorities in
    Engineering
New York, NY

Mercedes McGowen
Harper College
Palatine, IL

Judy Merlau
University of Illinois-Chicago
Chicago, IL

Carol Midgett
Brunswick County Schools
Southport, NC

Joyce Lyn Miller
Western Kentucky University
Bowling Green, KY

Dale Oliver
Humboldt State University
Arcata, CA

Albert Otto
Illinois State University
Normal, IL

Leigh Peake
Heinemann
Portsmouth, NH

Neil Portnoy
University of Tennessee-Knoxville
Knoxville, TN

Joan Prival
National Science Foundation
Arlington, VA

Marco Ramirez
Tucson Unified School District
Tucson, AZ

Patricia Reisdorf
Madison Metropolitan School District
Madison, WI

Pat O'Connell Ross
U.S. Department of Education
Washington, DC

Gerry Rossi
Salisbury State University
Salisbury, MD

Kay Sammons
Howard County Public Schools
Ellicott City, MD

Jack Schiller
Temple University
Philadelphia, PA

Marie Sheckels
Mary Washington College
Fredericksburg, VA

Betty Siano
National Board for Professional Teaching
  Standards
Southfield, MI

Marty Simon
Penn State University
University Park, PA

Erick Smith
University of Illinois-Chicago
Chicago, IL

Shirley Smith
Springbrook High School
Silver Spring, MD

Judith Sowder
San Diego State University
San Diego, CA

Cynthia Tocci
Educational Testing Service
Princeton, NJ

Alan Tucker
State University of New York at Stony
  Brook
Stony Brook, NY

Ginger Warfield
University of Washington
Seattle, WA

Rosamond Welchman
Brooklyn College
Brooklyn, NY

Gladys Whitehead
Prince George's County Public Schools
Accokeek, MD

Terry Woodin
National Science Foundation
Arlington, VA

Janie Zimmer
Howard County Public Schools
Ellicott City, MD

Pamela Zimmerman
Arizona State University
Tempe, AZ

Appendix E:
Transcript of Ball Videos

Figure 1. Class Seating Arrangement on 9/19/89

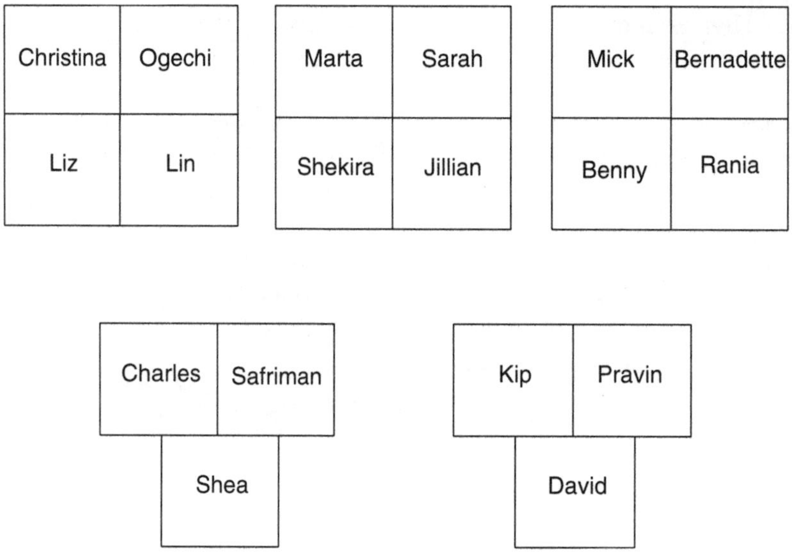

Christina	Ogechi
Liz	Lin

Marta	Sarah
Shekira	Jillian

Mick	Bernadette
Benny	Rania

Charles	Safriman
	Shea

Kip	Pravin
	David

1:03:38		*Ten minutes into class.*
86.	Ball	I wonder if someone can think of a number sentence that uses more then two numbers here. Just so we have a bunch of ideas of how we could do this. Who can make a number sentence that equals 10, but has more than two numbers adding up to 10?
87.	Kip	One plus one plus one plus one—
88.	Ball	Okay, wait-wait, slow down, I've got to h—to write it. One plus one plus one—

---

89. Rania	—one plus one—
90. Ball	I want Kip to tell me.
91. Kip	Plus one. Plus one. Plus one. Plus one. Plus three.
92. Ball	Okay, why does that equal 10? Why does that equal 10? Safriman?
93. Safriman	Plus one plus one plus one—
94. Ball	Sorry?
95. Safriman	That's just plus one plus one plus one.

1:04:43

96. Ball	Okay, can someone add to what Safriman is saying? How do we know that that equals 10? Rania? How do we know that that equals 10?
97. Rania	Because one plus one plus one plus one plus one plus one plus one and plus three equals 10.
98. Ball	Well then you're just sort of reading it, but how could you prove it to somebody who wasn't sure?
99. Rania	Because I counted it.
100. Ball	What did you count? What did you find out?
101. Rania	There's one and the next one is two and the next one is three, next one is four, next one is five, next one is six, next one is seven, next one is—seven, and then three more, eight, nine, ten.
102. Ball	Do you see the difference in Rania's second explanation? Did you see how she really showed us how it equals 10? The first time you just read it. And the second time you explained it. That was really nice. Okay? That's enough ideas for right now. I want you to write down as many different ones as you can and you—try to see if you can come up with some that you think nobody else in the class will think of.
103. Student	Can we work with each other?
104. Ball	You can work with other people at your table, but you should write it in your own notebook.

1:05:47   *Students work individually and in small groups for the next 30 minutes.*

1:36:30   *43 minutes into class.*

199. Ball	Let's see if we can share some of the things you can come up with. Look over your list, and pick a couple that you feel especially—are especially interesting. That you think other people might not have thought of or that you were pleased to get or something. And I would like you to listen to each other's. If you liked one that somebody else brings up you can add it to your list. Liz, do you have one that you like?
200. Liz	Yeah.
201. Ball	What is it?
202. Liz	100 divided by 10 equals 10.
203. Ball	Bernadette, could you hear Liz?
204. Bernadette	Yeah.
205. Ball	Okay, this is the time I want you to listening to other people. She said 100 divided by 10 equals 10. Liz can you explain that?

	Liz	What do you mean by explain?
	Ball	How do we know that that's right?
206.	Liz	Um, cause I have, like when I did 20 divided by, um—well I don't know really—
	Lin	I think I can explain it.

1:37:26

207.	Ball	Lin thinks she can explain this. Is there anybody else who thinks they can explain this? How do we know that what Liz told us is right? Sarah, you think you could explain it.
	Sarah	Um-hmm. I—I agr—
	Ball	Pravin and Kip can you be looking and listening right now?
208.	Sarah	I agree with Liz about what she said about the math sentence.
209.	Ball	Why do you think that's right?
210.	Sarah	I don't know . I just think it's right, for some reason.
211.	Ball	Lin?
212.	Lin	I had it—I agree with Liz too because I had it on my paper.

1:38:00

213.	Ball	But how do you know that it's right? Just because a couple people have it on their paper, doesn't mean it's right? Liz
214.	Liz	Lin said her mom taught her what—about dividing by, and so I believe Lin.
215.	Ball	Okay, so Lin told you and her mom taught her and so you believe her. Lin—.
	Rundquist	Liz has another reason too.
	Ball	You have another reason too Liz?
	Liz	Uh-uh.
216.	Rundquist	What did you think about that _____ the ones you told me.
217.	Liz	Um, well um, I have a lot of other ones, and like, if I had 20 divided by 2, Lin said it was right, so then—when I said that, she said it was right, so if I—if I have 10 divided—10 divided by 1 equals 10, and then I have it—and then I have like 50 divided by 5 equals 10, and Lin said that it was right, and so, like if you have 100 divided by 10 it would be right because—because if you went from like 5 then it would be 5 more, and then—cause 50 is 5 less than 100 so—so it would be 10 cause if it's 5 divided by—50 divided by 5 it would equal 10.

1:39:21

218.	Ball	Comments from other people? Bernadette?
219.	Bernadette	I have ano—I think I know what she's saying is, like the 50 she just put—she just plussed 50 plus 50 and made it into 100, 5 plus 5, made it into a 10, and then she divided it and put it into 10, made it 10.
220.	Ball	Is that what you're saying Liz?
221.	Liz	Yeah, sort of.

222.	Ball	Does anybody, um, have anything they could say that would help us know if we should believe this or not? Pravin and Kip? Lin, you think you have something that would help us believe it?
223.	Lin	Yeah.
224.	Ball	What?
225.	Lin	Cause see, really divided, those kind of problems are really the opposite of times.
226.	Ball	Uh huh.
227.	Lin	And like if—10 times 5, it would be 50. So, 50 divided in 5 would be 10.

1:40:20

228.	Ball	What does she mean 10 times 5 is 50. What does she mean by that? Anybody? Anybody have any thoughts about that? Jillian? What do you think? What does she mean 10 times 5 is 50?
229.	Jillian	When she writes it up there it looks like—like she writes, you know, if the number has three numbers she writes the first two numbers. And if it has two numbers, she writes the first number.
231.	Ball	It seems like maybe we should go on right now. I'm not sure that people—Rania and Bernadette—other people seem to be working on other things and I'm not sure that everyone is thinking about whether or not we should believe this. I'm not sure should—we should have included this on our list until we have some way of showing that we know that it's right. Like, remember before when Rania explained one plus one plus one plus one plus one plus one plus one plus three. She proved to us that it made sense. But right now we don't have any way of really knowing if these are right or not. And I'm not sure we should have them on our list unless we have a way to show that they make sense. Lin?
232.	Lin	I have one.
233.	Ball	Okay, I'm going to just put a bracket around this for right now. That doesn't mean that it's wrong, but until we have some way of deciding if it's right we're not sure. Okay? Who has something different?
234.	Student	Um, 1-200 take away 190 is 10.

Table 1. Class list as of September 19, 1990

NAME	GENDER	RACE	COUNTRY	ENGLISH PROFICIENCY	HOW LONG AT THIS SCHOOL[1]
Benny	M	White	Ethiopia	fluent	3 years
Bernadette	F	White	Canada	native speaker	just arrived
Charles	M	Asian	Taiwan	developing	2 years
Christina	F	African-American	U.S.A.	native speaker	1 year
David	M	Asian	Indonesia	developing	3 years
Jillian	F	White	U.S.A.	native speaker	3 years
Kip	M	African Black	Kenya	fluent	3 years
Lin	F	Asian	Taiwan	fluent	2 years
Liz	F	White	U.S.A.	native speaker	3 years
Marta	F	Latina	Nicaragua	beginning	just arrived
Mick	M	White	U.S.A.	native speaker	2 years
Ogechi	F	African Black	Nigeria	fair	3 years
Pravin	M	White	Nepal	beginning	1 month
Rania	F	White	Egypt	good	3 years
Safriman	M	Asian	Indonesia	developing	12 months
Sarah	S	White	U.S.A.	native speaker	2 years
Shea	M	White	U.S.A.	native speaker	2 years
Shekira	F	African-American	U.S.A.	native speaker	just arrived

[1]NOTE: This column reflects the length of time the child had been in this <u>school</u> as of 9/19/89.

9/21/89

1:22:38   *30 minutes into class.*

Ball has just asked Bernadette, Rania, Mick, and Benny to tell the class their idea from 9/19/89.

92. Bernadette   See, what we did is we would take any number, it wouldn't matter what number, say 200. And then we would minus, 200, then we would plus, 10, and it would always equal 10. So you could go on for, oh, a long, long time, just keep on doing that. You can get up to this.

Shea   How about 2000 ___.

Bernadette   And then you minus it, and then you plus it, and then it equals 10. So, since numbers they never stop, you could go on and on and on and on and on and on and on, and I got this one right here. It's—right here.

Pravin   On and on and on and on—

© Mathematics Teaching and Learning to Teach Project, University of Michigan

93.	Students	Whoa!
	Student	Let me see. Let me see.
	Student	Did you put _____?
	Student	Bernadette, we can't see it over here.
	Student	Sarah can't see.
	Ogechi	I can't see it anymore.
95.	Ball	Could you say what your idea was again? I want to write it down for us to think about.

1:23:45

With students' help, Ball writes Bernadette's idea on a poster.

1:26:50

119.	Ball	Okay. Now, I put a title on this piece of paper, it's important. I wrote, "Bernadette, Rania, Mick and Benny's Conjecture."
	Shea	What does that mean?
	Ball	Conjecture is an important word that we're going to use this year. A conjecture is when you come up with an idea, something you think is true, that you're trying to prove to other people. How did they prove to us that they think this is true? Who understands what they were doing, that tried to prove to us that the answers would go on forever? What did they show us? What did Bernadette do on the board to try to make you believe that this is true? Jillian, what did she do?
120.	Jillian	She wrote it up on the board until we thought that they were right.
121.	Ball	Well, what kind of example did she use? Do you remember what she showed?
122.	Jillian	She took away 200, and then that's zero, and then she added 10.
123.	Ball	Right. Table, um, 4, Ogechi and Chris—I know—and Shekira—
	Shea	That's 3.
	Students	3.
	Ball	3. The numbers are not matching the tables today. That's the problem. I'd like you listening to Jillian. She said she had a number—Bernadette had a number, then she took it away and that was zero, and then she added 10. Why does that—why does that help us to think that this is true? Why does that show that the answers would go on forever? I thought maybe people weren't sure about that. Can you—this group say anything more about why you think—oh, Sarah you think you know why that proves it?
124.	Sarah	Because numbers go on forever, and you can go like infinity take away infinity plus 10 equals 10. Because numbers go on and on.

1:28:42

9/25/89

1:00:00		*Three minutes into class.*
12.	Ball	Bernadette, you want to read what you said?
13.	Bernadette	We'd pick any number, it doesn't matter what number, say 200. Then we'd write, 200 minus 200 plus 10 equals 10. And it always equals 10.
14.	Ball	Go on, there's a little more there.
15.	Bernadette	And numbers go on forever and—and so you could go on and on.
16.	Ball	Actually, she said, "So you could go on and on and on and on, and on" is what she said. Do you remember that? Do the rest of you remember Bernadette explaining that?
	Students	Yeah
	Ball	She said you could take any number and you could minus that number, and then you could add 10, and it would always equal 10. I want to show you a way of writing what Bernadette said, and I'd like you to copy it down too. A way of writing—she had to use a lot of words to say what she said, didn't she? But it made sense to everybody. But there's a way she could write that that mathematicians would use to write her idea, her proof. And I want to show you how you could write that. She wanted to say "any number," didn't she? She said you could do this with any number, she just used 200 as an example, right? She could have used 50 as an example. She could have said—how would that one work? Could somebody tell me how it would work with 50? Kip?
19.	Kip	50 minus 50 plus 10 equals 10.
20.	Ball	Right. She could have picked 74. How would it work with 74? Christina?
21.	Shekira	Shekira.
22.	Ball	Shekira. Sorry!
23.	Shekira	74 take away 74, plus 10, equals 10.
	Ball	Shea, what other number could she have picked?
	Shea	Um, you—she could have picked like—like over a—over 10 million? Uh—
24.	Ball	Pick a number so we can write down one more example.
25.	Shea	10 million.
26.	Ball	10 million.
	Shea	Uh—
	Ball	Then what?
	Shea	Take away 10 million. Equal—plu—plus 10, equals 10.
1:02:14		
27.	Ball	Okay. But she was really saying to us any number—it doesn't matter what number. Do you see where she said that? Any number, it doesn't matter what number. And when mathematicians want to say

---

		that instead of saying any number, it doesn't matter what number, they just sometimes use another symbol to stand for that, and we could use x, for example. And you could say x minus x—and that means you're taking any number—any time you pick a number it would fill in the place for x. Any number minus that same number, plus what?
	Student	10.
	Ball	Plus 10, would equal what?
	Shea	10!
	Ball	That's what she was saying. She was saying, any number minus the same number, plus 10 would equal 10. And she also said something else. She said, you—there are—the numbers that you could use to fill in for x go on and on forever. That's the other part of what she was saying.

1:03:04

Pause in the tape, but the tape continues from where it stopped.

1:03:04

	Ball	She assumed you knew something. What did she assume you knew? What does everybody in this class understand that allows you to make all these examples from her proof? There's something you guys all know but nobody said because you all assumed it. Does anybody—can anybody figure out what you all know? There's something you all know that we haven't even had to say, when we looked at this. Rania?
29.	Rania	Numbers go on and on.
30.	Ball	That's one thing, but we did say that. I guess a lot of people know that numbers go on and on forever, but she did say that. There's something she didn't say that you all know, that makes this easy for you, that a kindergartner might not know. Something in this number sentence that you knew that we didn't even have to talk about, and in this one, and in this one. What was it? And in this one, and in x minus x plus 10—
	Student	Oh, I know.

1:04:00

	Ball	There's something you guys all know in this class that you don't even have to talk about because you all know it. Shekira, do you know what it is?
31.	Shekira	Anytime you take away a number, then you add a number, it's just gonna be a zero in there so—
32.	Ball	That's right. What you all know, and I'm going to write it here because it's important. Everybody knows—everybody in this class knows that x minus x equals zero. What do I mean by x minus x

		equals zero? You all know that, and it made this easy for you. Benny, do you think you know what I mean when I wrote that?
33.	Benny	Well like, any number—any—any number, um, plus, uh—
34.	Ball	Not plus, minus.
35.	Benny	Not—minus, uh, another number—
36.	Ball	Not another number—
	Benny	*x, x*—
	Ball	The same number. Any number minus the same number—
37.	Benny	Would be zero.

1:05:00

38.	Ball	Would be zero. Is that true? Does everybody in the class know that?
	Students	Yes
	Ball	You all knew that any number minus itself would be zero. Right? And that was part of her proof and you—she didn't even have to tell you that because you all assumed it. That was one assumption she could make. Okay? So this is a general way that she could write what she was saying. It's easier than writing all those words. And sometimes in mathematics we can find really easy ways to say very big ideas. Bernadette had a very big idea, and there's an easy way to write her big idea. See how short this idea—this is?
	Lin	Um hmm.

1:05:32

	Ball	Can somebody try explaining in their own words what that says? Looks kind of complicated but I bet everybody in here could explain it. Who'd like to try explaining what *x* minus *x* plus 10 equals 10 means? Could you try, Lin?
39.	Lin	Yeah.
40.	Ball	What?
41.	Lin	'Cause, *x* is like—you could pick any number, like, even in the thousands or millions—
42.	Ball	Right, and then what?
43.	Lin	Take away—you take away—the same number that—that you picked, and then—and then it would be zero 'cause all—cause any number take away the same number would be—be zero.
44.	Ball	Um-hmm. And then? There's some large part that you didn't finish explaining. Here you are at zero and then what?
45.	Lin	And then you plus 10, so there's 10.
46.	Ball	Okay. I'd like everybody to write down this idea that we talked about in your notebook. And write down the part about that we assumed, that everybody knew, too. Write down that everybody in this class knows that any number minus itself is zero. You can write it in that mathematical way instead of writing all those words.

1:06:35

_____

Appendix F:
Explanation of the Unit on Weight

(EXCERPTS FROM)
EXPLANATION OF THE UNIT
ON WEIGHT

EXPLANATION OF THE UNIT ON WEIGHT

I. OVERVIEW

Students have experienced the measurement of weight such as at the time of physical health check-ups to measure their body weight. We should remind them of such experiences to introduce the concept of weight for the first time in this unit. Although weight is a quantity unable to be measured in a direct, visible way like length and size, have the students realize that they can use an arbitrary unit and find how many units there are to find weight just like in length and size. It should be done through actual measuring of concrete objects, then have them understand the usage of the units of weight such as "g" and "kg."

Like a clock, a scale has graduations along the curve on its surface. Students sometimes have difficulty reading the measures. Also, the fact that weight cannot be determined by the object's size nor texture makes it hard for the students to understand weight. Thus, it is important to allow them to experience many occasions of actually measuring the weights and getting familiar with the concept.

II. GOALS

(1) To understand the concept of weight.
(2) To understand the units of weight, "g" and "kg."
(3) To be able to read a scale and measure various objects with a scale.
(4) To understand the relationship between "g" and "kg."
(5) To be able to add and subtract weight.

III. KEY POINTS OF INSTRUCTION

A. Concept and measurement of weight

Although this is the first unit of formal instruction on weight, children have had previous experience with weight in daily life and in various routine activities such as physical examinations.

Judging from outward appearance only, it is easier to estimate an object's length or volume than its weight. However, when determining weight, both indirect and direct approaches are possible: feeling the weight of the object in one's hands or placing it on a scale. It is also possible to numerically express an object's weight beginning with an arbitrary unit of measurement. A similar instructional method was outlined in the unit on Length and Measurement.

These basic ideas are important not only in order for students to understand the concept of weight, but also for them to understand its measurement. As in the instruction of length and volume, there are four steps for the instruction of weight:

1) Direct comparison;
2) Indirect comparison;
3) Measurement by an arbitrary unit;
4) Measurement by a universal unit.

Because weight is difficult to judge visually, it is important to focus on the necessity of a measuring tool. Students' subjective interpretations of weight (e.g., "heavy," "light") are replaced by the graduation indicated on measuring tools and visualized there. This leads to the introduction of a scale.

A scale is constructed to capture the force of gravity on an object's mass with visual movement. One example is associating an object's weight with the lengthening of a spring. Another example is converting the weight into rotational movement, observing the weight in relation to the number of degrees a scale's dial hand moves. This idea of measurement is much more difficult for students to learn compared to the measurement of length or volume. For example, it is easy to visually grasp the sense of an object's length by using a measuring tape, because the increments shown on the flexible tape are the same as those on a graduated ruler. But using a scale, an object's weight is indicated more abstractly—by the degree a dial hand has moved—so it is harder to get the sense of how much it weighs visually.

Because a balance scale makes it easier for children to understand the concept of weight and visualize the meaning of measurement, it is better to use a balance scale when first introducing the topic. However, because upper-dish automatic scales are used more frequently in real life, it is also important that children learn how to use and read them accurately.

As part of their study of the automatic scale, students in this unit will assemble several bags of sand with amounts such as 1kg, 2 kg, and 3 kg. This is so that students are exposed to both the physical experience and actual measurement of standard weight.

B. Introducing the unit of weight

There are three key points regarding the instruction of the weight unit.

1) Weight can be expressed using the number of standard units; it can be numerically stated and labeled.
2) It is more convenient to have two related units such as g and kg so that depending on the purpose one can determine the unit to use and can write the weight in simplest terms (e.g., 2 g rather than 0.002 kg).
3) 1 kg is equivalent to 1000 times 1g.

Because children are not particularly good at converting between these units, and converting is not encountered so often in daily life, it is extremely important to emphasize the relation 1 kg=1000 g.

The minimum graduation of an upper-dish automatic scale with the capacity of 1 kg represents 5 g, and there are 200 of these increments shown on such a scale. It follows then, that if the minimum graduation were 1g there would be 1000 increments on the scale. This may be one way for students to imagine the relation of 1 kg and 1000 g.

Also, it is advisable to tell the students that the "k" in 1 kg means "one thousand times." Teachers can remind students that a similar relationship was encountered previously with length (1 km=1000 m).

C. Sense of weight: Estimating standard quantity

Concerning the sense of weight, 1 kg and 1 g are the best standard quantities for students to become familiar with so they may begin to grasp the actual numeric amount certain objects weigh. Since there are various capacity levels for upper-dish automatic scales (e.g., 1 kg, 4 kg, 10 kg, etc.), depending on what the objects will actually weigh, it is also important to be capable of determining which scale to use.

For example, knowing roughly how much 1 kg weighs helps when estimating the weight of a 3-4 kg object since it is possible to guess that it would be 3 or 4 times heavier than 1 kg.

Another advantage of acquiring a sense of standard quantity is that, given a desired numeric amount and objects with an insufficient weight sum, students can estimate the additional amount needed to make up the difference. For this reason, teachers should provide an environment that includes many different objects weighing various standard amounts so that students have the opportunity to re-experience the weight of them at any time. For example, when assembling a bag of sand with the weight of 1 kg, teachers can keep an eye out for daily objects weighing 100 g or 500 g.

D. How to read graduations

It is harder for students to read graduations on a scale than to read graduations on a ruler, because a scale includes numbers such as 5, 50, 500; or 2, 20, 200; as well as 1, 10, 100 as the smallest graduations. However, it does not show numbers such as 3 or 70. Commenting on the contrast between the graduations on a scale and the ones on a ruler will lead to students' awareness about the structure of the base-10 system.

Be aware of the following points in order to use a scale correctly.
1) Put the scale on a level surface.
2) Before measuring, make sure that the hand points precisely at 0.
3) Check the maximum weight capacity of the scale, and do not put objects on it that seem heavier. (Before measuring, hold the objects and estimate their weight by hand.)
4) Place objects on the plate gently and take them away gently.
5) Face the dial straight on to read the graduation accurately.

It is also important to develop the students' ability to distinguish the characteristics of different scales and to choose a correct one according to their purpose. This can be done by having students actually use different scales to measure

the weight of various objects existing around them.

Next, the following steps should be taken in order to read graduations.
1) Check the maximum capacity of the scale (e.g., the graduation of 1 kg).
2) Check the graduations of large increment numbers.
■ How many graduations can these large increments be divided into?
■ What is the sense of physical weight represented by one of these large increments?
3) Check the smallest graduations.
■ How many graduations are there between two larger increments?
■ What is the sense of physical weight represented by one of these smallest increments?

Students should read from the large graduation to smaller graduations as outlined above. Also, if the dial hand points between two graduations, they should choose the number that is closest to the hand.

E. The importance of manipulative activities

Unlike the study of length or volume in first and second grade, it is hard to understand the conservation and additivity of weight. Since weight cannot be sensed visibly, and because many students may think an object's weight changes when its physical position or shape changes, it is difficult to illustrate the concepts through simple verbal explanation. It is therefore imperative to engage students in activities such as weighing a toy after changing its position and weighing clay after tearing it, then connecting it, etc.

Hence, we deal with several manipulative activities in this unit. For each activity, teachers should show a model experiment and should make sure every child is involved and gets frequent opportunities to use the scales.

The following are examples of manipulative activities.
1) Have students go to a sandbox and put 1 kg sand (which they have to guess) in a plastic bag and measure it on a scale. Most children at this age have not yet developed a sense of 1 kg of weight, so have them try to make the 1 kg bag by adding or removing sand many times. As an expansion of this activity, teachers can have the students make bags with 2 kg, 3 kg, or 1.5 kg sand, which will enhance their interest and motivation in their study of weight.
2) Let students try to make 2 kg by putting everyday objects on a scale. (It could be 1.5 kg or 3 kg, etc.) Given this assignment, students will likely begin to put objects on a scale randomly and soon become aware that they can make 2 kg more quickly with heavier objects. This activity will also help them develop a method of estimating an object's weight before measuring. Some students may even record the weight of each object and add to make the total weight of 2 kg.

Furthermore, teachers can show students how they can determine the weight of fruits in a basket if they subtract the weight of the basket from the total weight. This will help them understand the meaning of conservation and additivity of weight.

A. Section One
(2 hours):

Objectives for the first section:
To learn the concept of weight, the meaning of measurement, and the unit of weight [gram (g)].

Hour One and Two:
Goal: To understand the concept of weight and the unit of weight, the gram (g).

Materials:
Dictionary or books
A bucket with water
Large springs
Scale
Scissors
Compass (the type used to draw circles)
Glue
Pencil
Wooden blocks
1-yen coins

(Example of a proposal for teaching this section)

Topic 1:
"Which book is heavier? Which bucket is heavier?"
Activity: Present two kinds of books and two buckets of water.
Guidance: Let students compare the weights of both of the objects by holding one in one hand and another in another hand. Allow students to realize the importance of measurements of weights by letting them know that it is not necessarily possible to distinguish the weights of the objects just by holding them.

Topic 2:
"Which one is heavier? How can we compare the weight of the objects?"
Activity: Present scissors, compass, and glue.

Guidance: Have students discuss the different ways to compare the weights of the objects. Even though students may suggest using a regular scale, suggest that they use a justice scale indicated in the textbook.

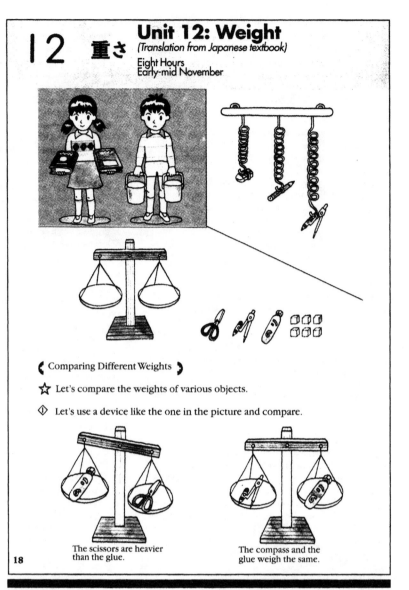

12 重さ Unit 12: Weight
(Translation from Japanese textbook)

Eight Hours
Early-mid November

❬ Comparing Different Weights ❭

☆ Let's compare the weights of various objects.

◇ Let's use a device like the one in the picture and compare.

The scissors are heavier than the glue.

The compass and the glue weigh the same.

18

Important Notes:
1. How to introduce the concept of weights:
Weight is a difficult concept for students to understand, compared with the concepts of length and volume, because (a) weight is hard to determine visually and (b) weight is not necessarily determined by the size and shape of the objects.

Therefore, it is important that more manipulative activities are introduced and that students measure the weights of objects by picking up the objects to feel their weights (direct comparison).

In other words, it is important for teachers to introduce them step-by-step to direct comparisons and indirect comparisons, leading to the use of universal units.

For the comparison of two objects, it is important to use objects that are tactually discernible in weight and objects that are not tactually discernible in weight, so that students can learn that they cannot measure the weight of the objects just by using their senses.

Editor's note: The Japanese teachers' manual includes—in a contrasting color of type, so as to be easily seen—the answers to each of the questions that appear in the children's text.

What is the difference in weight of a pair of scissors and a tube of glue? Let's use building blocks and compare them.

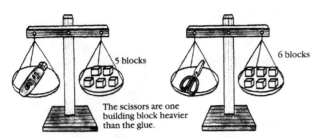

5 blocks

6 blocks

The scissors are one building block heavier than the glue.

It is possible to express weight using the number of units of weight. For the unit of weight, "gram" is used. One gram is written as "1g."

The weight of a 1-yen coin (*it's like a penny) is 1 g.

What is the weight of the compass?

Let's weigh it using 1-yen coins.

What is the weight of a tube of glue, a pair of scissors? Let's compare them using 1-yen coins.

19

---

2. The order of guidance for teaching weight:
It is important to include the following steps:
(a). Direct comparison (by using hands and justice scale);
(b). Indirect comparison (by using a regular scale);
(c). Arbitrary units (by using wooden blocks);
(d). Universal units (e.g., one gram).

3. Purpose of the unit:
The purpose of this unit is to remind students of the steps of measurement and weight, which are similar to those with the measurement of volume and length. Let the students realize the necessity of using arbitrary units and universal units.

Topic 3:
"Let's compare the objects using the justice scale."
Activity: Present a justice scale.
Guidance: Be sure to check if students know that when comparing two objects on a justice scale, the heavier side will drop down, and the lighter side will rise, and that if the two weights are the same, the two sides will remain even.

In the example on p. 18, the scissors is heaviest, and the compass and the glue have the same weight.

Topic 4:
"How much heavier are the scissors than the glue? Let's examine and find out by using wooden blocks."
Activity: Continue to weigh using the justice scale. This deals with step two on p. 19.
Guidance: First, allow students to realize the difference in the weights of the glue and the scissors. Second, get them to remember how they can measure the length by the number of units (i.e., make a certain unit and count how many units equal a certain length). Third, suggest that they use wooden blocks as units of measurement. Each block should be the same weight.

The glue in the textbook illustration equals five wooden blocks, whereas the scissors equals six blocks. Therefore, the scissors is one block heavier than the glue.

It may also be a good idea to suggest other items such as nails or paper clips as a unit of measurement. Then explain to the students that there is a unit of weight, a gram (g), and one gram is equal to one coin of one yen. One gram is written as 1g.

Topic 5:
"What is the weight of the compass? Let's measure it by using one-yen coins."
Activity: This deals with step three on p. 19.
Guidance: Let the students measure the weight of the compass by one-yen coins and finally represent the weight in terms of grams. Twenty one-yen coins equals twenty grams.

Topic 6:
"What are the weights of the glue and scissors, in terms of grams? Let's measure them using one-yen coins."
Activity: This deals with step four on p. 19.
Guidance: Let the students measure the objects and then share their findings with the class.

Reprinted with permission of the American Educator and Shing-ying Lee.

B. Section Two
(6 hours)

Objectives for the second section:
1. To learn how to read and use the units on a scale;
2. To learn the unit of weight, the kilogram, and that 1kg=1000g;
3. To learn how to select appropriate units and measuring devices depending on the objects;
4. To learn that weight has conservation and additivity.

Hour Three:

Goal: To learn how to read units of a scale.

Materials:
Scale with a horizontal platform (two types: 1kg and 400g)
Book (weight has to be less than 1kg)
Enlarged drawing of the face of the scale

(Example of a proposal for teaching this section)

Topic 1:
This deals with the asterisk and step one in the text on p. 20: "In order to measure weight we use a scale. How many lines are there between 0g and 100g, and how much does each line indicate in grams?"
Activity: Present the 1kg scale.
Guidance: Let the students understand the unit system of a scale before measuring the weights. There are three points:
- the largest units on the scale are 200g, 400g, 600g, 800g, and 1 kg;
- the smallest unit on the scale is 5g, with increments of 5g;
- the smallest unit on the scale is the least discriminable unit on the scale.

Topic 2:
"What's the weight of the picture book in grams?"
Activity: This deals with step two on p. 20.
Guidance: Show the enlarged drawing of the face of the scale, and let the students see that the picture book weighs 330g. Also, let them realize that 330g is lighter than 400g, and is heavier than 300g.
Exercise: Reading units on a scale
Read the weight of the scales a, b, and c in the textbook, which is on p. 20 of the textbook.

⟨ Scale ⟩

☆ A scale is used to weigh things. Let's use a scale and weigh a picture book.

◇ How many graduations are there between 0 and 100? How many grams is one graduation on this scale?

◈ What is the weight of the picture book?

◈ What is the maximum weight this scale can measure?

▯ Let's find out what weight each scale indicates.

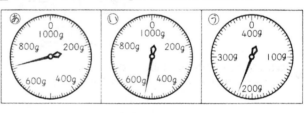

20

Important Notes:
- *Guidance for teaching students how to read units on the scale:*
  In the beginning, students are usually unfamiliar with reading units on the scale. So introduce the following basic steps in teaching:
  a. Let students read the large units on the scale, such as 200g or 1kg.
  b. Let students read the intermediate level of units. Let students see how many intermediate units there are in one large unit. Let them say what one intermediate level is.
  c. Let students read the smallest level of units.
  By following these steps, students can learn how to read the units correctly.

  In terms of reading units, students should learn first to read the larger units (100s). Then the intermediate units (10s). And then the smallest units (1s). Finally, to learn to put units together to equal the weight.

  In addition, students can also read the unit as being some number of units away from the maximum unit (e.g., 30g away from 400g equal 370g).

Reprinted with permission of the American Educator and Shing-ying Lee.

☆ When Deborah put the school bag on the scale, the hand of the scale pointed as shown in this picture. Let's find out the weight of the school bag.

To weigh the heavy objects, a unit called a **kilogram** is used.

1 kilogram is written as 1 kg.
1 kg = 1,000 g.

◇ What is the weight of the bookbag? How many grams is that?

◈ What is the maximum weight that this scale can measure?

When you use a scale:

① Put the scale on a flat surface.

② Make sure the hand is pointing at "0."

③ Find out the maximum weight it can measure.

④ After guessing roughly how much the object will weigh, place it gently on the scale.

⑤ Read the graduations from the starting point.

21

Hour Four and Five:
Goal: To learn the unit of weight, the kilogram, and that 1kg=1000g.

Materials:
Scale with a horizontal platform (two types: 1kg and 400g)
Bookbag

Topic 1:
"Let's measure the weight of the bookbags."
Guidance: Let students talk about their bookbags and let them estimate the weight of their bookbag.
    Teach them the units of weight (e.g., kg for heavy objects) and let them practice using the unit of kilogram.
    Let students understand the relation between 1kg and 1000g.
    Let students figure out what the bookbag in the textbook illustration weighs.

Topic 2:
"What is the maximum this scale (p. 21) would be able to measure?"
Activity: This deals with step three on p. 21.
Guidance: Let students know that the scale can measure up to 4kg. Let the students determine the minimum unit on the scale.

Topic 3:
"Let's list the points we need to be aware of when we measure weights."
Guidance: Let students know the right way of measuring weights and get them used to doing it.

■ *Sense of the weight of one kilogram:*
   Let students measure the weight of a liter of milk or juice, or whatever liquid they can find. Let them acquire the sense of weight for 1 kg by holding one liter of water, which equals 1kg.

Reprinted with permission of the American Educator and Shing-ying Lee.

EXPLANATION OF THE UNIT ON WEIGHT

Exercise one:
Let the students get the idea of the weight of 1kg.
"By holding a bag of sand that weighs 1kg, let's get an idea of the weight of 1kg." In addition, hold different objects and estimate the weight of each of the objects. Then find the exact weight by using a scale.

Exercise two: Reading the units on a scale:
■ Let the students learn how to read units in kilograms and in grams.
■ Get them familiar with reading the larger units first, and to figure out the weight by reading the smaller units.

Exercise three: Reading weight in grams (5200g), and in kilograms and grams (5kg 200g).

Hour Six:
Goal: To learn how to select appropriate units and measuring devices depending on the objects.

Materials:
Body scale
Spring scale
Automatic balance scale
Objects to be measured

Topic 1:
This deals with steps one and two in the textbook. Step one: "What kind of objects do you measure with these scales?" Step two: "Let's estimate the weight of the different objects and measure them with the scale."
Activity: Show the three different scales on p. 22 in the textbook.
Guidance: Let the students realize that there are different scales for measuring different objects.
Let them think of the kinds of objects they can use with the scales on p. 22 by thinking of the objects around them.
Let them realize that, before measuring weights, it is better to estimate the weight first, and then choose the right scale to measure the weight.

2 Take the bag of sand that weighs 1 kg and try to remember how heavy 1 kg is.

Hold various objects with your hand and guess how much each object will weigh. Then weigh each one with the scale.

3 Let's find out the weight that each scale indicates.

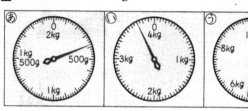

4 How many grams is 5 kg? How many kg and g is 1800g?

5 How many g is "3 kg 40 g"?

☆ Let's weigh the various objects using the scales.

◈ What kind of weight do the scales A, B, and C measure?

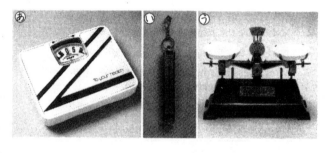

22

Supplementary problems
Let's find out the weight that each scale indicates:

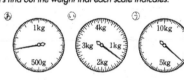

◈ Let's guess how much each object weighs, and then weigh each one with the scale.

☆ There are 2 pumpkins. The weight of each pumpkin was 900g and 800g.
What is the total weight of the two pumpkins?

◇ Let's weigh them and find out.

◈ What calculation do we have to do?

900 + 800 = 1700

1700 g = 1 kg 700 g   answer: <u>1 kg 700 g</u>

◆ What is the difference between the weights of the 2 pumpkins?

900 − 800 = 100   answer: <u>100g</u>

[6] 300 g + 500 g   8kg 200g + 5kg 400g

700 g − 200 g   4kg 700g − 3kg

[7] James weighs 26kg 900g. His brother is 5kg heavier, and his younger brother weighs 3kg 700g less than he.
What are the weights of James's younger and older brothers?

23

Hour Seven:
Goal: To learn conservation and additivity of the weight of an object.

Materials:
Automatic balance scale
Pumpkins

Topic 1:
"There are two pumpkins. One weighs 900g and the other weighs 800g. When you put the two pumpkins on one scale, what is the total weight?"
Activity: (Step one): "Let's measure the weight." "Add the weight of the two pumpkins and obtain the total weight of the pumpkins."
Guidance: Draw a number line similar to this:

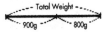

Obtain the total weight

Topic 2:
Activity: This deals with step two.
Guidance: Based on the results in step one, make an equation to obtain the total weight:
900g + 800g = 1700g
1700g = 1kg 700g

Topic 3:
"What is the difference between the two pumpkins in grams?"
Activity: This deals with step 2a.
Guidance: Make an equation and calculate it.

Topic 4:
The addition and subtraction of weights (problems 6 and 7 on p. 23).

■ *Conservation of weights:*
Suppose there is a kilogram clay ball. The weight of the clay won't change regardless of the shape of the clay. The number of pieces one divides the clay into also does not change the total weight. This characteristic is called conservation of weights.

■ *Additivity of weights:*
Suppose we add 3g of clay and 2g of clay. It is 3+2=5, which means there is a total of 5g of clay. This characteristic is called the additivity of weights.

Because it is believed that there are children who have not yet acquired the concepts of the conservation and additivity of weights, it is important to let children discover the ideas by shaping, cutting, and weighing the clay.

SPRING 1995   AMERICAN FEDERATION OF TEACHERS 23

Reprinted with permission of the American Educator and Shing-ying Lee.

Hour Eight:
Goal: Summary of this unit and more exercises.

Exercise one:
exercise for reading the units on the scale.

Exercise two:
exercise for reading weight in kilograms and in grams.

Exercise three:
ordering of weights, from heaviest to lightest.

Exercise four:
addition and subtraction of weights.

Exercise five:
exercise for selecting the appropriate units.

End of the Unit Exercise
まとめのれんしゅう

1 Let's read the weight that each hand is pointing at.

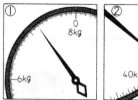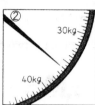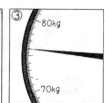

2 Let's figure out the numbers that go in the blanks.

$3 \text{ kg} = \square \text{ g}$ $4800 \text{ g} = \square \text{ kg} \square \text{ g}$

$1 \text{ kg } 600 \text{ g} = \square \text{ g}$ $9000 \text{ g} = \square \text{ kg}$

3 Which one is the heaviest weight and which one is the lightest weight? Let's put them in order from the heaviest to the lightest.
① (2500 g, 3 kg, 2 kg 800 g, 2 kg 90 g)
② (7900 g, 7 kg 500 g, 8 kg, 8400 g)

4 Let's calculate.

200 g + 500 g   5 kg + 7 kg 300 g

400 g – 200 g   7 kg 800 g – 3 kg 800 g

5 What unit is used for the weight below?

Weight of a (Japanese) arithmetic text 180 □

Weight of a large package to be mailed? 3 □

24

Supplementary Problems

1. Find out the numbers that fit in the blanks(□) and write the numbers down.

7kg = □g   (7000)
4000 g = □kg   (4)
2 kg800 g = □g   (2800)
8300 g =□kg □g   (8;300)
5 kg40 g = □g   (5040)
3050 g = □kg □ g   (3;50)

2. What units are used for the weights mentioned below:
   body weight   1 tomato

3. Calculate the problems.
   500 g +700 g   (1200 g, 1 kg200 g)
   4 kg + 8 kg   (12kg)
   6 kg800 g + 9 kg600 g   (16kg400 g)
   1300 g – 800 g   (500 g)
   7 kg400 g – 3 kg   (4 kg400 g)

Reprinted with permission of the American Educator and Shing-ying Lee.

Appendix G:
Excerpts from *Investigations*

ABOUT THE MATHEMATICS IN THIS UNIT

As suggested in the National Council of Teachers of Mathematics *Standards*, visualization skills are an important part of learning in mathematics and science. In fact, several mathematicians and engineers who reviewed this unit commented that it develops skills they have found essential both in college and in their jobs. The major goal of this unit, therefore, is to develop some basic concepts and the language needed to reflect on and communicate about spatial relationships in three dimensional (3-D) environments.

Visualizing a three-dimensional object by looking at a two-dimensional drawing is a critical spatial skill. This task is difficult because a two-dimensional drawing gives us only partial information about the object it represents. For example, the diagram below shows only three sides of the object. Because the picture is two-dimensional, it cannot capture all of the information contained in the actual three-dimensional object it represents.

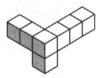

The next diagram, showing three views of the same object, presents even less information.

| Front View | Top View | Right Side View |

In this type of drawing, not only do students see only three sides, they have no information about how the sides are related or should be put together. To interpret either kind of diagram, students must use the partial information given to form a mental model of the whole object.

Figuring out what the whole object is, given partial information about it, is an important part of problem solving. It requires making inferences, generating and checking possible solutions, and reflecting upon and integrating information gained in previous solution attempts.

Another important notion for both geometry and spatial thinking is that objects look different from different points of view, or perspectives. But students must do more than recognize that this difference exists; they must also learn to visualize how objects look from different views. They develop this skill through problems like the three-views task, and problems in which they must figure out what views are possible at different points in given landscapes.

The NCTM *Standards* also recognize the important role of communication in student learning. This unit encourages students to devise ways to communicate effectively about three-dimensional objects. They explore common graphic methods used to communicate about such objects, for example, isometric and three-views drawings. They also develop suitable vocabulary for describing geometric figures.

To communicate well in writing, students must learn to step into the reader's shoes. In this unit, they see that to write a successful set of building instructions requires that the author see the construction process from the point of view of the reader. Thus, they must learn to read spatial descriptions from the point of view of someone who cannot see the object being described.

Because visualization skills have been neglected by traditional mathematics curricula, many students and adults find such tasks difficult. However, the ability to visualize improves with experience. Through repeated activities with concrete materials, like those provided in this unit, students' visualization skills will gradually increase. Keep in mind, too, that many spatial problems that are difficult to visualize can be easily solved if you build a

I-18 ■ *Seeing Silhouettes and Solids*

From *Seeing Solids and Silhouettes: Investigations in Number, Data, and Space* by Battista & Clements. © 1998 by Scott Foresman. Used by permission.

INVESTIGATION 1

Making and Visualizing Cube Buildings

What Happens

Session 1: Building with Cubes Students put interlocking cubes together to form cube buildings shown in drawings. They verbalize their strategies for building, and compare the sizes of the different structures.

Session 2: Making Mental Pictures After students are briefly shown a picture of a cube building, they construct it from memory by forming and inspecting a mental image of it. This activity gives students experience with visual organization and analysis of images, and more practice communicating about 3-D drawings and structures.

Mathematical Emphasis

- Developing concepts and language needed to reflect on and communicate about spatial relationships in 3-D environments
- Understanding standard drawings of 3-D cube configurations
- Exploring spatial relationships between components of 3-D figures
- Developing visualization skills
- Starting to think about problems related to volume

2 ▪ *Investigation 1: Making and Visualizing Cube Buildings*

From *Seeing Solids and Silhouettes: Investigations in Number, Data, and Space* by Battista & Clements. © 1998 by Scott Foresman. Used by permission.

The following activities will help ensure that this unit is comprehensible to students who are acquiring English as a second language. The suggested approach is based on *The Natural Approach: Language Acquisition in the Classroom* by Stephen D. Krashen and Tracy D. Terrell (Alemany Press, 1983). The intent is for second-language learners to acquire new vocabulary in an active, meaningful context.

Note that *acquiring* a word is different from *learning* a word. Depending on their level of proficiency, students may be able to comprehend a word upon hearing it during an investigation, without being able to say it. Other students may be able to use the word orally, but not read or write it. The goal is to help students naturally acquire targeted vocabulary at their present level of proficiency.

We suggest using these activities just before the related investigations. The activities can also be led by English-proficient students.

Investigation 1

cube building

1. As students watch, connect about eight cubes to make a structure of some sort. (It need not resemble a real building.) Explain that you are *building* with cubes, and that what you are making can be called a *cube building*.

2. Make two or three more different cube configurations, explaining that *cube buildings* can have many different shapes.

3. Challenge students to demonstrate comprehension of this term by giving them each about eight cubes and telling them to make a cube building. Have everyone display the finished buildings.

   Who has a cube building that looks like mine?

   Do you see a cube building made the same way as Luisa's?

   Who else has a cube building that is the same as someone else's?

Investigation 2

front, top, side, back

1. Display some small object (a doll, a toy car, an alarm clock) that has a clear front, top, side, and back. Walk around or turn the object as you identify the different views, motioning with a finger from your eyes to the appropriate part.

   If I look at it this way, I see the *top*.

   If I look at it this way, I see the *front*.

   From here, I am looking at the *side*.

2. Make a small, nonsymmetrical cube building. Place it next to the object you have been viewing, and relate the same words (*front, top, side, back*) to this cube structure.

3. Challenge students to demonstrate comprehension of these words by following action commands.

   Stand up when I point to the back of the [clock].

   Clap your hands when I point to a side of the building.

Investigation 3

instruction booklet, directions

1. Show and identify instruction booklets from several games, toys, or models. Make sure each booklet is placed on or next to the corresponding product.

2. Open the booklets and point out that the written text and diagrams are called *instructions* or *directions*.

3. Challenge students to demonstrate comprehension of these words by following action commands. Interchange the words *directions* and *instructions*.

   Pick up the instruction booklet for the model airplane.

   Point to the direction booklet for these building blocks.

   Point to the first instruction in this booklet.

Continued on next page

From *Seeing Solids and Silhouettes: Investigations in Number, Data, and Space* by Battista & Clements. © 1998 by Scott Foresman. Used by permission.

_____ , 19 ____

Dear Family,

For the next two weeks, our class will be doing a mathematics unit in 3-D geometry called *Seeing Solids and Silhouettes*. What your child will learn has very practical uses in daily life. When you read a floor plan, use a diagram to make a bookshelf, or sew a shirt from a pattern, you have to translate the words and drawings on a flat piece of paper into the actual object. This kind of "3-D thinking" also helps solve many problems in mathematics, engineering, and science.

Your child will be doing a lot of work with cube buildings—closely examining pictures of them, and then making the buildings with cubes. Your child will also work on writing clear instructions for making things with cubes.

We'll be talking about silhouettes, too. We'll look at shadows made by real objects, and try to match them with the objects. And we'll talk about different perspectives—that is, how things look from different angles, or different views.

If your child has any interlocking blocks, spend some time making simple buildings together. Look at what you build and try drawing them from different perspectives. If you're not very good at this, your child may be able to help, using strategies learned in class!

If your child builds models of any sort, talk together about the instructions that come with them. Are the words and diagrams clear? How could they be better? Any time that you're putting together a bicycle, a toy, or a piece of furniture, have your child help read and interpret the directions.

And if your child has never made something from a set of plans, encourage it—whether your child is a girl or a boy. Many people believe that either you're good at this or you're not. In fact, visualizing is a skill like anything else—the more you practice, the better you get!

Sincerely,

What to Plan Ahead of Time

Materials

- Sets of geometric solids that correspond to those on Student Sheet 6, Geometric Solids: 1 per group of 4–6 (all sessions)

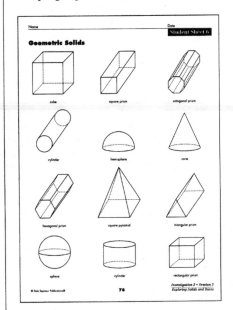

Other Preparation

- Duplicate student sheets (located at the end of this unit) in the following quantities. If you have Student Activity Booklets, copy only the item marked with an asterisk.

For Session 1

Student Sheet 1 (pages 1–3), Identifying Geometric Shapes in the Real World (p. 71): 1 per student (homework)

Family letter* (p. 70): 1 per student. Remember to sign it before copying.

- Use small adhesive labels to number the solids 1–12. For later reference, you might write the number of each solid beside the picture that corresponds to it on the Geometric Solids reference sheet. It is essential that all sets of models be numbered the same; for example, the octagonal prism in each set might be numbered 3. Also, if you mark each set with a different color, sets can be regrouped easily during cleanup time.

- If you plan to provide folders in which students will save their work for the entire unit, prepare these for distribution during Session 1.

Investigation 1: Sorting and Describing Solids ■ **3**

Geometric Solids: Types and Terminology

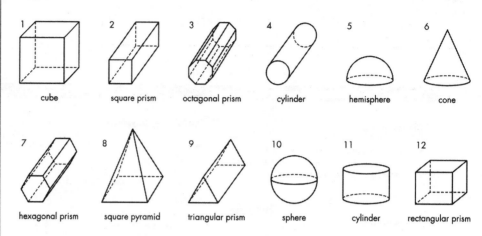

1 cube
2 square prism
3 octagonal prism
4 cylinder
5 hemisphere
6 cone

7 hexagonal prism
8 square pyramid
9 triangular prism
10 sphere
11 cylinder
12 rectangular prism

Types of Solids There are many types of geometric solids. Several, such as spheres, cones, and cylinders (figures 4, 5, 6, 10, and 11 above) have some curved surfaces. Others (figures 1, 2, 3, 7, 8, 9, and 12), called *polyhedra,* have only flat surfaces. (*Polyhedron* means having many flat surfaces, or faces.)

Two common types of polyhedra are prisms and pyramids. Students might say that prisms (figures 1, 2, 3, 7, 9, and 12) have "a top and bottom that are the same shape, and all the sides are [lateral faces] rectangles." Prisms are named by the shape on the "top and bottom"; hence, shape 7 is a *hexagonal* prism. Similarly, they might say that a pyramid (figure 8) has "a flat bottom and a point for a top, with all sides triangles." Pyramids are named by the shape that is the base (or "flat bottom"), in this case, a square.

Terminology It is not important that students memorize terminology (or acquire abstract definitions) for geometric solids at this grade level. However, you should use the correct terminology (along with terms invented by the students) to familiarize students with it. For instance, you might use the term *polyhedra* or a student-generated term such as *shapes with flat sides*

interchangeably, telling students that mathematicians call these shapes polyhedra.

Students will also frequently use *corner* for vertex, *line* for edge, and *side* for face. As long as they are communicating effectively, let them use the language they are comfortable with, while you continue to model the correct language. We will use the terms *edge* and *face,* but will generally use *corner* for vertex, both for polygons and polyhedra. You might, however, wish to use *vertex* [plural *vertices*] interchangeably with *corner.*

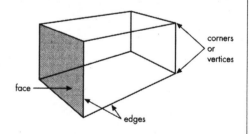

corners or vertices

face

edges

Talking to Students About Sorting

During the class discussion of students' sorting schemes in Session 1, this teacher is talking to the students in a small group about their grouping of polyhedra and non-polyhedra.

How are the shapes in this group [*pointing to the polyhedra*] the same?

Samir: The sides are all different. Some are rectangles, here are triangles, and some are squares. These are rectangles even though they are really skinny. [*The teacher notes that this student is focusing on what is different about the shapes in the group rather than what is the same.*]

Annie: They have points, edges, and are flat. This group [*non-polyhedra*] doesn't have them.

What do you mean?

Annie [*referring to a table to illustrate*]: This is a point [*touching a corner*]. This is the edge [*touching an edge of the table*]. It's flat [*placing hand down on the top of the table*].

If I had a shape that I wanted to add to this collection, what would it have to look like?

Students: The same thing.

How do you mean?

Jeremy: Points, corners, and sides. Because this one [*cone*] is not in the group. It has a corner and the bottom is flat, but it doesn't have sides that are flat. The sides are round here.

Later in the session, the teacher introduces the idea of sorting the polyhedra only (she has removed the non-polyhedra) into pyramids and prisms.

Now I'm going to sort these [*polyhedra*] into two groups [*pyramids and prisms*]. How are the shapes in the two groups different?

Liliana: This one [*points to pyramid*], when it goes up it gets thinner. All the other ones [*points to prisms*] stay the same shape.

Do you all agree?

Kate: This one [*points to pyramid*] is like a triangle and these are rectangles.

This figure [*triangular prism*] is triangular in shape. Why is it not in the group with this one [*the pyramid*]?

Khanh: This [*pyramid*] doesn't have as many sides. This [*triangular prism*] has a top and a bottom. These [*the prisms*] all have both.

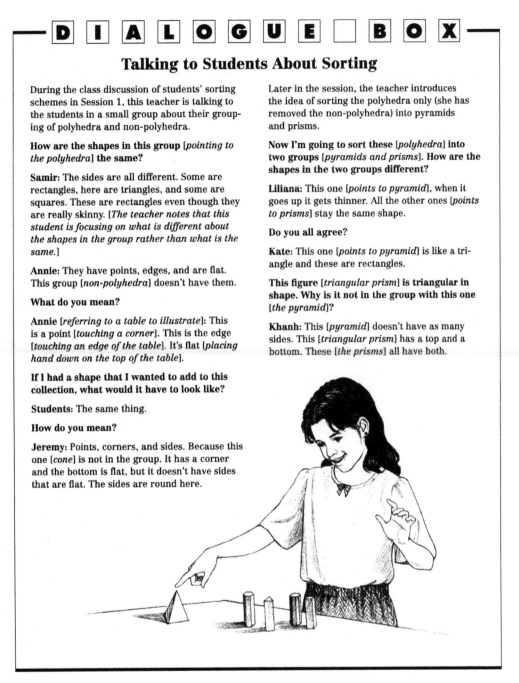

From *Exploring Solids and Boxes: Investigations in Number, Data, and Space* by Battista & Clements. © 1998 by Scott Foresman. Used by permission.

Discussing Student Strategies

The final activity in this session enables you to more closely observe the strategies students are using to predict the number of cubes that will fit in a box made from a pattern. This should help you better understand how individual students are making sense of the problems.

Show the Discussion Box Pattern transparency, and ask each student to predict how many cubes will fit in the box that it makes. Students write their predictions and a description of how they made the prediction. The **Teacher Note**, Strategies for Finding the Number of Cubes in a Box (pp. 43–44), includes some examples of students' written descriptions.

❖ **Tip for the Linguistically Diverse Classroom** Give each student who may have difficulty describing his or her prediction a copy of the Discussion Box Pattern. Students can mark on this sheet to show how they made their predictions. For example, two students might show their answers as follows:

You can easily tell from their markings that one student understands the problem and the other one still does not.

Follow up with a whole-class discussion, asking students to give their predictions and describe their strategies for making them. After all predictions have been discussed, fold a copy of the pattern and fill it with cubes to test the predictions. Ask students how to determine the number of cubes that actually fit in the box. Try the different methods suggested and have the students discuss any discrepancies.

42 ▪ *Investigation 4: How Many Cubes in a Box?*

Appendix H:
Mathematics Case Methods Project

Mathematics Case Methods Project
Teacher Preparation Content Workshop
National Academy of Sciences
Washington, DC

March 19-21, 1999

Introductory Packet

Carne Barnett
Director, Math Case Methods Project
WestEd
Oakland, CA

CHALLENGES TO OURSELVES AS PROFESSIONAL DEVELOPMENT DESIGNERS

How can we design learning professional development experiences that:

INCLUSIVE

Are inclusive and effective with teachers, regardless of their pedagogical views, knowledge, or skills.

PRODUCTIVE AND EFFICIENT

Have rapid, significant, and direct positive impact on the learning of teachers and their students—and on their ability to continue to learn from their own experiences.

MEASURABLE

Demonstrate a positive impact on students' understanding of mathematics which is measurable on a variety of instruments, including standardized tests.

OPEN TO CRITICAL EXAMINATION

Provide an environment that supports teachers questions themselves, each other's ideas, even the most highly regarded ideas of the mathematics teaching community.

TEACHER LEADERSHIP

Assumes that all teachers, regardless of their experience or pedagogical philosophy, should be given the opportunity to assume leadership roles.

Mathematics Case Methods Project, directed by Carne Barnett, WestEd © 2000.

WHY LEARN TO DISCUSS AND FACILITATE MATH CASES?

Mathematics

- To deepen our <u>own</u> understanding of the mathematics

Children's Thinking about Mathematics

- To experience the mathematics from our students' points of view

Mathematics Instruction

- To make informed teaching decisions by examining the benefits and drawbacks of various strategies

Language

- To understand the impact of oral, symbolic, visual, and written communication on the mathematics learning of all students

---

Mathematics Case Methods Project, directed by Carne Barnett, WestEd © 2000.

Case Discussion Roadmap
Summary
Mathematics Case Methods Project

- **Opening inclusion activity**
  Purpose: to build trust and support open discussion; participants may pass.
- **Starter Problem**
  Purpose: to stimulate thinking about the mathematics and student thinking; participants work independently; solutions may be presented during the discussion, but are not shared prior to the discussion.
- **Read or quickly review the case**
  If possible, participants read the case before coming to the discussion and begin to think about issues to discuss.
- **Facts**
  Purpose: to build common background about the case; collected quickly popcorn style without comments.
- **Issues written in question format**
  Purpose: to generate questions that will stimulate deep discussion; focus on the mathematics, child's thinking, instruction and materials, or language; participants
  generate issues in pairs.
- **Begin the discussion**
  The issues are read to the group; a volunteer chooses one of the issues and begins the discussion.
- **During the discussion**
  Participants build on and ask questions about each other's ideas; a few ideas are examined in depth; participants come to the board to make drawings or use materials to explain their ideas.
- **Closing inclusion activity**
  Purpose: to bring the group together for a brief reflection or appreciation of the experience; may be an oral or written reflection.
- **Process Check**
  Purpose: to allow participants to give feedback to each other on how well the group participated in the discussion; it is not an evaluation of the facilitator.

Mathematics Case Methods Project, directed by Carne Barnett, WestEd © 2000.

How could you show which is greater, 6/10 or 4/5 of a dollar?

Mathematics Case Methods Project, directed by Carne Barnett, WestEd © 2000.

Six-Tenths or Four-Fifths of a Dollar?

The math experiences of the 30 students in my fourth-grade class vary widely. Esmarelda, a recent immigrant to the United States, is Limited English Proficient (LEP) and has never had formal schooling. Chris is a gifted student who enjoys calculations and problem solving. Michael participates in my class, then later in the day goes to the resource room for additional math help. There are also 3 children with special needs, 4 other LEP students, and 12 extremely economically disadvantaged students.

Often, it seems, I teach a lesson 4 or 5 times before I feel comfortable moving ahead. Sometimes I worry that I'm beating a dead horse. For those students who catch on quickly I try to plan enrichment activities or set up activity centers. This year—my third year of teaching—I've been trying to include more math journal writing before, during, and after lessons. I also try to use concrete materials before explaining a mathematical concept to the class.

I recently introduced the class to fractions. They have learned how to identify fractions using diagrams such as the following:

2/3

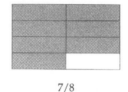

7/8

5/8

Each student made a fraction kit that allowed them to show and identify various fractions. The denominators of the fractions in the kits were 1, 2, 4, 8, and 16.

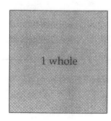

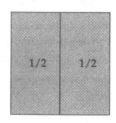

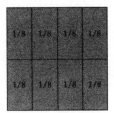

My beginning lesson had focused on identifying and orally naming various fractions.

"Place your 'whole' on the desk top," I said. "Show me $\frac{1}{4}$ of a whole by placing $\frac{1}{4}$ on top of it." The students responded by placing a "one-fourth" piece on the square representing 1 whole.

By the end of the lesson, they could successfully name and use the fraction kit to show unit fractions like $\frac{1}{2}$ or $\frac{1}{8}$ and nonunit fractions like $\frac{3}{4}$ or $\frac{5}{8}$.

1/2

1/8

3/4

5/8

The next lesson focused on equivalent fractions. I asked the students to figure out the answer to questions like how many eighths would be equal to $\frac{1}{4}$ or how many sixteenths would equal $\frac{3}{8}$. They used their fraction-kit pieces to determine the answers. By the end of this lesson, students were very familiar with the relationship among the fraction pieces and could solve simple equivalency problems without using the pieces.

I was then ready to have students learn how to compare fractions that have different denominators and numerators. Prior to beginning, I asked them to write about fraction equivalency in their journals, so I could assess their understanding of previous lessons and know what information I needed to cover. I asked them to answer this question:

Which would you rather have: $\frac{6}{10}$ of a dollar or $\frac{4}{5}$ of a dollar? Explain your reasons for choosing your answer.

From *Fractions, Decimals, Ratios, and Percents: Hard to Teach and Hard to Learn?* edited by Barnett, Goldenstein, and Jackson. © 1994 by Far West Laboratory for Educational Research and Development. Published by Heinemann. Reprinted with permission.

After reflecting, the students picked up their pencils and wrote.

Cindy's journal read: "If I had $\frac{6}{10}$, I would have 2 more than $\frac{4}{5}$. I would choose $\frac{6}{10}$ so I could have more money."

Chris wrote: "$\frac{4}{5} = \frac{8}{10}$. $\frac{8}{10}$ is greater than $\frac{6}{10}$. Of course, I'd take $\frac{4}{5}$ of a dollar. Wouldn't you?" He included an illustration:

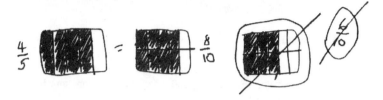

Esmarelda wrote: "No sé. $\frac{6}{10}$ es mas grande."

Nikki drew a picture to accompany her answer: "I want $\frac{6}{10}$. It is bigger."

Only 4 of the 30 students wrote $\frac{4}{5}$. Their journals gave me some hints about how they were thinking about fractions, but I was not sure how to use this information to plan our future work. Since the students were familiar with the fraction kit, I wondered if they would have answered differently if the question had been, "Would you rather have $\frac{3}{4}$ or $\frac{5}{8}$ of a chocolate bar?"

Suggested Reading

Behr, M. J., T. R. Post, and I. Wachsmuth. 1986. "Estimation and Children's Concept of Rational Number Size." In *Estimation and Mental Computation*, edited by H. L. Schoen and M. J. Zweng, 103–111. Reston, VA: The National Council of Teachers of Mathematics.

Cuevas, G. 1990. "Increasing the Achievement and Participation of Language Minority Students in Mathematics Education." In *Teaching and Learning Mathematics in the 1990s*, edited by T. J. Cooney and C. R. Hirsch, 159–165. Reston, VA: The National Council of Teachers of Mathematics.

PROCESS CHECK

Mathematics Case Methods Project

Rating Scale: 1   2   3   4   5

Strongly Disagree   Strongly Agree

Feedback to the group:

1. ____   Group members gave different points of view respectful consideration even when there was disagreement or the ideas were unpopular.

2. ____   I felt I had opportunities to comment, whether or not I contributed during the discussion.

3. ____   Members built on and contributed to each other's ideas. Members asked questions about each other's ideas.

4. ____   The group gave a high priority to discussing the mathematics and student thinking.

Feedback to the facilitator:

5. What is one thing that worked well?

6. What is one thing that might be tried next time?

Mathematics Case Methods Project, directed by Carne Barnett, WestEd © 2000.

Appendix I:
Biographical Information

Richard Askey is a member of the Program Steering Committee (PSC) and is Professor of Mathematics at the University of Wisconsin-Madison. He received his Ph.D. from Princeton University in 1961 and his M.A. from Harvard University in 1956. From 1958 to present, Askey has held various academic positions at the University of Wisconsin-Madison, the University of Chicago, and Washington University. His specialty is special functions. Askey is an Honorary Fellow of the Indian Academy of Sciences, Bangalore, and Fellow of the American Academy of Arts and Sciences. He currently serves on the National Research Council's (NRC) Mathematical Sciences Education Board (MSEB).

Deborah Loewenberg Ball is chair of the PSC and is Professor of Educational Studies at the University of Michigan. Her work as a researcher and teacher educator draws directly and indirectly on her long experience as an elementary classroom teacher. With mathematics as the main context for her work, Ball studies the practice of teaching and the processes of learning to teach. Her work examines efforts to improve teaching through policy, reform initiatives, and

teacher education. Ball's publications include articles on teacher learning and teacher education; the role of subject matter knowledge in teaching and learning to teach; endemic challenges of teaching; and the relations of policy and practice in instructional reform. Ball was the Coordinator for the Professional Development Action Conference held in conjunction with the Center for Science, Mathematics, and Engineering Education's (CSMEE) National Convocation on Mathematics Education in the Middle Grades. She is currently a member of the NRC's MSEB and Commission on Behavioral and Social Sciences and Education.

Carne Barnett is currently Director of the Mathematics Case Methods Project at WestEd in Oakland, California. She also has prior experience as a teacher in urban settings and as a teacher educator at the University of California, Berkeley, where her pioneering work with cases for teaching mathematics began in 1987. Her research focuses on the characterization and growth of mathematics teachers' pedagogical content knowledge, as well as on methods for using cases as a professional development tool. She has published journal articles and book chapters in the *Journal of Teacher Education, Teaching and Teacher Education*, the *Journal of Mathematics Teacher Education, The Case for Education*, and *Mathematics Teachers in Transition*. Barnett is the principal investigator of a National Science Foundation (NSF) grant whose central aim is to equip teachers with a stronger and more complex content knowledge base. She is also the principal investigator of a project to develop materials for students and support materials for teachers to improve students' understanding of rational number concepts

Hyman Bass is a member of the PSC and Professor of Mathematics at Columbia University, New York. He received his Ph.D. in mathematics from the University of Chicago in 1959. He has since been a member of Columbia University's Mathematics Department, which he chaired from 1975-1979. As an academic mathematician, Bass is involved in basic research, mainly in algebra and its interface with geometry, and teaching at all university levels. He is currently also engaged in education research in collaboration with Deborah Ball at the University of Michigan. He is an author of research and expository writings, active in the editorial aspects of scientific publishing, and engages in matters of educational and scientific policy. Bass has served as a member of or consultant to numerous national and international groups concerned with mathematical research and science. He has been a trustee of the AMS (of which he chairs its Committee on Education), of the Berkeley Mathematical Sciences Research Institute (as its initial Board Chair), and of the Institute for Advanced Study. He is currently a member of the National Academy of Sciences [where he chairs the Mathematical Sciences Education Board (MSEB) and has been a member of the Board on Mathematical Sciences], and of the American Academy of Arts and Sciences. He is President of the International Commission on Mathematics Instruction.

Virginia Bastable has been the director of the SummerMath for Teachers Program at Mount Holyoke College since 1993. Prior to that, over the course of a twenty-five-year career as a secondary school mathematics teacher, she earned a Masters in mathematics and an Ed.D. in mathematics education. Bastable has been working in the field of teacher education, designing and conducting summer institutes and academic year courses in both mathematics and mathematics education for teachers of grades K-12. She is currently working in collaboration with EDC, Inc., in Newton and TERC in Cambridge to create a professional development curriculum designed to allow teachers to engage with the mathematical ideas of the elementary curriculum and to examine the way students develop those ideas. This curriculum, Developing Mathematical Ideas, is published by Dale Seymour.

Gail Burrill earned an undergraduate degree in mathematics at Marquette University and her Masters in mathematics at Loyola University of Chicago. She was a secondary teacher and department chair in suburban Milwaukee, Wisconsin, for over twenty-five years and recently an associate researcher at the University of Wisconsin-Madison. She is currently at the National Research Council where she serves as program officer for the Mathematical Sciences Education Board. She is the immediate Past President of the National Council of Teachers of Mathematics. As an instructor for Teachers

Teaching with Technology, she conducts workshops around the country on using technology in the classroom. Her honors include the Presidential Award for Excellence in Teaching Mathematics and the Wisconsin Distinguished Educator Award. She was elected a fellow of the American Statistical Association. She is on the Advisory Board of the Woodrow Wilson National Fellowship Foundation and the National Board for Professional Teaching Standards. The author of numerous books and articles on statistics and mathematics education, she has spoken nationally and internationally on issues in mathematics education.

Rodger W. Bybee is Executive Director of the Center for Science, Mathematics, and Engineering Education (CSMEE) at the National Research Council, Washington, D.C. Between 1992 and 1995, he participated in the development of the *National Science Education Standards*, and from 1993-1995 chaired the content working group of that project. Prior to this appointment, he served as associate director of the Biological Sciences Curriculum Study (BSCS). Bybee was principal investigator for several NSF programs including an elementary school program entitled *Science for Life and Living*, a middle school program entitled *Middle School Science and Technology*, a high school program entitled *Biological Sciences: A Human Approach*, and the college program, *Biological Perspectives*. His work at BSCS also has included serving as principal investigator for programs to develop curriculum frameworks for teaching about the history and nature of science and technology and for biology education at high schools, community colleges, and four-year colleges. From 1972-1985, Bybee was Professor of Education at Carleton College in

Northfield, Minnesota. He received his Ph.D. in science education and psychology from New York University. His B.A. and M.A. are from the University of Northern Colorado with majors in both biology and fine arts and a minor in earth science. He has taught science at the elementary, junior and senior high school, and college levels. Bybee has been active in education for more than thirty years. Throughout his career, Bybee has written widely, publishing in both education and psychology. He is co-author of a leading textbook entitled *Teaching Secondary School Science: Strategies for Developing Scientific Literacy*. His most recent book is *Achieving Scientific Literacy: From Purposes to Practices*. Over the years, he has received awards for Leader of American Education and Outstanding Educator in America, and in 1979 was Outstanding Science Educator of the year. In 1989, he was recognized as one of the 100 outstanding alumni in the history of the University of Northern Colorado. Bybee's biography has been included in the Golden Anniversary 50th Edition of *Who's Who in America*.

Michaele F. Chappell is an Associate Professor of Mathematics Education in the Department of Secondary Education at the University of South Florida, Tampa, where she teaches methods courses for elementary, middle grades, and secondary preservice students, and graduate mathematics education courses related to trends in research and the practice of education. Chappell has worked on a number of mathematics education projects, including as an investigative researcher for the QUASAR Project. Chappell has been active in national, state, and local mathematics education organizations such as the National Council of Teachers of Mathematics (NCTM), the Association of Mathematics Teacher

Education, and the Benjamin Banneker Association; she has served in the role of board/committee member and officer in several of these organizations. During the past eighteen years, she has demonstrated her breadth of knowledge in mathematics teaching and learning through her teaching and presentations. She has been an invited speaker at conferences and has provided numerous teachers with professional development workshops.

Joan Ferrini-Mundy is Associate Executive Director of the Center for Science, Mathematics, and Engineering Education and Director, Mathematical Sciences Education Board, at the National Research Council. She is on leave from her position as a professor of mathematics at the University of New Hampshire, where she joined the faculty in 1983. She holds a Ph.D. in mathematics education from the University of New Hampshire. Ferrini-Mundy taught mathematics at Mount Holyoke College in 1982-1983, where she co-founded the SummerMath for Teachers program. She was the Principal Investigator for NCTM's Recognizing and Recording Reform in Mathematics Education (R^3M) project. She served as a visiting scientist at the National Science Foundation 1989-1991. She chaired the NCTM's Research Advisory Committee, was a member of the NCTM Board of Directors, and served on the NRC's MSEB. Ferrini-Mundy has chaired the Association for Educational Research (AERA) Special Interest Group for Research in Mathematics Education. Her research interests are in calculus learning and reform in mathematics education, K-14. Currently she chairs the Writing Group for Standards 2000, the revision of the NCTM *Standards*.

Bradford Findell is a Program Officer in the Center for Science, Mathematics,

and Engineering Education at the National Research Council, where most of his work is with the Mathematical Sciences Education Board. He holds a Master's degree in mathematics from Boston University and is completing a doctorate in mathematics education at the University of New Hampshire under Joan Ferrini-Mundy. His primary interests are in the teaching and learning of high school and undergraduate mathematics and in the preparation and professional development of mathematics teachers.

Alice Gill is currently Associate Director, Educational Issues Department of the American Federation of Teachers; she was an elementary teacher in the Cleveland public schools for twenty-four years. She coordinates *Thinking Mathematics,* a research-based professional development program for elementary/middle school teachers that she helped to develop during an NSF-funded collaboration between AFT and the University of Pittsburgh. This is part of the union's *Educational Research and Dissemination Program*. She also works on professional development and standards issues. Gill was a member of the advisory group for the Third International Mathematics and Science Study (TIMSS) Classroom Videotape Study report, advised on the Department of Education's *Attaining Excellence* TIMSS toolkit, and developed AFT's materials on TIMSS. She is a member of NCTM's External Relations Committee and on the Expert Panel for development of the Internet Learning Network that will be devoted to math and science.

Cathy Kessel is an independent scholar. She received her Ph.D. in mathematics from the University of Colorado at Boulder and has taught mathematics at Ohio State University, the College of Charleston, Vista Community College, Kaiser Hospital, and Mills College. She has worked as a researcher in mathematics education at the University of California and the University of Melbourne, as a textbook editor and researcher at Key Curriculum Press, as an assessment developer for New Standards, as an editor for Liping Ma's *Knowing and Teaching Elementary Mathematics*, as a curriculum developer at the University of California, and as an additional writer on the National Council of Teachers of Mathematics *Principles and Standards for School Mathematics*. Currently she serves on the Math/Science Network's advisory board.

Genevieve Knight is a member of the PSC and Professor of Mathematics at Coppin State College in Baltimore, Maryland. Knight has been a member of the Board of Directors of NCTM and Governor at Large for the Mathematical Association of America (MAA). She has served on commissions and committees for NCTM, the American Association of Colleges of Teachers of Education (AACTE), the National Council for Accreditation of Teacher Education (NCATE), and is currently a member of the Department of Education's Expert Panel on Science and Mathematics Education. Her work on behalf of equity issues as well as her interest in improving mathematics education have involved her in a variety of projects including the MSEB's Making Mathematics Work for Minorities project. Preparing aspiring future teachers to teach school mathematics; teaching mathematics majors the language of mathematics; and exploring how students learn, understand, and achieve are her primary interests. Knight received her Ph.D. from the University of Maryland.

Shin-ying Lee is an Associate Research Scientist at the Center for Human Growth and Development, University of Michigan. She is a developmental and educational psychologist. Her research focuses on the cross-national comparative studies of children's academic achievement, particularly mathematics achievement, and the contexts that relate to the attainment of academic achievement. This involves the comparison of the learning experience of students from Japan, Taiwan, China, and the United States. In her research, teacher interviews, classroom observations, testing of students, and analyses of curricular materials have been used to understand the mathematics teaching and learning processes. Lee is also developing a mathematics curriculum, M-Math, and works with teachers in elementary schools to initiate aspects of effective mathematics instructions based on their findings from the comparative research.

Jill Lester, currently the Assistant Director of the SummerMath for Teachers program at Mount Holyoke College, became a teacher-educator after many years working as an elementary school teacher. Ms. Lester has a B.S. in elementary education with a minor in psychology from Rhode Island College, an M.S. in elementary education from Southern Connecticut State University, and is enrolled as a doctoral student at the University of Massachusetts. In recent years, she has been working with both inservice and preservice teachers in the development and implementation of the Developing Mathematical Ideas Curriculum.

James Lewis is Professor and Chair of the Department of Mathematics and Statistics at the University of Nebraska-Lincoln. In 1998 his department won the

University of Nebraska's University-wide Department Teaching Award as the outstanding teaching department in the four-campus university system. His department also won a 1998 Presidential Award for Excellence in Science, Mathematics, and Engineering Mentoring. He was a principal investigator for the Nebraska Math and Science Initiative, Nebraska's NSF-funded SSI. He is a past chair of the American Mathematical Society's (AMS) Committee on Science Policy and currently serves on the AMS Committee on Education. He is chair of the Steering Committee for the Conference Board for the Mathematical Sciences (CBMS) Mathematics Education of Teachers Project and is co-chair of the NRC's Committee on the Preparation of Science and Mathematics Teachers. He received his Ph.D. in mathematics from Louisiana State University.

James Lightbourne is a Science Advisor in the National Science Foundation's Division of Undergraduate Education. Prior to his work at NSF, he was Chair of the Mathematics Department at West Virginia University. He received his Ph.D. in mathematics from North Carolina State University in 1976.

Liping Ma is an independent scholar. Her teaching career started when, as a teenager in rural China, she was asked to teach elementary school. During her seven years as an elementary teacher she taught all five grades of elementary school. Later she became the principal of the school, then the superintendent of the county in which the school was located. She received a Masters degree in education from East China Normal University and became an assistant research professor at Shanghai Research Institution for Higher Education. Her continued interest in education led her to graduate study at Michigan State University where she worked as a graduate assistant on the study that inspired her dissertation. She received her Ph.D. in curriculum and teacher education from Stanford University. As a McDonnell post-doctoral fellow at the University of California at Berkeley she revised her Ph.D. dissertation into the book *Knowing and Teaching Elementary Mathematics: Teachers' Understanding of Fundamental Mathematics in China and the United States.*

Carole Midgett is a National Board Certified Teacher who has taught first through eighth grades for nineteen years. She received her B.A. at Barton College (formerly Atlantic Christian College) and has done graduate studies at the University of North Carolina at Wilmington. Midgett holds certifications in gifted education and mentoring for preservice and novice teachers. She is a trainer of assessors for Performance Based Licensure in North Carolina. She is a Presidential Awardee in Elementary Mathematics. She has authored and co-authored articles in juried mathematics and research journals. Additionally, she has contributed to numerous publications on assessment, process writing, cognitive coaching, professional development, and Addison Wesley texts. Her presentations include state, regional, national, and international conferences. She served on the NCTM Assessment Addenda Writing Team and participated in the NCTM project to implement the geometry standards. She has served on state curriculum development projects and organized, coordinated, and directed numerous teacher enhancement projects in both mathematics and science. Currently, she serves on the Implementation Team of the Professional Development System at the UNC at Wilmington.

Marco Ramirez is an Assistant Principal at an elementary school. He received his B.S. in business and agriculture and his M.A. at the University of Arizona in 1983 and 1997. From 1987 to present, Ramirez has served on various committees for the NCTM, NSF, and NRC. Ramirez worked for Tucson Unified School District Title I / EXXON Mathematics Project conducting staff development for teachers before becoming an Assistant Principal.

Mark Saul is a member of the PSC and a teacher at Bronxville High School in Bronxville, New York. He has taught for over thirty years on the pre-college level, and has served as an adjunct professor for the City University of New York. He is also Director of the American Regions Mathematics League Russian Exchange Program. He received his Ph.D. in mathematics education from New York University in 1987. He was awarded the Sigma Xi Recognition for Outstanding High School Science Teacher, Lehman College Chapter, in 1981 and received the Westinghouse Science Talent Search Certificates of Honor, 1980-1983. He was recognized with the Presidential Award for Excellence in the Teaching of Mathematics of the National Science Foundation in 1984. He received the Admiral Hyman L. Rickover Foundation Fellowship in 1985, was a Tandy Scholar in 1994, and received the Gabriella and Paul Rosenbaum Foundation Fellowship in 1995. He became a Fellow, American Association for the Advancement of Science (AAAS), in 1997. He has extensive experience as a judge of mathematical competitions and with Russian mathematics education. He is a member of AMS and is active in the mathematics teaching standards revision. He has been continuously active in professional workshops, activities, and presentations, and has

authored over twenty publications. He is currently a member of the NRC's MSEB and the Committee on Science and Mathematics Teacher Preparation.

Deborah Schifter, a member of the PSC and a senior scientist at the Educational Development Center, Inc., in Newton, Massachusetts, has worked as an applied mathematician, and has taught elementary, secondary, and college level mathematics. Since 1985, she has been a mathematics teacher educator. She has a B.A. in liberal arts from Saint John's College, Annapolis, Maryland, an M.A. in applied mathematics from the University of Maryland, and an M.S. and Ph.D. in psychology from the University of Massachusetts. In 1988, Schifter became the director of SummerMath for Teachers, a nationally acclaimed mathematics teacher development program at Mount Holyoke College. In 1993, she moved to the Educational Development Center, where she is now creating a curriculum for teacher learning and directing programs to support the professional development of teacher educators, staff developers, and teacher-leaders. She co-authored with Catherine Twomey Fosnot *Reconstructing Mathematics Education: Stories of Teachers Meeting the Challenge of Reform*, edited a two-volume anthology of teachers' writing, *What's Happening in Math Class?* and co-produced with staff and participants of the Teaching to the Big Ideas project the professional development curriculum, *Developing Mathematical Ideas*.

Erick Smith is an Assistant Professor in Curriculum and Instruction at the University of Illinois at Chicago. In addition to teaching, his interests are in the ethics of teaching mathematics, the nature of mathematics in everyday life, and the preparation of inservice and preservice teachers for teaching mathematics in urban settings. He is particularly interested in the contextual aspects of the mathematics of teaching. For fifteen years prior to coming to UIC he was a strawberry farmer in upstate New York and for seven years a research associate at Cornell University on an NSF-funded project looking at the learning and teaching of exponential functions.

Olga Garcia Torres is a member of the PSC and an elementary teacher from a multi-age/multi-lingual classroom in Tucson Unified School District in Tucson, Arizona. She is also currently a math/science support teacher for a Title I Exxon Project for the Tucson district. She is a Presidential Awardee for Excellence in Teaching Mathematics and Science and her work for Arizona includes serving as a member of the State Department of Education Steering Committee for Curriculum Framework and Professional Guide Development. Torres' work outside of the classroom includes work with teachers on equity issues and teaching for understanding as well as video taping classroom practices and instruction for an NSF project.

Alan C. Tucker is the SUNY Distinguished Teaching Professor at the State University of New York at Stony Brook in the Department of Applied Mathematics and Statistics. He obtained his Ph.D. in mathematics from Stanford University in 1969. Tucker has been at Stony Brook since 1970. The applied math undergraduate major at Stony Brook, which he developed, regularly produces more graduates in mathematics, on a percentage basis, than any other U.S. public

university. His research interests are in combinatorial mathematics. He was a recipient of the Mathematics Association of America's National Award for Distinguished Teaching of Mathematics. He is author of the textbooks, *Applied Combinatorics* and *Linear Algebra*. Tucker has led a number of studies about collegiate mathematics including the 1981 CUPM Recommendations for a General Mathematical Sciences Program and two recent NSF-sponsored projects, Assessing Calculus Reform Efforts, and Case Studies in Effective Mathematics Undergraduate Programs. He was MAA First Vice President in 1988-1990 and has chaired the MAA Publications Committee and Education Council. He has been an external consultant/evaluator to fifty mathematics departments. He is currently project director of a large NSF grant for systemic change in quantitative instruction at a consortium of Long Island institutions.

Gladys Whitehead received her doctorate in mathematics education from Georgia State University in Atlanta, Georgia. She is a graduate of Florida A & M University and Florida International University. She has worked as a professor of mathematics at Prince George's Community College for the past ten years. She has taught the mathematics courses for elementary education majors. Gladys has been a consultant to public school systems since 1992 where she has provided inservice for elementary and middle school teachers of mathematics. She is currently on leave from the college to serve as the Supervisor of Mathematics to Prince George's County Public Schools.